D1521561

Advance Praise for *Becoming Who You Truly Are*:

"Written with a sensitivity and a sensibility that can only come from someone who has walked the inner path himself, *Becoming Who You Truly Are* offers us all the perfect morning reminders that we are not alone.

Parker shares his own personal journey with the openness of someone who has found a peace that eludes so many of the rest of us.

A perfect way to start each morning!"

—CLAY AIKEN,

singer, actor, and *American Idol* alumnus

"Patrick Parker opens his heart on a journey towards freedom and authenticity, not to boast about his experiences and mastery of the ongoing process of self-realization, but rather to lend anecdotes and analogies towards the human experience that is universal in all of us.

In contrast to the conventional, formulaic hodge-podge of wellness and self-help which we are familiar with, Parker's approach focuses instead on gratitude as the springboard of finding infinity in the singularity of experiencing the privilege of becoming who you truly are.

Truly a spectacular journey inward, with bountiful reflections of love, purpose, and salvation, all while learning to be present and accepting of oneself through every day of the year."

—HARDEEP PHULL, M.D.,

oncologist and physician wellness advocate

"Patrick Parker—an author who writes with a unique combination of soul and intellect!"

—JON GILLOCK,

concert and recording artist, author

Becoming Who You Truly Are

Daily Reflections for Wisdom, Peace, and Freedom

Patrick Parker

ANANDI KUTRA PRESS

ANANDI KUTRA PRESS

Oslo, Norway ◇ Houston, Texas

ISBN: 9798361954100
Library of Congress Control Number: 2023901181

Cover photo: S.B.P., Lofoten Islands, July 2021.

"The privilege of a lifetime is to become who you truly are."

-Carl Jung

This book is dedicated to my Best Friend and Ollie.

Thanks for going about your days alongside me, hand in hand, paw in paw.

◇ CONTENTS ◇

◇ JANUARY ◇

January 1
◇ COMMENCEMENT ◇

A few years back, I read that only one percent of people live an authentic, creative, self-actualized life.

At first, I disagreed with this notion.

But eventually, I saw that becoming who you truly are is indeed rare, because we live in a world where people of all classes and creeds are in a stressed-out 'survival mode.'

Therefore, the intention of this book is to relax your instincts and help you thrive by relaxing into the wisdom, peace, and freedom that come from living an authentic life.

I am certainly not an expert and I don't have definitive answers for you (after all, there is no formula to becoming who you truly are). All I can do is share what has worked for me and ask a few powerful questions here and there.

Writing this book has been an intentional, tender process of sharing stories from my life with the hope that they will inspire you to explore new depths within yourself.

So, as we commence on this auspicious day, may Saraswati, the Hindu goddess of music and wisdom, connect my heart to yours through my pen and these pages.

Hopefully, by the end of our year together, we will all be a little closer to dwelling in eternity and abiding in infinity!

January 2

◇ THE PRIVILEGE OF A LIFETIME ◇

I was experiencing career burnout when I came across a powerful quote by Carl Jung: "The privilege of a lifetime is to become who you truly are."

All of a sudden, my mission was as clear as day: to become who I truly am and help others do the same.

Jung's quote echoes a similar sentiment put forth by Marcus Aurelius almost two thousand years ago:

When you arise in the morning, think of what a precious privilege it is to be alive—to breathe, to think, to enjoy, to love.

Let's take a page from Jung and Aurelius over our year together.

Let's enjoy the privilege of being alive.

And, one day at a time, let's become who we truly are.

January 3
◇ WHAT ARE YOU WILLING TO LIVE AND DIE FOR? ◇

I believe that the best way to live life is by connecting to our truest self which resides deep below the thoughts and emotions of everyday life.

Our true self doesn't get swept away by the drama of current events because our true self remembers that *stars died* so we can be here today in conscious form.

When we connect with our most authentic self, we can get clear on our purpose.

Or, as the philosopher Søren Kirkegaard once wrote:

What I really need is to get clear about what I must do, not what I must know, except insofar as knowledge must precede every act. What matters is to find a purpose, to see what it really is that God wills that I shall do... to find the idea for which I am willing to live and die.

Living authentically and helping others do the same is the idea for which I am willing to live and die.

That's my 'why.'

But what is it that *you* are willing to live and die for?

January 4

◇ ONE FOOT IN REALITY, THE OTHER IN ETERNITY ◇

When we were in the process of designing a cover for this book, I completely missed the obvious.

Ironically, in a book that relies heavily on metaphors to depict inner experiences, I was oblivious that the book's cover image depicts the journey to becoming who you truly are!

A friend pointed out that in the cover photo, the sheep represent being well-grounded in the earth, going about their daily lives with their hooves firmly planted in reality.

Yet, simultaneously, the herd of sheep is right up against a magnificent backdrop of mountains that draw us upward to consider what's beyond.

Those infinite rocks inspire us to ask:

What are our lives all about?

How did we come here from above?

And how in the world do we keep one foot grounded in reality *and* remember the infinite and eternal that lies beyond the other side of the mountain?

Upon discussing those questions at length, my friend and I concluded that if it must be quite alright to be a sheep!

January 5

◇ LIFE IS HARD ◇

One of the greatest hooks in all of literature is the first three words of M. Scott Peck's classic book *The Road Less Traveled*: "Life is hard."

Peck goes on to say that once we accept that life is supposed to be hard, it gets a whole lot easier!

There seem to be two kinds of hardships in life.

The first kind of difficulty arises when we struggle against reality, creating calamity on top of the root problem.

A second, more honest type of adversity is the necessary pain that moves us forward toward a life and career worth having.

This 'honest hardship' is a deep inner journey where we go within and choose the legitimate pain of growth over the self-induced pain of staying stuck.

The deep inner journey is hard.

But I'd rather move forward than stay stuck.

I'd rather unlock the door to the promised land of the spiritual world than live as a beggar at the gate.

Life is hard.

Which 'hard' will you choose?

January 6

◇ MY FRIEND IN PARIS ◇

O n a beautiful January day in my early adulthood, serendipity introduced me to my Friend in Paris, who is one of the most celebrated figures in classical music.

After our meeting, I persisted in writing to him on a weekly basis because I knew that this special man had access to information that I craved.

We initially discussed the music of his *maître,* a mystical composer named Olivier Messiaen, but unbeknownst to me at the time, we were talking about so much more than music. We were talking about spirituality and about *life!*

Messiaen helped my Friend in Paris understand that the best parts of life are impossible to put into words.

Subsequently, my Friend helped me experience that the spiritual realm is underlying all we do and all we are, and all we have to do to gain access to the spiritual realm is to relax.

Now, that might sound simple, but it took me years of false starts to figure out what he was talking about.

However, once I got the jist of his idea, my life transformed, and I can't wait to share more installments about my Friend in Paris over the course of our year together!

January 7
◊ THE OTHER SIDE OF THE MOUNTAIN ◊

The cover of this book has a fog-capped mountain. While the effect is eerily exquisite in its otherworldliness, it also obscures part of the mountain.

Likewise, in each of us, there are parts of our inner mountain that we can't see, but we must explore what is hidden by the fog if we want to become who we truly are.

Acting in faith, we ignore internal, fearful chatter about the unknown landscape behind the fog.

When we are ready, we relax into infinity and eternity, and as a result, the fog slowly clears and a new terrain starts to emerge.

Sometimes our fear—and subsequently, the fog—returns.

But slowly, we come to discover and love the new aspects of our pastoral landscape as a clearer, more vibrant and holistic picture of who we truly are begins to emerge.

January 8

◇ TO SEE GOD IN THE FORM OF A PERSON ◇

On an otherwise completely normal January day, a historic event happened.

That moment will never be found in the annals of any book but this one, but nevertheless, a chance meeting in a hallway changed my life forever for the better.

Zuzu (the name her granddaughters gave her) instantly struck me as full of dignity and nobility.

Even though I barely knew her name, I intuitively knew I could ask her a loaded question.

And before she answered, she looked at me, took a breath, and said, "Oh my, we've got a live one here!"

Needless to say, Zuzu and I hit it off immediately!

The way we met reminds me of these words from the movie *Serendipity:*

Life is not merely a series of meaningless accidents or coincidences, but rather, it's a tapestry of events that culminate in an exquisite, sublime plan. If we are to live life in harmony with the universe, we must all possess a powerful faith in what the ancients used to call 'fatum,' what we currently refer to as destiny.

Zuzu became a mentor and friend, always inspiring me to be Patrick in my fullest glory.

And in return, I gave her hope for the future.

Zuzu's favorite quote, by the English poet William Blake, illustrates the expansiveness and vision she embodied.

That quote goes something along the lines of:

To see infinity in an hour,
To see the universe in a grain of sand.

To sum up her impact on my life, I would add one more line to Blake's brilliance:

To see infinity in an hour,
To see the universe in a grain of sand
And to see God through the form of a person.

Similarly, perhaps on this otherwise ordinary January day, a historic event will happen in *your* life.

Maybe you'll even see God through the form of a person.

January 9
◇ THE LAND OF BEYOND ◇

L ike the serene sheep grazing on the cover of this book, your current station in life may be quite comfortable.

But what if there's something *even better* in store if you are willing to go into the Land of Beyond that is on the other side of the mountain?

The Norwegian explorer Fridtjof Nansen once wrote:

We all have a Land of Beyond to seek in our life—what more can we ask? Our part is to find the trail that leads to it. A long trail, a hard trail, maybe; but the call comes to us, and we have to go.

Rooted deep in the nature of every one of us is the spirit of adventure, the call of the wild—vibrating under all our actions, making life deeper and higher and nobler.

Seeking the Land of Beyond may require giving up current comforts for the sore muscles and the dirtiness of climbing the mountain.

But the result is a new version of ourselves that is deeper, nobler, and more authentic!

January 10

◊ OUR HIGH AMBASSADOR OF CUTENESS ◊

I have a special two-year-old neighbor, and in this book I'll refer to him as our High Ambassador of Cuteness!

Now, clearly, this little guy's hero is his father. He walks like his dad, talks like his dad, even smiles like his dad, and as a child, I was no different from our High Ambassador.

When my dad would come home from working out in cold North Carolina winters, he would step onto the brick hearth of the living room fireplace. I would eagerly leap up to join him and we would stand with our backsides to the fire, hands clasping our lower backs.

As children, it's natural for us to emulate our parents, but our High Ambassador is not his dad, nor am I my father.

On the contrary, we were all made to be our own person.

Now, the process of individuating is quite messy and we often have to live from the pain of ego for years until we feel secure enough to soften into wisdom, peace, and freedom.

But I hope our High Ambassador of Cuteness will grow up and do the difficult, abstract work of becoming his own individual person.

And in the process, I hope he transforms into an Honest Prince of Authenticity; in fact, I wish that for everyone.

January 11

◇ SURE PROVISIONS ◇

The spiritual journey of becoming who you truly are is not a linear process that you can chart like the stock exchange, because often, the events that we perceive as losses and setbacks ultimately give us depth and strength.

For instance, when I was twenty-four, I worked in a low-paying, low-autonomy job for a difficult boss.

It was unpleasant, to say the least.

If I was one of those sheep on the cover of this book, it was as if my boss was a wolf coming to eat me!

However, looking back ten years later, I can see how the pain of that situation drove me to work hard on myself.

And one of the many spiritual returns on investment I received from that dark night of my soul was reworking the 23rd Psalm of King David into my own words:

My Shepherd will supply all my needs. We will relax together in a beautiful meadow and drink from the still waters of peace.

Together we'll slowly walk down the unique path leading to the special meadow I am supposed to dwell in, with the herd I am meant to abide with.

Even when I am terrified of what my Shepherd is asking me to do, I will take comfort in the fact that He is right beside me. He will caress my head with love and I will remember that all is well.

This human life is but a sojourn. But while I'm here, I'll hang my hat in the pastures of the blue-green hills of Earth. And my Shepherd will walk alongside me while I graze, always supplying sure provisions.

So, as we go about our day, let's remember that even when the wind is howling and the wolves are chomping at our heels, the world is a safe and loving place.

And the reason that the world is a safe and loving place is that our steadfast Shepherd will always be right alongside us to comfort, heal, and sustain us.

January 12

◇ WHAT'S IT ALL ABOUT, ALFIE? ◇

Throughout my senior year of high school, I had an incredible English teacher.

A world traveler, three-time cancer survivor, and widow, she found meaning in helping us discover the wit of Mark Twain, the transcendentalism of Emerson and Thoreau, and the wisdom of the English poets.

However, one of the most profound lessons she ever taught us was through the movie *Alfie.*

The plot centers around a man in London who lives a self-centered life until he faces the consequences of his womanizing.

At one point, the protagonist looks directly into the camera and asks, "What's it all about? You know what I mean."

Well, I don't know if we'll ever know what it's all about.

But I *do* believe that asking these big questions brings richness and meaning to life.

So, as you go about your daily life, consider: "What's it all about, Alfie?"

January 13

◇ THE MIRACLE OF THIS MOMENT ◇

You can't buy this moment.

This twinkle in time comes from beyond our physical realm, and *this very moment* is a special occasion, a sacred gift, a nonrenewable resource.

This moment only happens once in all the universe and it's happening *right now!*

So, try to enjoy the miracle of each moment in this once-in-a-lifetime day.

Wear a comfortable old sweater.

Dab on a bit of your favorite perfume or cologne.

Savor every bite of a home-cooked meal.

And listen to the sounds of love that surround us: the song of the magpie, the coo of a baby, the purring of a cat, the aria of the bubbling brook.

In all places and in each moment, love is freely flowing to us.

And all we have to do to receive that love is to intentionally enter into the miracle of this moment using the gift of our five senses.

January 14

◇ PEACOCK SQUAWKS ◇

I have a friend in Bangalore, India who is a shining example of what it looks like to do one's part in recreating the world.

My friend stays up all night in order to work for a software company in the U.S.

Then, by day, he's a wonderful dad and searches out the ideal land for his future ashram community.

My friend feels he is 'doing it all wrong' because he goes to bed just as the peacocks are coming down from the trees to squawk their song of praise for a new day dawning.

But I told him that his guilt is absurd because his life makes absolute sense for him, and anyway, peacocks have beautiful illogicisms of their own.

Their beautiful feathers slow them down and make them more vulnerable to predators, yet those same feathers strike awe and jealousy throughout the rest of the animal kingdom!

Therefore, I think it's more than okay to go to sleep as the peacocks start to squawk if that's what it takes to become who we truly are.

January 15

◇ ANSWERS IN THE BACK OF THE BOOK ◇

Imagine that you suddenly find yourself floating in the atmosphere, able to simultaneously gaze at Bali and Fiji, Madagascar and the Galapagos.

After observing the planet from on high with glee, you kick back and float on your back to look at the moon, when suddenly, you are surprised to see a massive monolith floating in outer space.

Presiding over the entrance is a spiritual leader sitting in lotus position.

He tells you that if you go inside the temple, you will feel a sense of unity and belonging in a way you can't conceive of on Earth.

You will know why you exist in human form, what you will do with your life, and how you will die.

And, you can even skip all the painful parts of being human and simply reside in the monolith as your truest spiritual essence.

Would you decide to go in and 'skip to the answers in the back of the book?'

Or, would you politely decline and return to Earth in order to fully embrace the mystery of being alive?

January 16

◇ LIFE ON LIFE'S TERMS ◇

Every human being on this planet is born with great birthrights.

However, the world is not perfect, life is unfair, and no one gets all the benefits they are entitled to.

For example, some of us are born with physical limitations or inherit mental illness.

Others suffer the pain of cold and distant families.

There are those of us who are born into economic hardship.

The litany of ways life is unfair could go on for pages.

Now, each generation recreates the world, and many people set out to do this by trying to make life more fair.

However, I think that accepting life on life's terms is important before we set about changing it.

And in that process, we'll remember that life's not perfect and life is not fair.

But it's not half bad, either!

January 17

◇ LOSING AN OUNCE ◇

When we die, we lose less than an ounce of our body mass.

There is no concrete explanation for this phenomenon, but science's best guess is that this anomaly is the soul leaving the physical body.

And that makes sense to me, because our souls are the part of us that existed before we were born and continue after we die.

Indeed, one day our bodies will pass away, but our souls will continue to live, because the soul has no beginning nor end.

So, weighing in at less than an ounce, our souls are virtually unmeasurable by the standards of this world, yet they are larger than this realm and expand beyond this epoch.

Each soul contains a multitude of oceans and valleys and sunsets and rainforests and dew-filled meadows.

Our souls are who we truly are.

January 18
◇ POETS, PROPHETS, AND SAGES ◇

Some of us hold onto the supernatural, unseen realm of life with such tenacity that we end up having a hard time making a go of it in the reality of the material world.

It's as though we are one of the sheep on the cover of this book that found a way to the Truth on the other side of the mountain; yet, as we return to regale our herd with the miracles we witnessed, our story simply doesn't compute.

It can feel highly invalidating, as though we are the boy who sees the Emporer with no clothes on.

And after brass tacks cut us enough times, we are often tempted to withhold the insight that comes from vibrating on a unique frequency.

So, do we just keep our mouths shut and feel separated?

Absolutely not!

That's enough to drive a person insane.

A better way is to heed the words of Carl Jung, who wrote:

Loneliness does not come from having no people about one, but from being unable to communicate the things that seem important to oneself, or from holding certain views which others find inadmissible.

It's hard for the poets, prophets, and sages of the world to sit with the loneliness that comes from being misunderstood.

But if the poets, prophets, and sages can learn to articulate their acumen in a way that others can understand and apply, then slowly, little by little, the world becomes more wise, peaceful, and free.

And the secret is: we all have a little bit of a misunderstood poet, prophet, and sage within us!

January 19
◇ BABY DEER ◇

One fine Saturday afternoon many years ago, I was driving around Houston, running errands and minding my own business, when all of a sudden—out of nowhere—serendipity struck!

As I walked through the sliding glass doors of a local store, I felt a tiny soul drawing me in.

Apparently, the city's animal shelter had set up shop for the day, and there, in the very last cage, was the world's most adorable pup!

We locked eyes.

His intense, dark pupils of love drew me in, possessed me, and let me know that I was his whether I liked it or not.

Ollie latched onto me: I never had a choice in the matter.

A twelve-pound baby deer of a dog totally knocked me out with a sucker punch of love right to my gut!

He's been running the show ever since, and I wouldn't have it any other way!

The moral of this story is that *amazing things come to pass* when we answer the call of serendipity and allow new souls to come into our lives and change us forever for the better!

32

January 20

◊ UNFOUNDED FEARS ◊

There was a lot of internal confetti and fireworks the day Ollie and I adopted each other.

He was so happy to get out of the rescue shelter cage, and I was delighted to have a new friend!

However, the party subdued as we got home and I quickly realized Ollie was easily scared by loud noises and sudden movements.

Admittedly, I'm a bit of a bull in a china shop, but I knew that I could learn to slow down, be gentle, and earn Ollie's trust.

Resolved in my new task to nurture Ollie, I felt true joy that first night when my new co-pilot in life joined me in bed and curled up in my arm.

As I smiled myself to sleep, I knew that so many of Ollie's fears were unfounded because I was there to protect him and take care of him.

Then, I realized that God must look at me, and at all of us, the exact same way.

Because just as I hold Ollie in my hands, God has the whole world, each one of us, in His hands.

January 21

◊ OVERCOMING THE INSIDIOUS THREAD ◊

An anonymous text taught me that fear is an insidious thread that weaves through the fabric of human existence.

In fact, it seems as though our whole individual and collective identity is shot through with fear.

And of course it's this way when most people, throughout most of history, have existed in an instinctual stress-response mode that allowed us to survive as a species.

But there's also a subplot in history: the people who stopped to examine their fears and instead act with love.

These are the people—the one in a million—that get to become who they truly are.

These are the heroes that we write books and make movies about.

Therefore, take a moment to imagine your life in the form of a movie plot.

Is fear preventing you from facing a challenging hardship?

Or, are you relaxing into love so that you can overcome the inevitable obstacles of life, and subsequently, progress into who you truly are?

January 22
◇ OIL AND WATER ◇

I am relatively sure that my Best Friend and I could set an all-time world record for the two people who are most different from each other!

He is from the East, I am from the West.

He is community-oriented, I am staunchly individualist.

He values security, I value creativity.

He is peaceful, I desire the dizzying anxiety of freedom.

He is the brakes, I am the gas pedal.

He is the pace horse, and I am the racehorse.

He is oil, I am water.

My Best Friend and I seem too different to mix, and yet we do, because I need his structure, order, and logic and he needs my creativity, emotional acuity, and intuition.

They say that you're not supposed to need anyone else to complete you; that you should be whole on your own.

But when my Best Friend and I synthesize the best parts of ourselves, the sum is much greater than the parts.

Because in the end, oil and water don't actually mix, but they *do* create beautiful, mesmerizing dispersions!

January 23
◇ MYTHS OR MEASUREMENTS? ◇

Since the Age of Enlightenment, humanity's emphasis on reason, logic, and the scientific method has led to truly remarkable exploration and discovery.

And while science is wonderful, an unintended consequence of innovation is that the world today tends to value material reductionism over spiritual expansiveness.

By material reductionism, I mean the mindset that if you can't measure something, then it doesn't exist.

And by spiritual expansiveness, I mean trusting in the power of unseen benevolent forces that can't be seen or put into words, yet are all around us, all the time.

For example, when we are in the mindset of material reductionism, we look at the cover of this book and quantify green grass, a big rock, sheep, and clouds. We see all the technical elements, yet completely miss the big picture.

However, through spiritual expansiveness, we see a magical landscape that invites us into eternity and infinity.

What I'm trying to say is that when we believe in the power of myth, we come to see that anything and everything—even the cover of a book—can contain deep Truth.

January 24

◊ PRETTY SOON, THIS OLD HEART OF MINE... ◊

Pretty soon, this old heart of mine, this heart that feels so deeply, that loves so fully, will stop beating.

My chest will cease to tighten during times of anxiety and ecstasy.

My eyes will no longer witness the majesty of the Oslo fjord, behold the eternal sunlight of Norwegian summers, or regard the love and care in my loved one's eyes.

Pretty soon, these hands and fingers of mine, which have been my breadwinners, will finally retire.

My belly will no longer be comforted by oatmeal or overjoyed by homemade desserts shared with friends.

My throat will cease to swallow thirst-quenching water on a hot summer's day.

And my skin will no longer absorb cleansing showers or essential oils.

Therefore, while I'm still here and this old heart of mine is still beating, I am resolving to delight each of my five senses in some way every single day.

After all, who knows if we get to keep our senses once we leave our human form?

January 25

◇ NEVER LET GO ◇

L ast night, the classic film *Titanic* came on cable television, and my Best Friend and I decided to watch a couple of scenes before making dinner.

The male protagonist, Jack, is a penniless yet free-spirited kind of guy, and at one point he says:

I love waking up in the morning not knowing what's going to happen or who I'm going to meet, where I'm going to wind up. Just the other night I was sleeping under a bridge and now here I am on the grandest ship in the world having champagne with you fine people.

Jack teaches the female protagonist, Rose, to be free: to think for herself and make the life *she* wants rather than marrying into money and high society.

Now, we can *all* relate to Rose in some way; we all have aspects of our life where we feel powerless.

But we don't need a Jack; we can save ourselves.

We just have to find the spark of authenticity within and never let go.

January 26

◇ FRANTIC DASHING ◇

A typical day's stress for many people in the world begins with leaping out of bed, dashing out the door without taking the time to have a decent breakfast, then slogging through backlogged rush hour traffic.

Already embattled from the morning commute, they frenetically blast through an intense and urgent workday, often sacrificing breaks and lunch.

Clocking out exhausted at the end of the day, they wearily merge back onto freeway traffic, unsure of exactly what they even spent the day doing.

Finally home, they fulfill the commitments of an overscheduled personal life until late in the evening.

Then, they go to sleep, wake up, rinse, and repeat.

In the words of a country song my sister and I loved to sing, this busy pace makes us feel like a dog on a toolbox in the back of a speeding truck, trying to hang on for dear life!

But I often wonder, how much of all this jostling and frantic dashing is devoted to the infinite and eternal?

I'm not saying we all need to quit attending to life's practicalities. I'm just saying that we all need to take time to relax into life and not just go as fast and hard as we can.

January 27

◇ SURVIVING REALITY ◇

D o you ever feel like you just can't do life, like reality is for the birds?

Well, life is hard for everyone, but it can be especially rough for those of us who hold on to our true selves and connect to the more mystical side of existence.

For example, Kirkegaard literally dropped dead when his inheritance ran out, because he realized he would have to put a hold on his writing and go make a living.

On the other hand, Jung had many of the same personality traits (and subsequent struggles) as Kirkegaard, but Jung fought for his life.

He found a way to balance what he called 'Jung 1' (the mystic) and 'Jung 2' (the scientist who was firmly planted in reality).

And by fighting for his life, Jung discovered many insights into the human condition that has helped millions of people, including himself.

How can you, also, find ways to honor the infinite, mystical side of your nature *and* develop a part of yourself that is rooted in surviving the practical realities of life?

January 28

◇ LIVING WITH AN OPEN HEART ◇

I really admire a man named Dwier Brown. As a movie actor, Dwier was Kevin Costner's character's father in *Field of Dreams*, and he deeply appreciates how his role in the classic movie has impacted countless lives.

Dwier once told me:

It's hard to live your life with an open heart: you're setting yourself up to be hurt and battered by the world. But that's no reason not to do it.

When you live with an open heart, you get to fully experience whatever it is that we're here to experience.

After all, it's 'just life' and this will all be over someday.

So you might as well go for it and have as much as you can and enjoy yourself as much as possible.

Indeed, I think that becoming who we truly are simply must involve living with an open heart while we fully enjoy whatever it is we're here to experience!

January 29

◇ WHAT YOU SEEK IS SEEKING YOU ◇

My friend in Bangalore (who goes to sleep as the peacocks wake up) once took an amazing picture of the starry firmament at Big Bend National Park in Texas.

He calls his masterpiece *What You Seek Is Seeking You* after a quote by the thirteenth-century mystic Rumi.

In the picture, my friend held up a lantern to the Milky Way to symbolize that he was seeking the infinite, the universe.

However, these days, my friend has decided to actively not seek.

In his words, "Seeking has led me nowhere. It's like putting the cart before the horse. So these days, I try to just be right here, right now, in this moment."

For years my, friend was seeking the universe.

In my early adulthood, I sought career advancement.

And Ollie seeks belly rubs and treats!

But what would it be like if we all dropped our illusions and quit seeking?

It's an interesting question to explore, because in the end, perhaps 'not seeking' contains the freedom to become who we truly are.

January 30

◇ THE WORLD IS A LOOKING-GLASS ◇

The way we look at the world shapes what we see.

If we look at the world with judgment, our fears are reinforced.

If we look at the world with curiosity, our options expand.

As William Makepeace Thackeray wrote in his classic novel *Vanity Fair:*

The world is a looking-glass, and gives back to every man the reflection of his own face. Frown at it, and it will in turn look sourly upon you; laugh at it and with it, and it is a jolly kind companion; and so let all young persons take their choice.

So, the world is a looking glass, and the way you view it shapes what you will see.

Which choice will you take?

January 31
◇ GOD IS LOVE ◇

My Friend in Paris often reminds me that God *is* love. Therefore, anything that is judgmental, angry, or fear-based is *not* of God.

And anything that is peaceful, joyful, trustworthy, safe, and harmonious *is* of God.

When we remember that God is love, we feel safe to become who we are.

We also feel safe enough to allow others to be who they are, even when that is very different from us.

And of course we feel safe, because what could be more comfortable than knowing we have a benevolent shepherd watching over us as we graze in the valley of infinity and eternity?

◇ FEBRUARY ◇

February 1
◇ THE DIZZYING ANXIETY OF FREEDOM ◇

Imagine that you are a sheep on the cover of this book and you suddenly find yourself transported from the valley up to the snow-capped peak of the fog-covered mountain.

With your hooves on the edge of the granite slab, you look down to the valley below, and you become nauseous and almost faint from your fear of heights.

Well, Kirkegaard believed that this gut reaction can also be activated when we realize how many ways there are to build a life, and he called this phenomenon "the dizzying anxiety of freedom."

If Kirkegaard is correct, then apparently, looking within yourself to see the boundlessness of possibilities you are capable of is much like standing at the edge of a mountain and looking down into the valley below.

So, what's the solution for this dizzying anxiety?

Well, most people find a cure in stepping away from the ledge and giving up freedom in exchange for security.

But I'd rather choose to believe that there is a benevolent shepherd watching over us as we push the limits of possibility and fully embrace the dizzying anxiety of freedom!

February 2

◇ WORK DOES NOT MAKE FREE ◇

When Zuzu visited Auschwitz, she was deeply impacted by three words at the entrance to the camp: *Arbeit macht frei,* which means 'work makes free.'

As Zuzu came face to face with this false promise, her palms started sweating and her heart began to palpitate.

She stood convicted.

Of course, Zuzu never suffered the horrors of Auschwitz.

But she had, up to that point, unknowingly lived her life programmed with the idea that salvation comes from work.

All of a sudden, Zuzu realized that everyone she knew operated under the assumption that life is a race and that one's output of work indicates how fast or slow they ran.

However, as she stood in front of Auschwitz, Zuzu had an instant spiritual experience like Moses in front of the burning bush. She realized that the promise of work leading to freedom was an illusion.

So, she found a new way to live.

She decided that rather than seeing life as a race to be run, she would view it as a journey to participate in.

With her new mindset, she still had goals. But she started to relax and enjoy each step in her life's journey rather than tying her identity solely to her career.

Likewise, as you go about your day, remember that you don't need salvation through work.

Work does not make free.

February 3

◇ TO DREAM THE IMPOSSIBLE DREAM ◇

Many of my childhood Sunday afternoons were spent cuddling up with my mom as we watched professional ice skating on television, happily allowing the balletic graces of the sport to enthrall us.

I still love figure skating, and over the last few years, a very special skater named Jason Brown has redefined the artistic side of his sport. He is twice as old as most of his competitors, and that added life experience has matured him into a true artist.

Jason recently skated to "The Impossible Dream" from *Man of La* Mancha, and his interpretation of the music embodied the courageous hero's journey I have tried to write about in this book.

Chill bumps cropped up all over my body as I watched him bring the inspirational text of the song to life:

To dream the impossible dream
to fight the unbeatable foe
To bear with unbearable sorrow
and to run where the brave dare not go.

To right the unrightable wrong
    and to love pure and chaste from afar
To try when your arms are too weary
    to reach the unreachable star.

This is my quest, to follow that star
    no matter how hopeless, no matter how far
To fight for the right, without question or pause
To be willing to march into hell
    for that heavenly cause.

And I know if I'll only be true to this glorious quest
That my heart will lie peaceful and calm
    when I'm laid to my rest.

And the world will be better for this
    that one man scorned and covered with scars
Still strove with his last ounce of courage
    to the unreachable star.

Indeed, let's spend our day today dreaming impossible dreams and reaching impossible stars!

February 4
◇ A FLOUNDER, THE MOON, AND THE MIND ◇

Many of my childhood weekends were spent with my family on the coast of North Carolina, and we loved to take midnight boat rides out into the waterway!

I especially loved when full moons illuminated life below the water's surface.

I felt so lucky to view the serene underworld where seaweed lazily danced with the current, crabs sauntered around, and flounders camouflaged themselves by resting in quietude on the seabed.

Unfortunately, one night our harmless boat got too close to a flounder and he reacted in fear by darting away. In the process, he kicked up a swirl of mud in his wake, as though the entire sea was his personal snow globe to shake up.

Like that flounder, our mind often tells us to act in fear, even when the people we perceive as dangerous have no intention of hurting us. And the fear-based reaction results in a confusing, muddy mess for ourselves and others.

A better strategy is to trust that the world is a safe and loving place and that all we need to do is rest in the seabed, abiding in our true nature, so that the entire landscape can be appreciated in all its moonlit glory!

February 5

◇ TRUSTING THE SHEPHERD ◇

L ike the sheep on the cover of this book, I can be mighty stubborn at times.

As a result, I have firsthand experience with the fact that there is a *stark* contrast between humbly submitting to God's herd versus willfully trying to steer life in my own direction.

Now, when I defiantly try to be my own shepherd, I get to feel proud and self-reliant, but the problem is that my best thinking tangles me up in a briar patch!

So, even though it means relinquishing the proclivity to just wander off whenever I want, I have learned from hard-earned experience to steer clear of briar patches and do things God's way.

And as I tune in to the instructions of the Shepherd and quit wandering off into danger, I feel a deep sense of wisdom, peace, and freedom.

After all, there's no better guide to trust in this life than the Shepherd of Truth who created us all.

February 6

◊ INTRINSIC MOTIVATION ◊

The prevailing consensus seems to be that in order to change and grow, we need to try harder, be more motivated, and 'do better.'

But I disagree.

I believe people need to find intrinsic motivation to change based on their vision of what it means to live with wisdom, peace, and freedom.

Personally, my greatest intrinsic motivation is my unborn child who is waiting to come down to *terra firma* and be held in my arms.

And for the last few years, this desire has motivated me to develop healthier habits around food, career, and emotions that would not have happened otherwise.

So, the source of our motivation matters.

External motivation inevitably burns out, but intrinsic motivation is inspired by the spiritual realm that is trying to shepherd us into wisdom, peace, and freedom.

So, are you forcing yourself to 'improve?'

Or, are you living into a compelling, infinite vision that elevates you into who you truly are and why you're here in this place and this time?

February 7
◇ THE NOBLE WORK OF PLAY ◇

We live in a world of frantic dashing, and in our busy society, we could all stand to slow down and put away our to-do lists.

It often seems counterintuitive to stop 'doing' with the mind and just 'be' with the heart, but taking time to relax and enjoy life is crucial to becoming who you truly are.

Luckily for me, the natural elements here in Norway have taught me to follow a slower, healthier pace.

It's stark and dark from December to March. During that time, my heart is nourished by knitting blankets for Ollie, going to winter markets, reading poetry, and other acts of quasi-hibernation.

Then, when the midnight sun of summer finally arrives, we truly appreciate our long-lost friend. It seems as though the whole neighborhood leaves work early each day to jump in the ice-cold fjord, camp out, and enjoy long walks!

Now, this may all seem like child's play, but I'm becoming more and more convinced that slowing down from the rat race and resting in childlike ease and grace is perhaps the most important work of all.

February 8
◇ THE HONEST GUYS ◇

No matter what difficulties comes my way, there is a deep place within me where peace, quiet, and stillness reside.

When I access that inner sanctum, it is as though I morph into one of the sheep in the idyllic meadow on the cover of this book.

And one of my favorite ways to 'turn into a sheep' is to put on a meditation tape by *The Honest Guys*, and during this most restful part of my daily routine, it feels as though the narrator is the very voice of love.

Now, I must admit that my perception of *The Honest Guys* is a bit idealized, but they simply see themselves as normal people going about the business of being human.

In fact, Siân Lloyd-Pennell, who writes the meditation scripts for *The Honest Guys*, once told me the intention behind their work.

She said:

We just want to help. When you're thinking of helping other people, you're not thinking of yourself, so that gives some space in what you create. It's just like somebody creating a nice meal with love for their family. We want to put out our content with the intention of serving others.

The Honest Guys have taught me that when we do the necessary internal work to become authentically human, we naturally gain an ability to serve others and recreate the world with a little more love than we found it.

February 9
◇ AGAINST THE GRAIN ◇

As Ollie and I walked toward the freedom of the fjord this morning, we had to make our way through well-dressed professionals converging from the bus stop to the nearby international office building.

It was a physical depiction of how a divergent, authentic life sometimes needs to walk in the opposite direction of others.

Of course, I myself was once one of those well-dressed professionals making a handsome salary, and my ego still longs for the perks of a 'traditional job.'

But in the end, I'd rather choose the dizzying anxiety of freedom over the frustration of taking someone else's path.

Now of course, sometimes it's hard to be different, and when I get insecure about how much I go against the grain, I remember these words by Bessie Stanley:

He has achieved success who has lived well,
laughed often, and loved much;

Who has enjoyed the trust of
pure women,

The respect of intelligent men and
the love of little children;

Who has filled his niche and accomplished his task;

Who has left the world better than he found it
whether by an improved poppy,
a perfect poem or a rescued soul;

Who has never lacked appreciation of Earth's beauty
or failed to express it;

Who has always looked for the best in others and
given them the best he had;

Whose life was an inspiration;
whose memory a benediction.

Plenty of people align beautifully with the grain, but sometimes, going with the grain isn't all it's cracked up to be. Sometimes, we have to create a new grain.

February 10

◇ TIME TAKES TIME ◇

The first time I tackled the complex process of baking croissants, I passed the beginning stages with flying colors! With each new step came more butter, more dough folds, and more waiting for the yeast to ferment. Finally, after almost twenty-four hours, it was time to bake my treat!

But frustratingly, after all the hours of mouth-watering anticipation, I just had to take the croissants out of the oven and taste them before they had time to rise properly!

It's a lesson I have had to learn over and over again: *time takes time.* It takes time for a croissant to rise into its flaky, tender glory. Likewise with us humans.

The spiritual teacher Henri Nouwen once wrote:

A waiting person is a patient person. The word patience means the willingness to stay where we are and live the situation out to the full in the belief that something hidden there will manifest itself to us.

Thus, the next time you feel irritable and want to rush, stay still and see what manifests. Maybe it will be a new part of your truest self. Or, at least, you won't ruin the croissants!

February 11
◇ WE'RE ALL A PIECE IN THE JIGSAW PUZZLE ◇

Each of the sheep on the cover of this book is positioned differently. Therefore, when they look up at the infinite rocks drawing them to the Truth beyond the fog, they all have a different viewpoint.

The same is true for us humans. We all see a piece of Truth that shapes our perspective on life, but none of us can see it from every dimension and angle.

None of us are able to see the whole picture (if we could, then we'd be God!).

Therefore, since we all see only a part of the whole, it's as though we are all jigsaw pieces in the puzzle of life!

Now, when our puzzle piece doesn't interlock with another, we often try to force an unintended interlocking.

We try to get others to see things our way, to fit them into our tabs and blanks.

But this strategy only distorts the Grand Picture.

However, by respecting differences—which means not trying to change others *and* not forcing yourself into a part of life you were never designed to fit into—the Grand Picture starts to emerge, which is much richer than the individual puzzle pieces could ever be on their own!

February 12

◇ GO YOUR OWN WAY ◇

A while back, a successful entrepreneur sent me his father's eulogy as an example of a self-actualized life.

I was touched by his essay and simply had to include it in this book:

My dad was the freest man I have ever known. Many people are held back by chains of fear: fear of the different, fear of the unknown, and the fear that comes from not trusting in yourself. But my dad was free to explore, create, and love.

My dad showed us that it is okay to be different. It takes guts and creativity to keep your sense of wonder in a world of people who want to settle for quick answers to life's big questions. My dad modeled what it meant to live free, to go your own way.

Like this man's father, we all naturally want to lead a life of special interest and value. However, it's rare to find a person who can become free enough to be different, to break the chains of fear, and to go their own way.

Will you be one of them?

February 13

◇ OLLIE'S PROS AND CONS ◇

Ollie's life in Houston was in many ways quite wonderful: he had his youth, a warm climate, and a stomach of steel that could withstand even the strangest foraging!

Here in Oslo, Ollie has new foes he never had to contend with in Houston: the evil snow of cold Tundra winters and stomach allergies that have come with aging.

On the other hand, Ollie's dad now works from home, and for a breed that tends to have an anxious attachment style, that's a major boon!

Ollie's pros and cons show me that as long as we're in this physical realm we call Earth, nothing will ever be perfect.

So, we can fight reality, or we can manage our expectations and accept both the pros *and* the cons of the people, places, and events in our lives.

February 14

◇ LOVE IS WHAT WE LIVE FOR ◇

Valentine's Day is a time set aside to shower a significant other with flowers and a nice meal out at a restaurant.

It's an external celebration of a very deep inner commitment two people have made to love one another.

But two of my favorite writers left us with insight into how to expand our definition of love past romance on a special occasion.

The Indian philosopher Krishnamurti said that love is something new, fresh, and innocent that can only be found in the present moment.

And M. Scott Peck wrote that "Love is the will to extend one's self for the purpose of nurturing one's own or another's spiritual growth."

Both of these quotes remind us that love takes many forms, only one of which is romantic. For example, love is present when we spend time with family, play and have fun, practice self-compassion, and volunteer, to name a few.

So, whether it is Valentine's Day or any other day of the year, there is nothing like feeling the fresh innocence of extending yourself for your own or another's growth.

Because love is what we live for.

February 15

◇ WHEN DOING NOTHING IS THE BEST SOMETHING ◇

According to the wisdom of Winnie the Pooh, sometimes doing nothing is the best something of all!

And in 2020, while the rest of the world was climbing up the walls of their homes in mandated lockdowns, Zuzu decided to treat her backyard like a Hundred-Acre Wood.

For example, during our weekly calls, she would regale me with delights of discovering doodlebugs with her granddaughters!

Zuzu's positive response to a difficult situation inspired me to similarly try and structure my own life into a Hundred-Acre Wood.

After all, I have everything I need and want right here in my little postage-stamp corner of the world (and also, the rat race will always be there if I decide to rejoin it!).

So for today, I think I'll just enjoy the serenity of my haven, because to reiterate our pal Winnie's wisdom, sometimes doing nothing is the best something of all.

And, if I may be so daring as to add do his sagacity: raiding the honey pot is almost *always* the second best thing of all!

February 16

◇ THE MAN WHO KNEW INFINITY ◇

I was taught as a child that math is a logical discipline, so imagine my surprise when I learned that philosophy and math have historically gone hand in hand!

Exhibit A: the great Indian mathematician Ramanujan.

Although Ramanujan had very little formal training in math, he used his intuition to crack 'unsolvable' problems.

Ramanujan drove his colleagues crazy because he could almost always find the right answer to problems that vexed the rest of the math community, but he couldn't prove how he arrived at the answer except to say something along the lines of, "An equation for me has no meaning unless it expresses a thought of God."

Well, I like that answer, and I think we would all do well to follow Ramanujan's crackerjack lead.

We can trust that our intuition, which is often called a 'gut feeling,' is telling us what is right and wrong for us, whether it makes sense to anyone else or not.

Ramanujan trusted his intuition as a way to access the unseen spiritual realm that is all of us, and as a result, we remember him as the man who knew infinity.

May we all come to know the same.

BECOMING WHO YOU TRULY ARE

February 17
◇ ONE ATOM, COLLOSAL DIFFERENCE ◇

Did you have a classmate in grade school that read poetry during math class?

Well, that kid was me!

In my adult life, I have finally learned that math is the poetry of the universe, and that physics asks big questions about our existence.

So, I've tried to make up for lost time regarding math and science, and I recently learned about antimatter.

When matter and antimatter meet, they annihilate each other and only energy remains.

However, in the first moments of the Big Bang, matter outweighed antimatter by just one molecule, and everything that exists today comes from that one particle!

That one atom, over billions of years, changed the course of the cosmos, the galaxy, the planet, *us*.

Thus, as *The Honest Guys* say, despite what you may have heard or what you may think, you are not insignificant in the long arc of the universal story.

Your authentic life changes the destiny of the universe, just as one tiny atom did billions of years ago.

An atom of matter 'mattered,' and so do you!

PATRICK PARKER

February 18

◇ TEMPEST IN A TEACUP ◇

I was having tea with Zuzu when she suddenly came up with a powerful metaphor of 'the tempest in a teacup.'

The tempest is the emotions and fears that result from being alive on this planet, and the teacup is you.

Fearful thoughts and emotions intensify the tempest as you realize that the tempest is within you, bigger than you, threatening to break you.

One way to deal with the tempest in your teacup is by trying to control the size of the tempest.

That's what most people do, to no avail.

You simply can't control the external factors of life that create the tempest.

So, instead of letting the tempest break you, you expand your teacup by remembering you are bigger than what you experience on a day-to-day basis.

At your deepest core, you are not a teacup that can be shattered by emotional tempests.

Rather, you are actually an ocean that the storm can dissipate in.

You are not a teacup. You are an ocean.

You just are.

February 19

◇ GENTLE NUDGES ◇

It is absolutely impossible to change others if they are not willing to do their own inner work.

Therefore, the only way to influence any situation in life is to become willing to do things differently yourself.

So, what is willingness?

Zuzu once told me that willingness is not a die-hard commitment so much as it is a gentle energy, a quiet voice.

She told me that what I become willing to do today may not be the overarching purpose of my life; it's not an absolute, but just a gentle nudge in the direction life naturally wants to flow.

When she was near the end of her life, Zuzu wrote to me:

I am willing to explore daily the will of God. I'm no longer going to say 'God, here's my plan, now bless it.' Rather, I'm going to consider: what would it be like to never do another thing unless it is the will of God?

Zuzu's conscious dedication to willingness allowed her to make the most of her last days in human form.

Likewise, what could willingness create in your life?

February 20

◇ LIFE IS AN ADVENTURE! ◇

My Friend in Paris often reminds me that life is an adventure!

Now, the word adventure usually conjures mental images of cowboys, astronauts, and adrenaline junkies.

But really, an adventure is any undertaking into unknown territory.

Let's take my Best Friend's nephew as an example: he recently came to visit for a few days, and at one point I said, "It wasn't so long ago that I met you at your parents' house in India over semolina. Did you imagine that ten months later, you'd be in graduate school in Wales and visiting your uncle and I in snowy Norway?"

He grinned from ear to ear as he realized just how fun his life was, and we talked late into the night about how much he had grown as a result of going into unknown territory.

By definition, an adventure transforms you as you have new experiences, but you don't have to jump out of a plane (or move to a new country like my friend's nephew) to have an adventure.

In fact, sometimes the best adventure of all is just sitting still and exploring the unknown territory within yourself!

February 21

◇ IT IS WELL WITH MY SOUL ◇

If there ever was a nineteenth-century Elijah, it must have been the Chicago lawyer Horatio Spafford.

Successful by all accounts, Spafford's character was put to the test when he lost his wealth (which was tied up in real estate) in the Chicago Fire of 1871. Soon after, his daughters tragically drowned when their passenger ship sank.

Penniless and bereft, Spafford immediately set out to reunite with his wife in Europe. And as his voyage approached the location where his daughters perished, he let healthy sadness flow through him, and as a result, penned one of the greatest lyrics of the Christian faith:

When peace, like a river, attendeth my way,
When sorrows like sea billows roll;
Whatever my lot, thou hast taught me to say,
It is well, it is well with my soul.

None of us know what tomorrow will bring.

None of us are in control of the winds of fate.

But no matter what comes, we can choose to say, "It is well with my soul."

February 22

◇ STARS, BLACK HOLES, AND ELVIS ◇

When I visited Graceland many years ago, I learned that Elvis never wanted fame as much as he wanted to make music and buy a house for his mama.

But unfortunately, he got vaporized by people who wanted to control him.

The authorities of the day wanted him to quit shaking those provocative hips, and when he refused, they drafted him into the U.S. Army and shipped him overseas.

Meanwhile, his manager saw him as a rainmaker to work like a hound dog in order to have a huge payday.

They say Elvis died of an overdose, but in my mind, it is as though he was a bright, shining star that got sucked into the orbit of a black hole (the black hole being the people who co-opted him when he simply wanted to share his voice with the world).

Now, even though the world is a safe and loving place, there are still black holes out there that want to overtake us and suck us into their vortex.

And the only real protection we have from those forces is to go on the inner journey so that we stay in the gravitational pull of wisdom, peace, and freedom.

February 23

◇ COZINESS ◇

Norwegian winters have a mystical, almost forlorn effect.

The sun has flown south for the winter with the geese, and the moon is on duty around the clock, even at midday.

The stars are spectacularly clear, yet at the street level, there is fog around the street lamps à la Harry Potter.

The ground is a sheet of ice threatening to topple you at any moment, and the cold wind instantly chaps your skin.

No wonder, then, that Norwegians have a special word to describe the feeling of arriving home after a venture into the bleak midwinter: *koselig.*

Koselig is similar in meaning to the English word 'cozy,' but it seems to have a deeper intimacy and warmth.

My favorite *koselig* routine after coming in from the cold is to take a hot shower, put on my pajamas, grab a cup of hot chocolate, and open up a good book. This experience soothes both my body and my soul in the coziest of ways!

I think we could all stand to take a little more time to warm our souls with coziness, no matter where in the world we live or what season it is.

Therefore, how will you give yourself coziness today?

February 24

◇ THE MARIANA TRENCH OF THE SOUL ◇

Our conscious mind, where we experience daily thoughts and feelings, is like the surface of the ocean.

Our unconscious mind, on the other hand, delves miles below the swells of everyday tides.

And at the farthest recesses of our unconscious self, we all have a Mariana Trench of the soul, where we shove painful emotions.

But no matter how hard we try to keep our feelings in the chasm, they will eventually float to the surface.

Emotions refuse to stay dormant in the abyss because they have something important to teach us, and we need to hear their messages in order to become who we truly are.

Most of us go to extraordinary measures like drinking, overspending, and overworking in order to keep these emotions suppressed. But the crux of the issue is that we can never run from the emotions in the Mariana Trench. After all, they are inside us, and we can't outrun ourselves!

A better way is to allow these emotions to rise to the surface, until, like magnificent humpback whales breaching the waters of the ocean, they surface and we can appreciate their beauty and significance.

February 25
◇ THE KEYSTONE TO FREEDOM ◇

If you ever get a chance to visit the French Gothic glory that is Chartres Cathedral, look upward to the keystones that connect the arches of the ceiling.

Keystones are the central supporting structures that lock ancient cathedrals together; they are the crucial elements that allow the sacred spaces to stand the test of time.

Likewise, the idea that I am not the benevolent shepherd, but rather just one sheep grazing in the landscape of life, is the central keystone that holds my life together.

The original architects of Chartres Cathedral trusted the keystones to hold resolute for centuries to come.

Likewise, we can trust that the benevolent shepherd that resides on the other side of the mountain will care for us as we graze in infinity and eternity.

February 26

◊ JAR OF TEARS ◊

Every couple of weeks, I catch up with a good friend of mine at a local cafe.

It's like my own personal episode of *Frasier*!

Therefore, I'll refer to her as my Coffee Companion.

My Coffee Companion traverses the connection between the mind, heart, and body like no one else I've ever met, and her calling in life makes me think of how Jesus performed healing miracles with the power of touch.

A while back I was having a lot of neck pain, and my Coffee Companion told me that stress often manifests as physical pain, so she took me to her office and tenderly touched very sensitive parts of my neck and shoulders.

And somehow, she got me crying like a baby.

Afterward, my Coffee Companion showed me a tiny chalice on her desk that was a replica of a tear jar from antiquity. She shared that the ancients deeply revered tears, and when they cried, they would hold the jar up to their eyes to honor and preserve the healing power of tears.

That day, I learned that it's okay to cry when we need to cry and our tears are not a sign of weakness. Rather, tears are healing and precious power, and they are to be revered.

February 27
◇ MUSINGS FROM MONTY PYTHON ◇

John Cleese of *Monty Python* fame once gave a brilliant speech on the 'two modes' of creative work and life, which he called the closed mode and the open mode.

The closed mode is a task-oriented mindset of getting things done and checking items off the to-do list; it's a serious energy that doesn't suffer fools.

The closed mode is valuable for task completion, but it is stressful because it is accompanied by the feeling that there's a lot to be done and not enough time to do it all in.

The open mode, on the other hand, is more childlike: it is the realm of rest and play which allows us to feel relaxed, expansive, and easygoing. The open mode naturally allows creativity to surface, whether it's a preschooler playing with modeling clay, a monk meditating, or newlyweds honeymooning in the Hebrides.

The grand finale of Cleese's speech was that we need the open mode to create dreams *and* we need the closed mode to bring those dreams into reality.

So, as you go about your day, how can you artfully balance these two modes in order to keep one foot in infinite eternity and the other foot grounded in reality?

February 28
◇ THE PURPLE THREAD ◇

Let's take a time machine back to first-century Rome! Upon arrival, we find ourselves in a throng of people dressed in white togas.

Yet one man has a purple thread running through his garment, a strand that is more valuable than gold.

The bearer of this unique toga just happens to be the philosopher Epictetus. He shares with us that purple represents felicity and mystery. This rare color can only be made from the dye of shellfish, and the small trim on his garment alone required the dye of ten thousand clams!

Before we leave, Epictetus also shares that the color purple is a metaphor for his life's journey when he declares:

I desire to be the purple thread, that small and shining part which makes the rest seem fair and beautiful...why should I attempt to be like the many, and if I am, then how shall I remain purple?

On the trip back home, you and I extend the metaphor when we agree that *everyone* has a purple thread within, and that we are *all* worth more than our weight in gold!

◇ MARCH ◇

March 1

◇ "DEAR MARCH, COME IN!" ◇

In the words of Emily Dickinson, "Dear March, come in!... trifles look so trivial, as soon as you have come."

A strange bird by society's standards, Dickinson confined herself to writing in her room and walking her dog Carlo in the woods near her home.

This aloneness allowed her to see the world in an altogether very unique way, facilitating an exploration of her inner 'undiscovered continent.'

Thus, when her poetry speaks of prisons, castles, and corridors (to name but a few symbols she uses) she is not describing physical objects, but rather, internal landmarks in her undiscovered continent.

Each poetic symbol helps her describe her authentic self residing underneath everyday thoughts and emotions.

I wonder, then, on this inaugural day of March, what it might be like if we welcomed March into the external landscape, and we welcomed *ourselves* to go into our inner landscape?

March 2
◇ THE TAILOR ◇

The day Zuzu died, the only coherent thought I had was "I have to buy a new suit for her memorial service."

Thus, I found myself standing paralyzed in grief at the entrance of the local tailor. Luckily, he was accustomed to bereft clients and knew just what to do.

With tender loving care, the tailor picked out a beautiful gray suit with a maroon shirt and a dark blue tie. As he took my measurements for alterations, we hardly spoke a word, yet our hearts were having a full-on conversation, and I am forever grateful for his help in completing one of the hardest errands of my life.

My feelings about this man are best said by Helen Keller:

I believe there are angels among us, sent down to us from somewhere up above. They come to you and me in our darkest hours, to show us how to live, to teach us how to give, to guide us with a light of love.

Thanking the tailor would have cheapened the moment.

But I will repay him now by asking: what has someone done for you that you really appreciate and will never forget?

March 3
◇ THE BOOK OF LIFE ◇

L ife is like writing a book.
The first twenty-odd years pull together the developmental building blocks needed to write a first draft.

Then, we edit our book of life with decisions regarding where to live, who to marry, and our vocation.

The story is continually revised as age takes us deeper into life through internal practices and external adventures.

Unfortunately, many lives become unfinished stories because people get stuck at an obstacle (like an addiction, or losing a loved one) and give up authoring their lives.

In these moments, we must summon the strength to overcome the obstacle we face by going within, because no matter what life throws our way, we can create an inner sanctum as serene as the cover of this book.

Externally, the pastoral landscape may turn into an Artic winter, but in our inner realm, the benevolent shepherd always provides sunlight, grass to graze, and water to drink.

Thus, when we go within to solve external obstacles, we turn the page of our life story and go just a little further than we've ever been before in the unique book of our life.

March 4

◊ THE SONG I CAME TO SING ◊

Just as birds narrate the dawn and dusk of each day through their warbles and trills, we sing the song of our lives through our actions.

But there is one big difference between us and birds.

I've never heard a magpie sing the murmuring dove's song or a raven hoot the owl's aria, yet so many of us don't sing our own song. We sing someone else's song, or worse yet, we don't sing at all.

As the great Indian poet Tagore once wrote:

The song I came to sing remains unsung to this day.
I have spent my days in stringing
and in unstringing my instrument.
The time has not come true,
The words have not been rightly set;
Only there is the agony of wishing in my heart...

You may be agonizing over whether or not to sing your own unique song. But birds have no such timidity, so follow their lead: perch on your limb, puff up your chest, open your beak, and *sing your song!*

March 5

◇ PARIS BAKERY TOUR! ◇

Two years into writing this book, I came down with a major case of writer's block. Realizing I needed to self-prescribe a cure, I booked a trip to Paris, a city that has inspired some of the greatest art of all time!

Upon arrival, I made record time to the awe-inspiring Stohrer Bakery. This historic *pâtisserie* was founded centuries ago by the pastry chef of King Louis XV, and to this day, it retains its original French classic interior design!

After spending way too much time ogling the beautiful desserts, I decided to purchase the most beautiful croissant I've ever seen in my life. And at the last moment, I also grabbed a mouth-watering *chocolate éclair caramel salé,* which is much easier to eat than it is to pronounce!

I was blown away by how the bakers brought together basic ingredients like flour, butter, and sugar to create world-class treats, and I realized that as an author, my 'basic ingredients' are personal experiences that I can share to illustrate spiritual principles. Writer's block cured!

Stohrer Bakery inspired my creativity, but inspiration is all around us, no matter where in the world we are.

How can you seek it today?

March 6
◇ THE MAGICAL FORCE OF CREATIVITY ◇

Creativity has inspired humans to meet the challenges of being alive on an uncertain planet since the inception of our species.

This magical force is fundamental to being human: to create is almost as instinctual as the fight or flight response.

Simply put, creativity is a thread that runs through the fabric of human existence.

Siân Lloyd-Pennell of *The Honest Guys* once told me that the secret ingredient to the magical force of creativity is time.

She said:

So many people have their nose to the grindstone. But if they just had more time, they would act, sculpt, become great cooks, or beautifully decorate their home.

So, as you go about your day, make sure to give yourself the time, space, and relaxation to allow an intuitive thought to springboard you into creative action!

After all, creativity helped our ancestors survive, and now it can help us become our truest, most actualized selves.

March 7

◇ TENDER CARESSES ◇

You are here.

You are alive.

You are breathing.

Touch your forehead with the spirit of your ancestors.

Contemplate what you looked like before your grandmother was born.

Gently touch your feet.

Softly rub your belly.

Delicately trace your fingers along your arms.

These tender caresses underscore that you are worthy of dignity and respect and that you appreciate and value yourself.

Just as a mother calms her child with soothing tones, we can honor who we truly are through tender caresses.

So, as you go about your day, remember:

You are here.

You are alive.

And you are breathing.

March 8
◇ CHANGED FOR GOOD ◇

I spent a good chunk of my high school years as a pianist for community musical theater productions, and the single most powerful scene that I encountered during those years was "For Good" from *Wicked*.

The power of friendship is beautifully illustrated through the duet's lyrics:

I've heard it said that people come into our lives
for a reason, bringing something we must learn.
And we are led to those who help us most to grow
if we let them and we help them in return.
Well, I don't know if I believe that's true
but I know I'm who I am today because I knew you.

Like a comet pulled from orbit as it passes the sun,
like a stream that meets a boulder halfway
through the wood.
Who can say if I've been changed for the better?
But because I knew you I have been changed for good.

Over the fifteen years since my high school days, I occasionally come back to this song, and as I hum the tune, a montage of people who have shaped my life plays like a movie reel in my mind's eye.

Now, in some ways, this book is like a written description of that movie reel: it's a collection of stories about people, places, and experiences that have changed me for good.

For example, my friendships with Zuzu and my Friend in Paris have allowed me to revel in all my creative glory; their companionship has changed me as though I am a comet pulled from orbit as it passes the sun.

And the gentle support I receive from my Best Friend, Ollie, and my Coffee Companion is like the stream that meets the boulder halfway through the wood.

I've received so much love from these special friends I write about, and hopefully, you have your own friendships that you could fill up an entire book with!

So, as you go about your day, consider: who are the people that, simply by virtue of being your friend, have changed you *for good*?

March 9

◇ HOLI HAPPINESS ◇

Holi is one of the most important festivals in the Hindu faith and it celebrates the arrival of spring and the blossoming of love. People celebrate it by meeting with friends and family and laughing as they playfully throw colored powder at one another!

This past weekend, my Best Friend and I participated in a Holi festival at a nearby temple. As an American in Norway attending an Indian festival, I was afraid I would feel out of place. But that was all nonsense.

Everyone welcomed me with open arms and we smiled, laughed, and danced to the live music. My senses were sucker-punched as we threw powdered color all over each other, sending my tiny brain into a delirium of happiness!

And somehow, as the powder covered our clothes as though we were a collective Jackson Pollock painting, the God in each of us emerged.

The happiness of Holi brought a feeling of buoyant lightness that allowed me to open up and expand into new frontiers of curiosity and creativity.

Likewise, how can you create your own mini-festival of happiness in your daily life today?

March 10

◇ ROPING THE WIND ◇

Trying to get to the heart of purpose is impossible. It's like trying to rope the wind.

And although purpose is impossible to quantify, it's obvious that purpose drives us.

Otherwise, why would humans stand on their tippy toes at the ballet, flip onto a four-inch-wide piece of wood at the Olympics, fling themselves out of perfectly good airplanes, walk a tightrope over waterfalls, launch a rocket toward the moon, or spend years writing a book without any guarantee it will ever be read?

I don't think any of us truly understand why we're passionate about the things that matter to us, but the passion and purpose are there for a reason!

So, trust that your heart's desires are from God, because by following your purpose, you are recreating the world in a way that helps the entire universe raise its consciousness.

And, as a postscript: who am I to say that it's not possible to rope the wind after all?!

March 11

◇ THE HUMAN ZOO ◇

As you travel the journey of your life, you will undoubtedly meet people who will tell you that you are wrong to think, feel, and believe as you do.

Do not listen to them!

People will subtly—and sometimes not so subtly—tell you to blend in and camouflage yourself, to be a chameleon.

Do not listen to them!

Instead, believe that you are worthy, exactly as you are.

You have unique strengths and talents.

You have a special way of understanding and navigating the world that you can share with others as you choose.

And, you deserve to embrace the preferences you have; they are there for a reason.

So go ahead and cherish the one-of-a-kind details about yourself.

After all, we would never go to a zoo or an aquarium if all the animals looked and acted the same way; that would be boring!

Just like those animals, we are all unrepeatable miracles.

So let's live from our truest selves, in all our fullest glory!

March 12

◇ NATIONAL TREASURE ◇

A few nights ago, I was nostalgic for yesteryear memories, so I rewatched *National Treasure*.

The protagonist of the story, Ben Gates, tries to solve a mystery the Founding Fathers of the United States left on the back of the Declaration of Independence.

According to legend, the map should lead to unsearchable riches. But at the low point of the movie, the treasure hunters lose hope as their efforts lead to an empty room.

And at that point, Ben's father says:

This room is real, Ben. And that means the treasure is real. We're in the company of some of the most brilliant minds in history because you found what they left behind for us to find, and understood the meaning of it.

Likewise, we must remember that we are in the same room as the most brilliant minds in history, and we call that 'room' Planet Earth!

Our ancestors have left us clues to unfathomable treasure if we take the time to understand their wisdom.

And the treasure is to become who we truly are.

March 13
◇ WAKING UP TO THE BIRDS SINGING ◇

The spiritual writer Anthony de Mello once said that rather than putting slippers on to protect our feet, we want the whole world to carpet itself!

But these days, I think I put my slippers on more often.

Case in point: this morning I happily began my day to the tune of my friend Mr. Magpie. On the other hand, years ago, the murmur of Dr. Dove on the roof of my Houston apartment simply embroiled me.

The birds sang then and they sing now. The only difference is my perspective. Rather than being annoyed, I am in awe. The birds wake me up each day, and they've also woken me up to beauty.

As de Mello went on to write:

Spirituality means waking up. Most people, even though they don't know it, are asleep. They're born asleep, they live asleep...they die in their sleep without ever waking up. They never understand the loveliness and the beauty of this thing that we call human existence.

Thank you, Mr. Magpie and Dr. Dove, for waking me up.

March 14

◇ LITTLE IS MUCH ◇

I grew up in rural North Carolina, where southern gospel music is as common as oxygen, and many childhood weekends were spent at outdoor 'sings,' where we'd picnic while male quartets and a pianist, all in matching suits, sang about heaven and sinners saved by grace.

While I have not carried all those ideas into adulthood, one of my favorite lyrics remains as relevant today as it did a continent and a lifetime ago:

In the harvest field now ripened,
  there's a work for all to do;
Hark, the Master's voice is calling,
  to the harvest calling you.
Does the place you're called to labor
  seem so small and little known?
It is great if God is in it, and He'll not forget His own.

No matter how small and little-known your vocation is, remember, that as the lyrics go on to state, "Little is much, when God is in it!

March 15

◊ COMPASSIONATE ACCOUNTABILITY ◊

One day when I was six years old, I rode my black Mongoose bike to my Uncle Chris's auto repair shop. I was interrupting his day but he didn't mind; after all, I was flaunting my childhood cuteness in full glory!

Uncle Chris never had children of his own, so he had plenty of love to give his nieces and nephews, and on this particular morning, I was so excited to spend time with him that I accidentally spilled the juice box he gave me.

Oops!

All of a sudden, my happiness turned into fear of reprimand, but rather than getting upset at me, Uncle Chris smiled and handed me a couple of paper towels.

He gently said, "I think you need to clean it up. Here, let me show you how. Let's do it together."

When we finished, I gave him a hug, hopped on my bike, and went on my merry way!

Uncle Chris didn't let me off the hook, but he also didn't punish me.

Thirty years later, that memory still serves as a powerful reminder of what happens when we combine compassion with accountability.

March 16

◇ THE MARVELOUS MUDPUDDLE ◇

This morning, Ollie and I groaned at the cold rain awaiting us outside. We both wanted to stay abiding in the eternity of sleep, but the requisites of reality (also known as Ollie's bladder!) beckoned.

And as Ollie did his usual pee 'n play ritual, I *saw a mud puddle*. I didn't pass it by, and I didn't turn it into a metaphor or apply some deeper meaning to it.

I just saw it.

I saw cigarette butts lining a filthy, stick-laden mudpuddle interrupted by footprints.

Then, I watched magical droplets of water fall from the sky; some of the beads rebounded from the surface, while others expanded gorgeous ripples.

Noticing this marvelous mudpuddle was an absolute delight, served *gratis* from the Universe, and today, I hope that you also *really see* the ordinary, oft-overlooked parts of life.

Whether it's a mudpuddle, a stick floating in the river, or leaves flying in the wind, marvelous delights are all around.

We just need to take notice!

March 17

◊ QUASI-MEDITATION ◊

I used to think that meditation was elitist.
In my mind's eye, I pictured a snobby, well-to-do person in a luxurious studio, sitting cross-legged in designer tights on a custom-made cushion.

Needless to say, I had contempt prior to investigation!

Unfortunately, my prejudice prevented the peace that comes from contemplation.

However, I became more open to meditation when I read how the brilliant poet Mary Oliver 'meditates, sort of.'

In her collection of poetry entitled *Blue Horses,* she writes:

I just lay down while distance and time
reveal their true attitudes.
They never heard of me
and never will or never need to.

Of course I wake up finally thinking
how wonderful to be who I am,
made out of earth and water,
my own thoughts,
my own fingerprints,
all that glorious temporary stuff.

If you're like I used to be and you disdain the concept of meditation, then consider trying Mary Oliver's version.

Just lay down, close your eyes, and reflect on what distance and time are revealing to you.

And, take time to remember how wonderful it is to be *you,* experiencing all this glorious temporary stuff!

March 18
◊ GUILT TAX ◊

Once upon a time, I was camping in the backwoods of Louisiana when my path crossed with a couple my age.

Over campfire tacos and Topo Chicos, one of my momentary companions shared that he had launched a start-up software company that had become a cash cow.

But he had only begun to tell me the story of his success when his embarrassed girlfriend quickly interjected with her plans to give away the vast majority of his new wealth.

His body posture visibly tightened as her philanthropic vision turned the joy of his work accomplishments into guilt-ridden resignation.

On the long drive back to Houston, I thought long and hard about the interaction, and here's what I came up with.

I think that wanting to help other people is really honorable, but, I think it is *dishonorable* to give money away because you're trying to appease someone who has turned your accomplishment into a burden.

If we can give to others in an anonymous, guilt-free way, then good on us.

If we can't, better we just skip the guilt tax altogether and keep the money.

March 19

◇ FLOATING UNDER THE MOON ◇

Moving to Houston was one of the most exciting decisions of my life, but the sights and sounds of a major city were initially overwhelming.

So, upon making my first friend, I packed up the car and we went camping on Galveston Beach to get away for the weekend.

As we floated on our backs in the Gulf Coast under a full moon, it somehow felt as though we were the only two humans in the entire universe.

We marveled at the vastness of the sky, the empty darkness of the ocean, and how they melded together.

We felt so teeny tiny in comparison!

We didn't know it, but we were talking in metaphor about how life is less scary when you have a friend by your side.

Likewise, as we go about our year together, consider this book as a friend by your side as *you* float under the moon.

I hope that the time we spend together will help you get out of fear's grip and instead relax into wisdom, peace, and freedom so that you can inevitably contribute your unique gift to the recreation of the world!

March 20

◇ THE GRATITUDE SPRINGBOARD ◇

I recently heard a cancer researcher named Dr. Roland Griffiths speak about coming to terms with his own personal diagnosis.

Like all terminal patients, Dr. Griffiths and his wife went through anxiety, depression, resentment, and even good old-fashioned denial.

But none of those struck him as pleasant places to reside, so he decided to quit wasting his remaining time on Earth, and instead, he began to use the knowledge of his imminent passing as a springboard for gratitude.

Dr. Griffiths spoke with the rhetoric of a poet when he shared:

[The fact that life is a precious gift] is something we all know. It's something really remarkable that we find ourselves as these highly evolved, sentient creatures, walking the Earth's surface, talking, in the middle of culture.

But what's going on here? What's the backstory behind this? How do we account for this?

For me, when we contemplate those questions, gratitude comes up.

So, my choice became to deeply practice gratitude and use the so-called 'problems' that arise from a cancer diagnosis...in a way that reflects back a reminder that each moment is precious. Each moment is unretrievable. And that's what this diagnosis has been like for me. It's a gift, it's a blessing.

If a dying man can give thanks for his cancer diagnosis, then surely the rest of us have no excuse to balk at exercising gratitude.

So, let's take inspiration from Dr. Griffith's life, and, as he so eloquently said, let's springboard into gratitude and remember that life is a precious gift.

March 21

◇ OLLIE'S MASTERCLASS ◇

Ollie knows not a stranger, whether puppy or person! He prances everywhere he goes and he is not ashamed to dance on his hind legs in exchange for pats on the head and belly rubs.

In response to his friendliness, Ollie has a large following of devoted neighbors who give him lots of tender loving care.

Indeed, in *How to Win Friends and Influence People,* Dale Carnegie writes:

Why not study the technique of the greatest winner of friends the world has ever known? Who is he? You may meet him tomorrow coming down the street. When you get within ten feet of him, he will begin to wag his tail. If you stop and pat him, he will almost jump out of his skin to show you how much he likes you.

Let's all take a masterclass from Ollie.

Let's show others how much we like them.

And, let's stand out for our ability to be kind and loving toward all, just like Ollie!

March 22

◇ THE TWO ROCKS ON MY DESK ◇

At the suggestion of my Coffee Companion, I keep two stones on my work desk. One is ordinary and the other is decorated with an Indian mandala.

The 'plain rock' represents reality: details, planning, and family responsibilities.

The 'creative rock' represents vision, expansion, infinity, and eternity.

Each day before I begin work, I put the plain rock in my left hand and the creative rock in my right. I slowly move my hands up and down as though the rocks are on a fulcrum. The equal weight of the rocks reminds me to strive for a balance of creative *and* practical energy throughout my day.

As I work on various projects, I pull a rock forward that represents the energy behind what I'm doing. The goal is for both rocks to spend equal time in the foreground by the end of the day.

This measuring system allows me to balance the two energies of reality and eternity as I work toward recreating the world with wisdom, peace, and freedom.

As you go about your day, consider how you, also, can keep a healthy balance between eternity and reality.

March 23

◇ A CONFEDERATE SOLDIER'S PRAYER ◇

I grew up near a Civil War site called Bentonville Battleground, where Union and Confederate troops fought for four bloody days in 1865.

Every March, my parents took me to reenactments of the battle, which was a great way to make history come alive, learn about the complexities of war, and better understand the nuances of our nation's history.

Each year we toured the Harper House, which was used as a field hospital, as well as the war trenches and the Confederate cemetery.

But my favorite part of that childhood experience was a poem they taught me, which was discovered folded in the pocket of a fallen Confederate soldier.

This unknown soldier wrote:

I asked God for strength, that I might achieve,
I was made weak, that I might learn humbly to obey.
I asked God for health, that I might do greater things,
I was given infirmity, that I might do better things.

I asked for riches, that I might be happy,
  I was given poverty, that I might be wise.
I asked for power, that I might have the praise of men,
  I was given weakness, that I might feel the need of God.
I asked for all things, that I might enjoy life,
  I was given life, that I might enjoy all things.
I got nothing that I asked for,
  but everything I had hoped for.
Almost despite myself,
  my unspoken prayers were answered.
I am among men, most richly blessed.

This prayer has resonated with me for many years now, and I have carried it in my heart all around the world.

But rather than telling you what this prayer means to me, I'd like to ask you: how can these words help you relax into infinity and abide in eternity on your journey to becoming all that you truly are?

March 24

◇ BEAUTIFUL EVENING ◇

In my first career as a classical musician, the stars aligned for a serendipitous meeting with a stunning singer I would go on to collaborate with for over a decade.

My life changed in our first meeting as she handed over the sheet music to a beautiful *chanson* by Claude Debussy and her beautiful voice seared the words of the poem into my heart:

When at sunset the rivers are pink
and a warm breeze ripples the fields of wheat,
All things seem to advise content
and rise toward the troubled heart.

Advise us to savor the gift of life,
while we are young and the evening fair,
For our life slips by, as that river does:
it to the sea—we to the tomb.

As the river goes to the sea, so we go to the tomb. And on the way to the tomb, savoring the gift of life with the people we meet—like my dear friend—is what makes life rich.

March 25
◇ ROOTS AND WINGS ◇

Many of us choose to leave our hometown. We cut off our roots in order to fly, not realizing that we can have both roots *and* wings.

But no matter how far our wings take us away from our roots, we all have an origin story, and it's important to acknowledge and connect with this story because we can't move forward into who we truly are until we accept the past.

So, before you go about your day, take a moment to write down where you are from.

Who are the people who shaped your childhood?

How would you describe your hometown, family, and community to someone who has never experienced it?

What were your favorite childhood foods?

Which traditions did your family celebrate?

What were your favorite things to do as a child?

What memories do you cherish?

Whether your wings took you a few miles from the home you grew up in, or you ended up halfway around the world like I did, reconnecting with your roots is always powerful.

Tomorrow, I will share where I am from.

March 26
◇ I AM FROM ◇

I am from a North Carolina home
   nestled in a forest of pine trees
   between blue beaches and Smoky Mountains.

I am from majestic red cardinals and
   squirrels in trees and
   deer in the backyard and
   catfish in the pond.

I am from community pig pickin's and
   tea so sweet you can't stand it and
   grandmother's twenty-layer chocolate cakes and
   Mama Andy's cupcakes and
   maw-maw's biscuits and
   community fish fry's and
   fall harvest sales and
   turkey shoots.

I am from blue-collar small business owners who
    go to church on Sunday morning,
    volunteer at the fire department,
    and vote every election no matter what.

I am from "Bless your heart!" and "I declare!" and
    "Y'all come on over anytime!"

I am from a small country church between Four Oaks
    where Mrs. Janice played the altar call
    softly and tenderly,
    her music going straight to my heart and
    nourishing me in a formative way.

And I am from a community I had to leave
    in order to be myself and
    fulfill my identity and my dreams.

Now, I am in a foreign land that I have made my new home:
    a land of midnight suns and fjord horses,
    of northern lights and polar bears,
    of nature, peace, and quiet.

Now, I make my home with someone who is from
    Ganesh and
    Samosas and
    Rangoli and
    Sacred Cows.

Now, I am an adult in the world living a big, free life,
    but I carry the little boy who lived in that
    home by the pond in my heart.
    I am never without him: anywhere I go, he goes.

I am from stars that died in order to give me life.

I am from me.

Where are you from?

March 27

◇ "YES MA'AM, MISS MAJESTY!" ◇

When the COVID-19 lockdowns went into effect in 2020, my high-paced work life slammed on brakes in a "Do not pass go, do not collect two hundred dollars" sort of way.

Well, I had been in the rat race so long that I had forgotten how to slow down and be human, and one day during the lockdown, I was particularly stir-crazy and headed over to Oslo's beautiful Vigeland Park.

It was a gorgeous spring afternoon, so I sat down to have lunch and watch a swan float by the bridge of sculptures.

Suddenly, this regal creature interrupted the eery quiet as she flapped her wings and expanded into the sky just two feet over my head. It took my breath away!

I nodded my head and said, "Yes ma'am, Miss Majesty, I hear you loud and clear."

Miss Majesty reminded me that the world was not over and I was not dead. We were all just taking a rest as we floated during the lockdown, and the time to flap and soar would come again soon.

And now, Miss Majesty wants me to ask you, what do you need more today: to float, or to flap?

March 28

◇ ME, THE MAGPIE, AND THE SPIRIT OF THE TIMES ◇

Earlier today, Mr. Magpie flitted down from the sky and perched on the park bench I was occupying with Ollie and unashamedly ripped me away from the pages of an intriguing book with his beautiful melody.

At first I was a little annoyed, but suddenly, the magic of Norway sprinkled some pixie dust on me, and I could understand what Mr. Magpie was saying!

He sang, "Hey, Patrick! I've been looking for an amazing treasure I've heard about. I can't remember what you humans call it, but it's vast. It covers the entire world. It's blue, but sometimes it has white spots that wisp over it. At night, it becomes dark, but there are twinkling yellow lights in it. Do you know what I'm talking about?"

With perplexed amusement, I answered, "Do you mean the sky?

He chirped, "Yes, that's it! Where can I find the sky?!"

I responded, "Oh Mag, you were just in it before you flew down to sing me your song."

Mag rolled his eyes and said, "That's just air, dummy," and flew away to ask someone else.

Sweet, ignorant Mag helped me realize that it's hard to clearly see something you've been surrounded by your whole life.

And just as my two-toned little friend didn't realize he had been in the sky all along, we often don't realize basic things about our existence.

Indeed, asking a human to realize the environment he lives in is like asking a bird to identify the sky or a fish to recognize the ocean. We just don't think about the impact of the *zeitgeist* because it is as ubiquitous as the air we breathe.

However, it's important to become aware of the environment around us, because the spirit of the times directly affects our life's journey.

Jung summed up the impact of the *zeitgeist* well when he wrote, "We are born at a given moment, in a given place, and like vintage years of wine, we have the qualities of the year, and of the season in which we are born."

And sure, to have the qualities of the *zeitgeist* is fine.

But *even better* is to carve out who you truly are amidst the spirit of the times.

March 29
◇ VALUATIONS◇

Who is worth more, an antelope or a lion?

Most of us would say lions, because they are higher on the food chain.

However, without the antelope, the lion would starve.

Who is worth more, a sloth or a peacock?

Many would say the peacock, because their feathers can be exchanged in the free market, yet the sloth is virtually the only species that has no natural predators. Thus, wouldn't it be shrewd to observe the sloth's nature and discern what makes him an outlier in the food chain?

And what is worth more, a billion dollars in your bank account, or a newborn baby?

Well, the answer to that question is a no-brainer to that baby's mother and father.

Although these comparisons may sound a little absurd, we often unconsciously compare ourselves to others in similarly wacky ways.

But the truth is that comparisons are simply not helpful because we are all worth the same. I am worth no more—and, I am worth no less—than you are. Therefore, comparisons are a moot point.

So, as you go about your day, remember that your skills and abilities are *not* a measure of how you stack up against others.

Instead, remember that, just like the peacock's feathers or the antelope's speed, our skills and abilities are simply tools to aid us in our quest to recreate the world as a byproduct of becoming who we truly are.

March 30
◇ HUMBLE AMBITION ◇

A friend of mine once waited for hours after a Green Day concert hoping to meet his heroes.

When the bandmates finally left the arena to board their tour bus, they were undoubtedly exhausted.

Still, they signed autographs and chatted with my friend on the tailgate of a pickup truck, just like normal guys enjoying a small town Saturday night.

The humble ambition Green Day embodies is founded upon the knowledge that a person does not have to be distinguished to be useful and happy.

As an anonymous book says:

Serving others, meeting obligations, accepting and solving the challenges of life, understanding that in God's eyes we are all equal: these are the satisfactions of right ambition.

How can you use humble ambition to serve others?

March 31

◇ PEAK LIFE EXPERIENCES ◇

Have you ever had one of those peak life experiences? Perhaps it was learning to read *See Spot Run* as a tiny tot, or sailboating on a beautiful summer day as an adult.

In these moments, we experience what is true at all times: that the world is okay, that all is as it should be, and that we are full of well-being.

Therefore, try to carve out time today to create a peak life experience that makes life worth living.

It could be 'big,' like finally taking that dream vacation.

Or it could be 'small': something as simple as savoring your lunch or noticing the blade of grass next to your foot.

Whether it's hugging a friend, enjoying a home-cooked meal, helping someone in need, or sharing your creativity, the inspiration of peak life experiences gives us verve.

So, no matter what peak experience you consciously choose to create today, I hope it fills you up and connects you with infinity and eternity!

◇ APRIL ◇

April 1

◇ PLEASURE'S PURPOSE ◇

As soon as I finish writing these paragraphs, Ollie and I will step outside and enjoy the spring sunshine with my neighbors; after all, how can I say no to Mr. Magpie calling my name from the window near my desk?!

Here in my community on the outskirts of Oslo, we enjoy winter's transition into spring by picnicking at the fjord, riding bikes to the sailboat harbor, and playing pickup volleyball games.

And of course, dusk always beckons 'last call' dog walks!

Entering into these pleasant experiences can seem like a waste of time under the mentality of 'work makes free.'

However, relaxation and leisure are actually the foundation of a sustainable work energy that doesn't lead to burnout.

In fact, taking time to soften and loosen up through pleasure allows us to go back to work with a sense of ease and grace that ultimately leads to more creativity and productivity.

So, as you go about this beautiful spring day, how can you relax into the pleasant experiences of life?

April 2

◇ SWEET SILENCE, CALM SERENITY! ◇

We all have tens of thousands of thoughts per day. Some thoughts are helpful, while others are downright distortions. But, like emotions, none of our thoughts are who we truly are.

The emotions and thoughts that occur in everyday life are like the waves at the top of the open sea: sometimes gentle swells lope in, and at other times violent tidal waves threaten to destroy everything in their wake.

In contrast, the true self resides in a deeper part of the sea. This domain is not so dictated by the arsis and thesis of tides. It is still and settled, beyond disruption.

This authentic state of being is best described by the poetry of an aria composed by Handel:

Sweet silence...calm serenity!
Even my soul is delighted by this peace
that reminds me of what awaits us in eternity.

Indeed, when we dive under the constant waves of everyday thoughts and emotions, and instead, rest deep within our true selves, we can relax into peace and serenity.

April 3

◊ GOD'S NAME ◊

The first thing we do once we leave Mother's womb is breathe.

Likewise, our last act before our spirit leaves our physical body is an ultimate sigh, a collapse of respiration.

Therefore, breath is one of the few Deep Truths that connect humans of all generations and geography.

And interestingly, in Hebrew, God's name literally means 'breath.'

I like that notion because it means that every time we breathe, from the moment we enter the world to the final curtain call, we are saying God's name (not bad as far as branding goes!).

So, when you get tight and stressed today, focus on God's name: your breath.

Take a nice big breath in through your nose, hold it for a second, then exhale out slowly through your mouth.

Pause and feel the emptiness of your lungs, then repeat the cycle a few times.

God's name matters because tuning into our body's natural ability to breathe helps us relax into the wisdom, peace, and freedom that will guide us to who we truly are.

April 4

◇ PRISON OR PARADISE? ◇

Like everyone who has ever lived, I sometimes have to do things I don't want to do, and at times, meeting the obligations of adulthood has felt like a prison sentence.

But my Coffee Companion has given me a different perspective: she believes that the only difference between being in prison and being in paradise is our mindset.

She suggested that we brainstorm historical figures who maintained their humanity, dignity, and creativity throughout unjust situations that were much worse than anything I will ever face.

Our list included the letters of St. Paul, Viktor Frankl's *Man's Search for Meaning,* and Olivier Messiaen's *Quartet For the End of Time,* to name but a few.

We decided that if these wrongfully imprisoned men could find the freedom to create great art, then the prison of my mind's resentment is peanuts in comparison!

So, these days, when I start to feel imprisoned, I check reality. I remember the powerful figures who found a way to thrive amidst actual oppression.

And with that perspective comes a mental jailbreak from resentment to the paradise of acceptance and peace.

April 5

◊ YOU CAN BE COMFORTABLE IN A COFFIN ◊

The deep inner journey of becoming who you truly are is iconoclastic. It's like standing up to the rest of the world and saying, "Two plus two does not equal four. Two plus two equals the moon."

And meaning it!

Divergence and new ideas scare people, therefore, many humans refuse the call of the uncomfortable Hero's Journey.

And for those of us who do accept the call, there are many difficult trials to endure before we can emerge on the other side of inner work with all its new insight and richness.

But, as Zuzu often said, "You can be comfortable when you're in a coffin."

So, choose to take the road less traveled into the deep inner journey.

You'll have to trudge at times, but you'll manage well by remembering that you are heading toward happy destiny.

It will be uncomfortable, but you can be comfortable when you're in a coffin.

April 6

◇ PHILOSOPHY'S WATCHWORDS ◇

Socrates said, "Know thyself."

Nietzsche believed that "One's own self is well hidden from one's own self; of all mines of treasure, one's own is the last to be dug up."

Shakespeare wrote, "To thine own self be true."

And that great Dane Søren Kierkegaard journaled:

One must first learn to know himself before knowing anything else. Not until a man has inwardly understood himself and then sees the course he is to take does his life gain peace and meaning; only then is he free.

And, of course, Carl Jung proclaimed that "The privilege of a lifetime is to become who you truly are."

Clearly, there's a theme of self-actualization throughout philosophy.

But do these thinkers go deeper into *how* to get there?

In some ways, yes.

However, they also knew that it would be impossible for future generations to inherit their answers in a way that would ring true.

They understood that the spiritual realm is an individual, experiential process and that there is no formula for life.

But boy, oh boy, did they give us a vision that inspires us to explore and discover our own insights through their watchwords!

April 7

◊ OLLIE'S ANKLES ◊

One of my biggest regrets is that I sometimes take Ollie's ever-present love and affection for granted. This week, however, I had a moment where I woke up from all that.

I cuddled with Ollie on his sheepskin rug and hand-fed him his favorite treat: baked sweet potato!

I watched Ollie's velvet-soft tongue turn to the shape of a platypus bill as he licked the food from my fingertip.

I felt his tiny teeth scraping under my fingernail for the last morsel of treat, which is one of the best feelings on Earth!

And I noticed Olle's ankles, which took me back in time thirty thousand years as I imagined a guy not so different from me, cuddling with his dog in their shared dwelling.

Together yet separately, humans and dogs have lived together year after year, century after century, millennia after millennia.

And Ollie and I are so grateful to be one small part of this subgenre of the Universe's story!

On second thought, maybe it's not a subgenre. Maybe dog and man living life together is the central tenet of the universe's quest for actualization.

April 8

◇ ODE TO BRUCKNER ◇

In my early twenties, I spent many Saturday nights at Severance Hall, home of the world-famous Cleveland Orchestra.

And on one special evening, my life changed as I experienced a symphony by Anton Bruckner for the first time.

My ears, my imagination, and my *life* opened up!

I walked on air for several days afterward, because somehow, that symphony connected me to a power greater than myself.

And the timing couldn't have been more serendipitous, because I was in desperate need of guidance as I contemplated major decisions about my future.

Luckily, those glorious melodies and harmonies firmly indicated that the next chapter of my story would take place in Houston, where I lived out a miraculous decade of my life.

So, one glorious Saturday night fifteen years ago, I found Truth through music and it changed the trajectory of my life.

Likewise, where can you find Truth in *your* day today?

April 9

◇ ALL IS WELL! ◇

It is a spiritual axiom that, despite all evidence to the contrary, all is well!

As Anthony de Mello says in his book *Awareness,* "Most people never get to see that all is well because they are asleep. They are having a nightmare."

And the nightmare is our fearful instincts.

Our instinctual hypervigilance to danger allowed us to survive the formative years of our species, but it doesn't help us thrive in the modern world, because, contrary to common belief, the fear instinct is less relevant today than ever before.

In fact, the Swedish physician Hans Rosling wrote:

The image of a dangerous world has never been broadcast more effectively than it is now, while the world has never been less violent and more safe.

I try to live every day awake from the nightmare.

I consciously choose to ignore all the messengers of impending doom and believe that, despite all evidence to the contrary, the world is a safe and loving place.

April 10

◇ YOU CRADLE ME IN YOUR BOSOM ◇

Sometimes my emotions become so intense that I can't separate my authentic self from my feelings.

In these moments, I'm lost, and my only reprieve is to pray:

God, help me relax and take it easy. Let me remember that you cradle me in your bosom and swaddle me in my body's five senses. Let your love flow through me so that I can be comforted, and as a result, be of maximum effectiveness to others.

Upon saying 'amen,' I have new wiggle room to choose love over fear, to choose my true self over my ancient instincts, and to respond wisely rather than react impulsively.

Similarly, what might happen if, when confronted with big emotions, you also take pause and pray until you are able to relax into wisdom, peace, and freedom?

April 11

◇ THE SWANS OF LEIPZIG ◇

Halfway through my doctoral degree, I was burnt out and ready to quit when Providence herself unexpectedly rang me up on the phone and invited me to live in Leipzig, Germany for six months!

I ended up being housed in a beautiful park, and on my daily walks, I watched swans tenderly caring for their baby swans, and as the flowers bloomed, so did I!

As nature slowly helped me relax into wisdom, peace, and freedom, I began to be grateful.

Rather than resenting how hard and long my doctoral program was, I appreciated that it allowed me to experience Leipzig. I came to see how each professor, even the ones I disliked, had something valuable to teach me. And eventually, I moved back to Houston and finished my degree, which created financial stability.

Leipzig taught me that nature is a powerful balm that can heal the soul.

Therefore, I hope you can make time today, to go outdoors and appreciate the goodness of God's nature.

Because apparently, baby swans and flowers can help us become who we truly are!

April 12

◇ A PORTAL TO THE REALM OF LASTING VALUE ◇

Just like the sheep on the cover of this book need to fill their bellies by grazing on grass, we need to fill our souls through the food of music and art.

Music and art are a portal to the realm of lasting value. Great artists knew how to dwell in infinity and abide in eternity. Resting in that energy gave them the wisdom, peace, and freedom to create immortal works of art that were a natural byproduct of their authentic lives.

These artists saw and heard Truth.

Then, they produced art in an attempt to help *us* experience the spiritual information they had access to.

So, before you put your head on your pillow tonight, find time to appreciate a creative relic of Truth from yesteryear. Read a sonnet, learn about the Arts and Crafts movement, or listen to a Chopin nocturne.

Taking a moment in your day to appreciate art will allow you to rest in infinity and abide in eternity, so that, like the great artists, you can do your part in recreating the world.

April 13

◊ THE COSMIC VACATION ◊

A few years ago, my Best Friend and I decided to take a road trip to northern Norway. We knew that driving through curving mountains and precariously narrow roads would be exhausting. But we trusted that the destination would be worth the work.

Eventually, we arrived at the magical land that they call Lofoten Islands, where we took the photo for the cover of this book.

And we chose that photo because Lofoten inspired some powerful questions that led to the genesis of this book:

Just as our trip to Lofoten was a vacation from our everyday life in Oslo, what if being human on Earth is like a cosmic vacation for our immortal souls?

What if there's a waiting list a mile long to get here and experience the adventure, whether we arrive as pauper or prince?

What if we're all stardust, and our creative acts in this life are a by-product of our celestial essence?

And what in the world are we supposed to do while we're docked Earthside on this cosmic voyage of the infinite and eternal?

Well, perhaps we're here to learn how to be frustrated, confused, and stressed.

Perhaps those pain points are opportunities to transcend and expand, leaving Earth with more character and heart than when we arrived.

And perhaps, somehow in this life, we become who we truly are more than we ever could in any other part of the universe.

The trip to Lofoten was arduous, but it was completely worth the life-changing, soul-affirming experience.

Similarly, perhaps we come to Earth anticipating that life will be hard at times, but we gladly sign the terms and conditions because we know that this life is an experience like no other.

This cosmic vacation that we share together is an absolute privilege.

And the privilege of this lifetime is to become who you truly are.

April 14

◇ BRINGING DREAMS INTO REALITY ◇

The initial, visionary steps of bringing a dream into reality are expansive, inspiring, and downright fun!

And of course, the final stages of completing what we set out to do are joyful and satisfying.

But the middle part is a long, hard road that must be traversed in order to bring our dreams into reality. And it can be easy to lose faith when we're in that purgatory-like daily grind and aren't sure if anything will ever materialize from our effort.

Luckily for me, I've had people in my life who have encouraged me to continue down the road to my dreams, even when the going gets tough.

For example, my primary care physician here in Oslo is part doctor, part philosopher, and when I first met her three years ago, she wanted to know more than just my medical history. She also wanted to know my hopes for the future.

I hesitantly shared my dream of putting down roots in Oslo, raising a family, and figuring out how to make an entrepreneurial living as a coach, speaker, and author.

I also told her that although Zuzu's passing clarified these goals, I had no idea how to make it happen.

She gently smiled at my uncertainty, leaned back in her chair, and said, "Patrick, I've been doing this job for twenty-six years, and I can't tell you how many times I've seen people envision a dream, hold it passionately in their heart, and then bring it into reality. Sometimes realizing a dream comes quickly, sometimes it comes slowly. But it always comes if the desire is from our authentic self and if we work for it."

Well, three years later, I have to look back and say that my physician's prophecy was true!

And although I could technically quantify how I achieved my goals, the truth is that there was a logic-defying force underlying the process that had its own timetable and its own momentum.

So, today, let's dream big and rest assured in my physician's prophecy that, even when we're in that difficult middle stage of bringing dreams to reality, there is *always hope* if the dream is from our authentic self and if we work hard for it.

April 15
◇ BE PRESENT FOR WHAT DESTINY PRESENTS ◇

My Best Friend once told me that when a baby is born in India, she is briefly left alone so that the gods can come down and write destiny on her forehead.

This ritual of *teeka* imprints all the strengths, weaknesses, trials, and triumphs her life will entail.

The destiny that the gods present is the accumulation of deeds done—or left undone—in previous places and times her soul inhabited.

In other words, becoming who she truly is in this life requires resolving unfinished business from past lives.

So, as you go about your day, be present for what destiny presents to you.

Complete your unfinished business.

And become who you truly are.

April 16

◇ WHERE WISDOM REIGNS ◇

Wisdom is not just for sages and prophets.
In fact, wisdom is the mixture of three garden-variety ingredients: experience, knowledge, and good judgment.

But if wisdom is comprised of such ordinary qualities, then why does it seem so elevated and elusive?

Well, wisdom requires holding the two opposing forces of emotion and logic in the same hand.

Now, managing the competing interests of emotion and logic is like a parent caring for two quarreling siblings.

However, if we can withstand the internal discomfort that comes from synthesizing emotion and logic into wisdom, the resulting insight can lead us in the direction of who we truly are, what we really want, and what matters most.

April 17

◇ FLOCKMATES ◇

Just as the sheep on the cover of this book find safety in numbers, we need like-minded, kindred spirits to nurture us.

If we find ourselves in a flock that doesn't suit our needs, we end up settling for making small talk about the weather or complaining about current events rather than truly sharing our thoughts and feelings.

However, if we're willing to risk finding a new flock, we might just cultivate decadently rich friendships with a few close confidants.

And that's exactly what I have experienced since moving to Norway!

Slowly, I have developed a small flock of people who, like me, are trying to balance seeking the spiritual realm while also attending to the practical realities of life.

Of course, having a grip on both spirituality and reality is a rare feat, and when I find someone that can do both, I hold onto them and I don't let go!

So, those are the qualities I desire in my flock of friends.

Now, it's your turn to consider: what qualities do *you* desire in *your* flockmates?

April 18

◇ PHASE CARDS ◇

Recently, a neighbor of mine was telling me that it is heartbreaking to hear his newborn baby cry, but luckily, his pediatrician provided a pamphlet explaining the developmental phases of infancy.

The Phase Card taught my friend that no matter how well he cares for his baby, there will be inevitable all-night crying sprees because of imperceptible brain development.

This information allowed him to center and ground himself during long, tear-filled nights with his son.

That got me thinking that perhaps we adults need to create a Phase Card for ourselves. It can prepare us for the moments of life when we'll want to throw a temper tantrum, and instead, be our own soothing parent.

On my Phase Card, I wrote that my biggest stress in life is the feeling that there is too much to do and not enough time to do it in.

I also wrote down the antidote to this feeling: naptime!

So, at some point, consider making your own Phase Card; it's a great way to forecast difficult times ahead and create a plan to manage stress through wisdom, peace, and freedom!

April 19
◇ IT'S THE LITTLE THINGS ◇

Lately, Ollie has been having some health problems. His stomach squeaks and creaks just like when my bike gears need WD-40!

So, my Best Friend, Ollie, and I went to the veterinarian this morning.

After receiving marching orders for Ollie's care, my Best Friend said "Let's not rush back home. There's a beautiful park across the street and I think Ollie deserves a reward for being a good boy at the doctor's office."

I happily agreed, and we sat under an old oak tree while Ollie dashed in large figure-eight circles around the lawn.

In the distance, we saw kids doing the noble work of play, which inspired us to dream up plans for the future.

Eventually, Ollie wore himself out and the three of us took a napF, half in the sunlight, half in the shade, on a gloriously simple day.

Over and over, Ollie reminds us that it's the little things, like a clean bill of health, the gift of sunlight, and companionship on a beautiful day, that make life heaven on earth!

April 20

◇ THE COSMIC BABY BLANKET ◇

Do you remember my friend in Bangalore who goes to sleep when the peacocks squawk?

Well, quite a few years ago, he confided in me that he and his wife were expecting their first child!

I was beyond thrilled and wanted to express my goodwill toward his family, so I bought a spool of light blue yarn made from Nordic alpaca wool.

I learned how to knit and made a soft, warm blanket to smoothen the baby's transition from the water of the womb to Earth's air.

As the trees blossomed into their spring costumes and Mr. Magpie sang his song, I sat on my balcony and infused as much love as I could muster into each stitch.

I felt so honored to be part of the divine tapestry of life by welcoming a babe to his cosmic vacation!

When I told Zuzu what knitting the blanket meant to me, she playfully laughed and said, "No one thinks like you!"

But really, anyone can think like me. All it takes to knit a cosmic baby blanket is the willingness to find spiritual meaning as you go about the tasks of your daily life today.

April 21

◇ LOVE YOUR DUTY ◇

For the past few years, I have lived out my calling of helping others become who they truly are.

I love what I do and I *love* being self-employed!

However, the downside of entrepreneurship is that the paychecks aren't always steady.

Therefore, I occasionally have to do temporary projects I'd rather not do during lean times.

I used to really resent these experiences, but over time, I've acted myself into a new way of thinking.

I've accepted that, for whatever reason, humans need to work and make money.

And, I try to be grateful for the opportunity to contribute to society, and in return, get my basic needs met.

My shift in thinking was due in part to my Coffee Companion telling me that she once heard a monk say "Love your duty."

The monk advised that instead of rushing through chores we dislike, to be fully present for the duty of whatever person, place, or thing is right in front of us.

A few days after my Coffee Companion taught me to love my duty, I came across these brilliant words by Helen M. Luke:

We hurry through the so-called boring things
in order to attend to that which we deem
more important, interesting.
Perhaps the final freedom will be a recognition that
everything in every moment is 'essential'
and that nothing at all is 'important.'

Today, let's all remember that everything is essential, even the things we'd rather not do.

Let's go love our duty.

April 22

◊ DAUGHTERS OF THE MOON ◊

I never understood what people meant when they said they could talk to their loved ones from beyond the grave, and yet there I was, regularly feeling Zuzu's presence in the trees as I walked Ollie along the bayous of Houston.

Once I moved to Norway, I no longer felt Zuzu's presence in the trees, but pretty quickly, I found her once again in the full, bright moons of Oslo winters.

Initially, I wondered if there was something about my geographic relocation, or perhaps the passage of time, that made our connection 'zoom out.'

Then, one day, I came across an idea that let me know that I experience her in the moon for a very specific reason.

Life tenderly got my attention when I read that Carl Jung believed the antidote to the restlessness and vacillation of life is to remember that we are daughters of the moon.

I believe Zuzu brought that passage to me and connects with me through the moon because she wanted to do her part to make that idea come alive in today's world.

So, before you go to sleep tonight, look up at the sky and remember that whether it makes sense or not, we are *all* daughters of the moon.

April 23
◇ VERTICAL HORIZONS ◇

My Best Friend is very horizon-focused. He is squarely set in reality and takes care of the needs of the people he loves. He values his family above all else.

On the other hand, I am very vertical. I tend to focus on developing my unique self and following my calling.

And although each of us gravitates toward our predispositions, we have come to learn that verticality and horizontality are not a zero-sum game.

Instead, we are both determined to learn from each other and find a way to grow as tall as Mt. Everest while stretching as wide as the Atlantic.

It's a daily effort, two steps forward, one step back, but finding the vertical horizon is worth the work!

April 24

◇ THE PALACE AND THE GUEST HOUSE ◇

A s I made my paces through the massive Palace of Versailles in France, I was keenly aware that I was only a guest on grounds that were the property of a different place and time.

On my walk, I thought of Rumi's most enduring poem, in which he compares our human body to a house, and emotions as guests who come and go from the house.

Rumi wrote:

This being human is a guest house.
Every morning a new arrival.
A joy, a depression, a meanness,
some momentary awareness comes
as an unexpected visitor.
Welcome and entertain them all!

Even if they are a crowd of sorrows,
who violently sweep your house
empty of its furniture,
still treat each guest honorably.

He may be clearing you out for some new delight.

The dark thought, the shame, the malice,
*   meet them at the door laughing,*
*   and invite them in.*

Be grateful for whoever comes,
*   because each has been*
*   sent as a guide from beyond.*

Just as I entered the Palace of Versailles, walked around, and eventually left, emotions come and go. They are not permanent residents. Therefore, there's no reason for us to deny their entry.

Indeed, if we can find the strength to welcome even the most painful emotions into the home of our physical bodies, they will make way for new joys within our life and work.

Because each one has been sent as a guide from beyond.

April 25

◇ THE RAINBOW IS THE POT OF GOLD ◇

I love cold, rainy days like today. There is just something *so cozy* about sitting on the balcony in sweats and reading a good book while listening to the rain.

Just a few seconds ago, I put down my novel to take in our picturesque view of the sailboat harbor, and a double rainbow revealed itself and winked at me!

I curiously started to wonder if there might be two pots of gold at the end of a double rainbow, and it was then that I realized that it must be human behavior to focus more on the pot of gold than the rainbow itself.

For example, many people strive for a job promotion for the extra money, when they are actually more suited for the role they already occupy.

So, perhaps there is no pot of gold at the end of the rainbow; maybe the payoff is simply enjoying the beauty life has to offer.

And as we go about our day, let's strive for more than just the pot of gold.

Let's enjoy the rainbows as we make our journey through life, because the rainbow *is* the pot of gold!

April 26

◇ BACK IN THE WOMB ◇

On the rare occasion that I get to go to the gym during its empty mid-afternoon hours, I get to experience a blissful combination of reality and eternity.

On the one hand, I'm taking care of the practicalities that my human body needs as I move, stretch, and activate my muscles. On the other hand, I love the expansive sensation of sitting alone in the sauna after a workout during these ghost town afternoons.

As I ladle water over the hot rocks and hear the sizzle as steam rises, I feel the bamboo bench beneath me and my nostrils burn from inhaling a heat worthy of the Amazon.

Something about this sensual experience shuts off my ever-quacking mind. It is as if I regain the peace of being back in my mother's womb. Even the crown of my head feels lovingly touched by the steam, reminding me of how it felt to leave my mother's body and enter the world.

I have been so blessed to find a way to turn on my body while turning off my mind, and I think the world would benefit greatly from more of us finding ways to self-soothe to the point that we feel 'back in the womb.'

April 27

◇ WANT TO HAVE A CATCH? ◇

F*ield of Dreams* actor Dwier Brown once told me that
when he signs books for people at baseball parks across
America, he writes "Want to have a catch?" before his name.

Dwier writes this because he believes that, just as
two people playing catch give and receive the ball, a good
conversation involves two people giving and receiving love,
divine energy, and inspiration.

Dwier said, "When I share myself fully with you,
hopefully, it's an invitation for you to share back with me."

Likewise, I hope that as we share this book and go about
our days together this year, we will have a catch together!

April 28

◇ THIS TOO SHALL PASS ◇

Each spring, my Best Friend, Ollie, and I take the gorgeous train ride from Oslo to Bergen.

This world-renown voyage includes almost two hundred tunnels, each of which is like a vintage View-Master toy: in other words, you never know what lies on the other side of each tunnel!

For example, before entering the mountain ahead, you might be traveling through the midst of the frozen tundra.

Then, somehow, the tunnel transports you to a new landscape with waterfalls, heavenly sunbeams, and sheep grazing next to sparkling water.

Experiencing all four seasons in one day along this train ride reminds me of the old saying, "This too shall pass."

Winter passes into spring.

Crying turns into laughing.

Conflict transforms into peace.

And death creates new life.

So, as you go about your day, remember that whatever you're going through, "This too shall pass."

April 29

◇ BABY ON BOARD ◇

I will never forget my first experience on an Indian highway.

As my Best Friend drove me from the airport to his childhood home, I took in scenes of people working in fields, small children selling fruit by the side of the interstate, and men packed like sardines in the back of work trucks.

I was humbled by the hard work everyone was doing just to put food on the table each evening.

Then, my brain completely short-circuited when I saw a young man and his wife on their motorcycle. They were helmet-free, sandwiched between two large transfer trucks, with an infant nestled in his mother's bosom!

My Best Friend saw my reaction, bobbed his head, smiled gently, and said "Patrick, they're fine. India's fine. You don't have to worry about them. They don't need saving."

One day at a time, I try to remember what I learned in India: that everything is fine, that all is well, and that I don't need to worry. I don't need to place my judgments and preferences on the way other people live their life. I only need to relax into infinity and eternity and do my small part in recreating the world.

April 30

◇ HEAVEN'S SHIRE ◇

There is a hamlet smack dab in the middle of Norway that is home to one hundred people, yet five hundred goats! Barely a blip on the map, this enchanting little community they call Undredal just might be Heaven's address.

My Best Friend, Ollie, and I decided to spend this past weekend in Undredal, and once we settled into our bed and breakfast, we explored the five-street village in less than an hour! We were amused by Europe's smallest firehouse, which barely qualifies as a shed, and we prayed in Scandinavia's smallest stave church.

After lunch and a nice nap, I decided I would try some ice cream made from the milk of the village goats while Ollie sunbathed on the dock nearby. As I enjoyed my snack, I felt the wind on my lips and the sun on my face and looked at the beautiful mountains framing the picturesque scene.

It was all just *absolute bliss.*

Have you, also, had a moment where you felt like you were in Heaven's Shire?

If so, take a moment to close your eyes and mentally return to that moment, and let Heaven's Shire provide you with spiritual information about how to live your life today!

◊ MAY ◊

May 1

◊ THE ERROR OF WAITING FOR HEAVEN'S REWARD ◊

I was recently swapping memories of doctoral studies with a colleague and we both made fun of ourselves for falling prey to the delusion that postponing happiness and suffering for a piece of paper would magically bestow a Heaven-like lifelong happiness once we could put 'Doctor' in front of our name.

We both believed that the blood, sweat, and tears of jumping through (often arbitrary) hoops would end with a golden light coming down from heaven and angels singing a Hallelujah Chorus!

Yet after overcoming the difficulties of matriculating, we were left alone with ourselves, thinking, "This is it?"

Neither of us ever stopped to consider what our hearts were saying about what we were doing. We simply resigned ourselves to suffer through an invalidating environment in hopes that we might be happy in the future.

As a result of our disappointment, we now make sure to regularly check in with ourselves and ask, "Is how I spend my time and energy what my heart wants?"

After all, heaven's reward is not in the future.

Because heaven is right now!

May 2

◇ YOUR TURN ◇

I have struggled over crafting today's reflection and have not been able to get it up to snuff.

Consequently, I'm going to cry 'Uncle!' and let you help me out on this one.

All I have for you today is a powerful question that I, myself, have thought about for years.

I think this question is universal, but the answer is highly personal, and only you can author the answer that you need to read.

Therefore, I hope you will take the time to reflect on this question, and perhaps jot down some responses you have in the margins of this book.

So, here goes the question: what would the world be like if more people, including you, were more deeply engaged with their innermost creativity?

May 3

◇ PROGRESS, NOT PERFECTION ◇

The principle of 'progress, not perfection' is embodied in the ancient pilgrimage site of Chartres Cathedral located about eighty kilometers southwest of Paris.

In this sacred edifice, thousand-year-old headless angels and armless Apostles of Christ abound along the massive, beautifully ornamented choir wall.

Meanwhile, the incomplete restoration of the cathedral's stone walls and columns creates a two-toned effect: the soot-stained segments stand in stark contrast to those parts which have been restored to their original white hue.

As I walked through the magnificent space, I realized that if a sacred house of prayer like Chartres Cathedral can be an imperfect work in progress, then so can I.

Cathedrals, like people, are not finished works of art. They are living, breathing organisms that need maintenance and tender loving care, just like us humans.

So, as you go about your day, remember that life is not about perfection, it's about spiritual progress toward love.

May 4

◇ GRATITUDE, NOT GUILT ◇

In my work and my life, I often wax poetic about becoming who you truly are, but in India, I witnessed many people simply trying to meet their basic daily needs.

As we traveled from my Best Friend's childhood home to his sister's ashram, I was overwhelmed by what I perceived to be hardships.

I watched women line up to fill clay pots with water from the community well and carry them back home on top of their heads.

From my comfortable car seat, my heart broke as we passed people living in tents, breaking their backs to harvest sugarcane for a few rupees per day.

And as we neared a toll booth, a sweat-drenched man tried to sell us strawberries amidst the sweltering heat of eight lanes of traffic.

My Best Friend could tell that I was getting emotionally riled up, so he gently said, "Patrick, guilt doesn't help anyone. Some of these people are quite happy because they are focused on what truly matters: family. Don't look at their lives through the interpretation of American standards. It's a whole different system here."

I remembered that I was a guest in a foreign land and I should thus heed his cultural insight, so I closed my eyes in a much-needed reprieve from the sensory overload and took a deep, calming breath.

I quickly filed through my internal Rolodex, trying to figure out what emotion I could call up to assuage the guilt, and the only emotion that answered my call was gratitude, an ever-faithful Hail Mary pass when all else fails.

As gratitude coached me through a mindset shift, the emotion of curiosity came around and turned the conversation into a conference call.

And all of a sudden, I was asking a million questions about how my Best Friend saw the same set of external circumstances in such a different way.

Staying in guilt would have kept me locked into my existing frame of reference. But gratitude, and the resulting curiosity, expanded my understanding of the situation.

So, consider taking a lesson from my trip to India. The next time you feel guilty about something, try to shift to a mindset of gratitude and curiosity.

Gratitude, not guilt.

May 5

◇ MOTHERS ◇

The things that are most true in this life are the things that can be found in every culture, in every generation, in every religion, and in the story of every human who has ever lived.

This kind of profound Truth is rare, but it is powerful.

Case in point: everyone has a mother.

In our first nine months, we are nurtured by her womb and umbilical cord.

Once we go from her womb's water to the arid realm of Earth, she fills the stomach with milk, relaxes the body with comforting touches, and calms the soul with reassuring words.

And as we develop through childhood, she makes it safe to go out and seize the day. After all, it's easier to take risks when we know she'll be there to bandage a scraped knee in childhood, or to mend a broken heart when young love doesn't go our way.

So, let's all take a moment to reflect on the love our mother gave us, because without her, we would not have had the chance to be here and experience this amazing adventure we call 'life!'

May 6

◊ A PLACE BEYOND FOREVER ◊

I have always believed that there is life after death, but I actually *experienced* this Truth once Zuzu passed.

And as a result of Zuzu continuing our conversations from beyond the grave, I now see that the space between life and death is not a concrete boundary so much as a porous line.

For example, while she was alive, Zuzu used her phone to call me and ask questions that helped me explore life, and now, she uses dreams to continually provoke me to new spiritual depths.

In these dreams, she asks me questions like:

What if graves are gateways, and we live on, not as physical beings, but as spiritual information?

What if there is a deeper reality in which space and time do not exist?

What if there's a place beyond forever, even beyond infinity and eternity?

And what if, in that place beyond forever, our loved ones are waiting for us to connect with them, so they can live on as spiritual information and help us become who we truly are?

May 7

◇ FOOD, GLORIOUS FOOD! ◇

One of my favorite activities is eating delicious food! I have enjoyed waffles in Brussels, crepes and croissants in Paris, bratwurst in Hamburg, krumkake in Oslo, Tex-Mex in Houston, prime rib in Dallas, idli in Ichalkaranji, crawfish and gumbo in New Orleans, and pierogies in Cleveland.

Not to mention the chicken pastry, pecan pie, sweet tea, and deep-fried southern comfort food of my hometown!

Food is a thrice-daily chance to light a candle, set a beautiful floral arrangement on the table, cook a hot meal, and eat it one glorious bite at a time.

Food is an opportunity to hear the crunch of bread and the slurp of soup.

To smell the butter and caramelized onions.

To see the vibrant colors of summer fruit.

And to feel a variety of textures, from the silk of melted chocolate to the soot of cornstarch.

So, as you go about your day, remember that you deserve to invest the time and attention required to make an event out of one of the great pleasures of this lifetime: food, glorious food!

May 8

◊ BALANCING ACCEPTANCE AND CHANGE ◊

One of my heroes is the psychologist Dr. Marsha Linehan, and for several decades now, her life skills class has been the gold standard in the world of personal development.

Perhaps the reason her class is so effective is that it stems from skills she had to patchwork together to solve her own struggles.

In her teen years, psychiatrists damned Dr. Linehan as a lost cause, yet she refused to cede her soul to the back ward of a mental institution. And while she accepted her diagnosis, it was clear that her doctors had no idea how to help her. So she decided that she would figure out how to help herself and then help others as well.

By balancing acceptance of her issues *and* seeking to change her life, a sick person found her own cure. How often does *that* happen in the annals of world history?!

You, also, can find your cure to whatever is blocking you from a life of authenticity by identifying what you need to accept versus what is in your power to change.

Balancing acceptance and change can get you out of hell and even create heaven on earth!

May 9

◇ NO SUCH THING AS AN UNDESIRABLE ◇

As I strolled along downtown Oslo's Akerselva River last Sunday, I overheard a tour guide saying, "You'll see some undesirables on the river banks drinking and doing drugs. Just ignore them. They're a part of city life."

Something about the statement rang quite ignorant to me, yet only minutes later I encountered a shabby-looking man that must have been one of the 'undesirables' the tour guide spoke of.

I watched the shaking man struggle to light up a pipe that was not for tobacco or even marijuana.

And as my heart focused into view, I realized why the label 'undesirable' seemed so false to me.

This man was *not* undesirable.

He simply wasn't free.

It was a gorgeous heaven-on-earth sort of day, yet this man was crouched over in the hell of a once-novel and curiosity-provoking drug that now enslaved him.

Nevertheless, he is not undesirable.

He's a child of God, just like me and just like you.

So rather than judging him, I wish for him to be free.

In fact, I wish for us all to be free.

May 10
◇ WHERE ANGELS LEAVE NO DUST PRINT ◇

The eight-year-old Patrick within me fondly remembers being delighted by the cleverness of Ray Bradbury in his classic science-fiction novel *Fahrenheit 451*.

After all, how often does an author write a story about a society that burns books?!

Bradbury's book encouraged me to seize the day when he wrote:

Stuff your eyes with wonder. Live as if you'd drop dead in ten seconds. See the world. It's more fantastic than any dream made or paid for in factories.

Almost thirty years later, as Ollie curled up on my stomach and we sunbathed by the fjord, I opened up Bradbury's memoir entitled *Zen in the Art of Writing*.

Once again, he completely stole my heart with a powerful message that "Creativity is plunging forward where angels leave no dust print."

Let's all heed Bradbury's advice and endeavor to stuff our eyes with wonder, live as if we'll drop dead in ten seconds, and plunge forward where angels leave no dust print!

May 11
◇ RECREATION RATHER THAN PROLONGATION ◇

It is each person's responsibility to hand down their wisdom to the next generation.

But unfortunately, well-intentioned parents and teachers shoot themselves in the foot when they go about this noble task by using prolongation rather than recreation.

Prolongation is about telling the next generation what to believe by indoctrinating them with so-called answers.

A better way is to teach the next generation how to recreate the world for themselves.

We can do that by asking them questions and then allowing them the freedom to explore life and discover their own path.

In other words, in the quest to give to others, we have to make sure that we are helping them become who *they* truly are, not who *we* are!

For example, many years ago, I was playing one of my favorite pieces of music for my Friend in Paris and nervously asked for his feedback.

I said, "You're the greatest musician I've ever met. But what if I prefer my way of interpreting this composition and disregard your suggestions?"

He said, "Patrick, you *must* do it your way! All I can do is give you insight into my way, which might help you see *your* way a little more clearly."

I can only hope that I go through my life with the humility of my Friend in Paris, gracefully asking questions and sharing how I came to my conclusions, all the while giving others the freedom to find their own way.

How can you do the same?

May 12
◇ STALLIONS AND RIDERS ◇

A woman I deeply admire once shared that within each of us, there resides both a powerful Lippizaner stallion and a talented rider.

Lippizaners naturally kick up their heels and sling mud in untethered freedom. However, once a young stallion enters dressage schooling, his highly-skilled rider spends at least six years harnessing the stallion's natural strengths.

When it comes time to perform, the rider must be in control, making sure he doesn't give the horse too much rein. The stallion can kick up his heels in the pasture later, but in order to perform the intricate choreography of Viennese dressage, his vitality needs to be concentrated.

Well, my mentor's point was that some of us let our inner stallion run free to the point that our lives become unbridled.

Others of us, however, are such strict riders that we break the spirit of our inner stallion.

So, as you think about this metaphor today, consider: how can you harmoniously attune your inner stallion *and* your inner rider so that your contribution to the world is just as stunning as Viennese dressage?

May 13

◇ OPENING THE TREASURE CHEST ◇

My earliest memory involves sitting on my dad's lap and playing the piano while my mom cooked dinner in the adjacent room.

That moment was like opening up a treasure chest!

Thus, from an early age, my soul understood that there was profound depth to uncover and explore in the arts.

As I grew into a society that is often focused on the current moment, I was mesmerized by the idea that classical music transcends generations through epic narratives and big questions about who we are and why we're here.

It's undeniable that great art beckons us out of the ordinary experience and into the unknown spiritual realm; it connects us to a deeper frequency that helps us understand life, ourselves, and others in more meaningful ways.

To put it another way, by looking to the enduring spiritual value of great art and music, we can kiss the very lips of Truth.

So, as you go about your day, open the treasure chest of music and art to move past everyday thoughts and emotions and connect to the unseen, free-floating energy of life!

May 14
◇ "OH, YOUR SHOES!" ◇

Many years ago, my Best Friend and I were on an elevator at a large corporation in Houston, and we held the door for two impeccably dressed women who made us look like street rats in comparison.

As the elevator ascended, they both scanned each other head to toe, then one woman flipped her hair and said to the other, "Oh, I just *love* your shoes! Where did you get them?"

The second woman clutched the pearls around her chest and said "Thank you so much, I bought them at a new boutique nearby. Let's go shopping there sometime!"

As the second woman got off the elevator, the first woman whispered, "I hate that bitch and her shoes too."

My friend and I looked at each other, stunned, and then we burst out in uncontrollable laughter!

Since then, when he and I are together and hear people say things they don't mean, we look at each other, say "Oh, your shoes!" and crack up.

The moral of the story, you ask?

Say what you mean, and mean what you say.

Otherwise, you might just end up the butt of an inside joke!

May 15

◇ THIS TOPSY-TURVY WORLD! ◇

L ast weekend my neighbor and I took a canoe trip to his favorite campsite in all of Norway.

As we gently paddled through the crystal clear waters, I marveled at the beautiful rocks, which my friend mentioned came from a nearby volcano.

Surprised, I asked, "How can it be that there is a volcano in a land of snow and ice?"

He laughed and said, "Patrick, *everything* came from a volcano at some point. And if that doesn't blow your mind, just look at those mountain peaks in the distance. The rocks crowning those mountains once lined the depths of the ocean floor!"

My head spun as I realized that we live in a topsy-turvy world where molten lava shapes frozen landscapes and the deepest part of the ocean can become the tips of mountains.

And, just as fantastical, is the Truth that your life can play a part in recreating the entire world if you do the courageous inner work of becoming who you truly are.

May 16

◇ IF YOU CARRY RESTLESSNESS IN YOUR HEART... ◇

The Hindi movie *Zindagi Na Milegi Dobara* (which translates to "You Only Live Once") is a comedy about three friends who are unhappy and restless.

So, they go on holiday to Spain, where they make a pact to face their fears through the extreme sports of scuba diving, skydiving, and running with the bulls.

Each friend swears that if he actually survives, he will make a major life change.

The financier will choose love over money.

The copywriter will publish his secret tome of poems.

And the friend who is engaged will cancel his wedding and find true love.

In the final scene, as bulls chase the three friends through the streets of Pamplona, the poetry of Javed Akhtar is heard in the background, which sums up the entire movie in a chill-bump-inducing way:

If you're carrying restlessness in your heart,
    you are alive.
If you're carrying the lightning of dreams in your eyes,
    you are alive.
Like a gust of wind, learn to live free,
    learn to flow like the waves that make a sea.
Let your arms be wide open to every moment you meet,
    may every moment gift you a new sight to greet.
If you're carrying wonder in your eyes,
    you are alive.
If you're carrying restlessness in your heart,
    you are alive.

As you go about your daily life, remember that if you have restlessness in your heart, it means you are alive.

Listen to the restlessness.

Honor it.

And like the three friends in the movie, make changes that are necessary so that you may live free like the wind, flow like the waves, and live with arms wide open.

May 17

◇ HAPPY BIRTHDAY, NORWAY! ◇

Every Seventeenth of May, the citizens of Norway celebrate their country's birthday!

After dressing auspiciously in traditional Nordic dresses and suits called *bunads,* families and neighbors gather together for a breakfast feast that includes heart-shaped waffles and cinnamon rolls.

Then, around noon, children process in a large parade down Karl Johans Gate, which is Oslo's main thoroughfare.

Eventually, the kids pass the King's Palace and wave to the royal family sitting on the balcony.

Afterward, ice cream abounds until tiny tots and adults alike groan with bellyaches!

Festival days are fun because we set aside time and energy to celebrate traditions by living in a novel way for one day. And as a result of the day's uniqueness, we feel ease and grace that leads to spontaneous creativity!

But actually, every day can be a celebration, we just need to wake up each morning and consciously find ways to seize the day.

So, how can you intentionally cultivate feelings of excitement and freshness on this once-in-a-lifetime day?

May 18

◇ THE DOOR THAT LEADS TO NOWHERE ◇

On a beautiful lane in a quaint neighborhood, my Friend in Paris has turned his abode into an exquisite monument to Beauty.

Sublime relics from the Art Nouveau movement adorn his home, including silk embroideries, elegant vases, and artwork of dragons, cranes, and owls.

But my favorite part of my friend's home is the Door That Leads To Nowhere in the middle of his living room.

My friend once shared that various houseguests have ridiculed his Alice-in-Wonderlandesque door, but I get it!

To me, the Door That Leads To Nowhere is the very embodiment of Beauty.

Like the Door That Leads To Nowhere, Beauty may seem non-functional or without purpose.

And yet, Beauty is one of the most necessary things in the world, because it expands us and makes us think!

Thus, sometimes a Door That Leads To Nowhere actually leads to infinity and eternity!

So, as you go about your day, seek to find your own Door That Leads To Nowhere, and let turning the handle expand you into new realms of wisdom, peace, and freedom.

May 19

◇ ANGER ON THE EVENING NEWS ◇

On any given night, turn on the television and you're bound to see a news commentator who acts as the final word and deed on affairs of the day. Agree with them, and you're good; disagree with them, and you're bad.

Flip the channel, and you'll see someone else preaching the opposite view. Once again, agree with them, and you're good; disagree with them, and you're bad.

Well, I think all that anger and noise is just one big diversion; it's just a bunch of people who are trying to do anything and everything to avoid the deep inner journey.

And while it can be intoxicating to enter into debates of the day, succumbing to the fray leads to stress and fear.

Conversely, it is much more fulfilling to enter into the wisdom, peace, and freedom of the inner journey and engage the instinct of creativity rather than the instinct of fear.

So, consider avoiding the news cycle, just for today, and see if I might have a point.

And don't worry, if you turn the news off, they'll still be upset and angry when you come back to them!

May 20

◊ THE COWBOY IN ME ◊

An old country song states, "I've got a life that most would love to have, but sometimes I still wake up fighting mad."

The singer goes on to chalk up his bad mood to fate and sings, "I guess that's just the cowboy in me," but I disagree. I think all our emotions are caused, even if we don't understand why.

There are plenty of mornings when I, also, wake up on the wrong side of the bed. After all, it's impossible to cross every 't' and dot every 'i' before sleeping, so it's natural that sometimes we wake up angry over unfinished business from the day before.

But it's important to remember that the way we wake up is not just something uncontrollable that we shrug our shoulders over.

Rather, once we acknowledge the mood we wake up with and listen to the message it contains, we can tidy up undealt-with baggage and then proceed merrily about our day.

May 21

◇ I AM THE UNIVERSE IN A GRAIN OF SAND ◇

I am the universe in a grain of sand.
I hear the thunder of creativity,
  I smell the colors of time,
  and I see heaven in a wildflower.

I touch my forehead with the spirit of my ancestors and
  contemplate what I looked like before my grandmother
  was born.

I am made of moondust on Neil Armstrong's space suit,
  from the water that Jesus turned into wine,
  and from lava that lined the bottom
  of the Mariana Trench,
  before transforming into the peak of Mt. Everest.

I am the universe in a grain of sand.

May 22

◇ THE LONELY PLACES ◇

No one can tell you how to become who you truly are, because there is no formula or cookie-cutter approach. However, we can find people who live life in a way we admire. We can take cues from their wisdom and see if their life lessons can shed light on our unique journey.

For example, I am inspired to take time to reflect when I remember the words of the Norwegian explorer Fridtjof Nansen, who wrote:

The first great thing is to find yourself and for that, you need solitude and contemplation—at least sometimes. I can tell you deliverance will not come from the rushing noisy centers of civilization. It will come from lonely places.

The rat race of society seduces us with promises of external rewards, but Nansen is saying that the greatest prize of all is to go within and find yourself.

So, as you go about your day, how can you leave the noise of modern life and find the deliverance that comes from quiet, lonely places?

May 23

◇ ZUZU'S SOUL SISTER ◇

Summer Sunday evenings are a busy time at my favorite little clearing at the fjord. I usually enjoy watching the adults barbeque while the kids take their sand buckets to the shoreline. But today, there was one group of people that just really got my goat.

They were dressed in, shall we say, 'free-spirited' and 'new age' clothing, and it seemed as though they were worshiping a tree when I first arrived.

My first reaction was to roll my eyes and mutter some not-kindergarten-approved words under my breath.

But I quickly realized that my life's sinister villain, Mr. Judgment, was showing up, and I decided to instead try and open my mind and heart to these people.

At the same time, I started hearing them making primal sounds. Well you'd think that would have activated my judgment even more, but actually, Zuzu taught me the value of making primal sounds to clear emotions.

And all of a sudden I went from scoffing at the leader of the group to admiring her for being Zuzu's soul sister.

And as I watched the leader guide her group through the meditation, I felt closer to Zuzu than I had in a long, long time.

Then, I saw how she cared for a baby who started crying, as well as the parent of the baby, in the middle of their meditation.

I admired the way Zuzu's soul sister nurtured the parent and child while also continuing the guided meditation. Her heart was open to life on life's terms, and as a result, she flexibly met the unexpected turn of events with ease and grace.

Now, if I had stayed in my judgment and walked to another part of the fjord, I would have missed out on the chance to feel Zuzu's presence. Instead, I did the hard work of opening myself up, and as a result, I got a heaping dose of love and connection from Zuzu.

So, as you go about your day, I hope you can identify when you're being judgmental, and instead of closing down your mind, open up your heart. Every time I do this, my wisdom, peace, and freedom increase, and I bet the same will be true for you!

May 24

◊ THE BEST GIFT MY MOM EVER GAVE ME ◊

The year was 1993, and all the authorities in my life were backing me into a corner called kindergarten.

However, I was not on board.

I liked my momma, and I liked home

After weeks of scowls and protests, my mom finally brokered a deal with the five-year-old terrorist in her life.

She knew books were my passion, and she promised that if I went to school, by year's end I would be reading all by myself!

It was a deal I could not refuse.

Reluctantly, and with fat tears rolling down my cheeks, I resigned myself to school, trusting in my mother's unfailing word.

Now, let's fast forward to my final day of kindergarten: my mother's promise had soured.

Learning to read just wasn't in the cards for me yet.

Shouts of "You lied to me! How could you treat your son this way?!" could be heard from three doors down.

I had my mom and my teacher bawling by the time I was finished with my guilt trip. After all, hell hath no fury like a five-year-old scorned!

But I have to say that my mom more than made amends.

In fact, the greatest gift my mom ever gave me was our weekly trips to the public library, where sweet old librarians who might as well have been goddesses gave me a magical plastic card I could swipe in exchange for two armfuls of books!

My mom did quite alright by me. She pushed me to do the things that would prepare me for the future, like going to public school and participating in organized sports.

But at the same time, she validated my natural personality by allowing me to enjoy activities that weren't normal for boys in my hometown: things like going to the library and taking piano lessons.

And now that I think about it, perhaps even more than all those library trips, the greatest gift my mom ever gave me was teaching me how to balance uncomfortable activities that stretch me alongside comforting, affirming hobbies.

And now that I am an adult, I can take over her responsibilities and continue to balance the necessary parts of life with the parts of life that fill me up.

What was the best gift your mom ever gave you?

May 25

◇ SIMPLY THE BEST ◇

This morning I woke up to the news that Tina Turner had passed away after a long life of seeking freedom.

After spending years in an abusive marriage to a husband who literally owned her likeness, she divorced him and lost everything but the rights to her name.

The inner courage to start over from scratch came from applying Buddhist philosophies, and her personal development led to superstardom in the 1980s.

But eventually, she needed even more freedom and retired in the year 2000, starting a new life in Switzerland.

During this new chapter of peace and well-being, she once told a reporter:

True and lasting happiness comes from having an unshakeable, hopeful spirit that can shine, no matter what. That's what I've achieved, and it is my greatest wish to help others become truly happy as well.

Well, Tina certainly made millions of people happy.

And, if we follow her example, her life story can also help us become more free.

May 26

◇ WHEN THE AMBASSADOR WASHES DISHES ◇

Today our High Ambassador of Cuteness and his parents came over for tea and homemade Neapolitan cake.

And although our Ambassador enjoyed the food, he was much more interested in the dishwasher than in our adult conversation!

With one hand he munched on cake. With the other, he opened and closed the dishwasher door with the rambunctiousness of a happy, healthy two-year-old.

Then, he suddenly had a "Eureka!" moment and gave himself a work promotion from door opener to dish emptier!

As he picked up a heavy glass casserole dish, my instincts went into overdrive. I went to yank it out of his hand, but instead, I found myself saying, "Wow, thanks for your help, but I think it'll be even better if we do it together!"

He smiled with delight as he contributed to his little community, and I loved fostering his growth rather than telling him, "No, that's for grown-ups."

I taught him healthy boundaries, he taught me patience.

My hope for your day is that you also experience the joy of extending yourself for the nurturing and growth of another (and by proxy, yourself)!

May 27

◇ SPIRITUAL PARENTS ◇

One of the top honors of my life was when Zuzu's husband asked me to speak at her memorial service.

The event never happened due to the worldwide pandemic, but preparing my remarks was a much-needed Balm in Gilead during my grief journey.

I've interspersed some ideas from her eulogy throughout this book, but perhaps the most poignant way to encapsulate our relationship was written by M. Scott Peck in his classic book *The Road Less Traveled*.

In describing his relationship with his mentor, Peck gave voice to my feelings about Zuzu when he wrote:

I was able to hear much of what this great woman said, precisely because I was willing to do the work of listening to her.

My listening to her was an act of love. I loved her because I perceived her to be a person of great value worth attending to, and I loved myself because I was willing to work on behalf of my growth.

Since she was the teacher and I the pupil, she the giver and I the receiver, my love was primarily self-directed, motivated by what I could get out of our relationship and not what I could give her.

Nonetheless, it is entirely possible that she could sense within her audience the intensity of my concentration, my attention, my love, and she may have thereby rewarded.

The chance to meet someone who can be your spiritual parent—like Zuzu or my Friend in Paris—is as rare as Haley's comet. Most people are lucky to find even one in their lifetime, but somehow, I got two!

Based on my experience, I can say that you will know your spiritual parent when you meet them. At that moment, follow your heart and persist in cultivating a relationship.

If you can do that, and they are also open and willing, then I can almost guarantee that your life, their life, and dare I say the course of the universe will change to a direction that is just a bit more true and authentic.

May 28

◇ ADMIRATION PASSES, LOVE ENDURES ◇

Combine the popularity of authors Danielle Steel, Stephen King, and Nicholas Sparks, and you come close to rivaling the Indian phenomenon that is Chetan Bhagat!

Why is he so popular?

Because he represents a generation of Indians who are individuating from traditional familial expectations.

Chetan himself walked this path. He endured the most competitive engineering and business schools in India before deciding to diverge from expected norms.

When Chetan decided to live the life of a writer, there was no fame or money guaranteed.

The material success that came his way was just a by-product of choosing to live his life in line with his talents and values.

In fact, it may be that Chetan would prefer not to have fame at all.

For example, in the preface to his wonderful novel *Half-Girlfriend,* Chetan wrote:

Don't give me your admiration. Give me your love. Admiration passes, love endures. Also, admiration comes with expectations. Love accepts some flaws.

Chetan is telling us that when we do what others expect of us, we might get admiration. But fulfillment from external validation will inevitably fade away.

However, a more enduring process is to create from the depths of who you truly are, and subsequently, receive love from a community of people who appreciate the byproducts of your creativity.

Admiration passes, love endures.

May 29

◇ SINGING IN THE RAIN ◇

Today my neighbor and I were sweating through a bike ride into the city center when suddenly, out of nowhere, it started raining cats and dogs!

The rest of the city ran for cover, but we were already drenched, so what was the point?

Soaked to the bone, we continued our bike ride, laughing, shouting over the roar of the downpour, and singing in the rain at the top of our lungs.

In a word, we were *free*.

The experience brought back childhood scenes of singing in the rain: spinning in circles with Buttercup, our family Collie; playing in mud puddles with my cousins; and sitting in the back porch swing with my dad during a flash flood.

Anyway, as quickly as the downpour came, it receded. Normal city life resumed and we no longer owned the road, so we dismounted our bikes at a nearby food truck to wring out our clothes and grab a bite to eat.

As we ate lunch, a beautiful rainbow revealed itself to us, and that rainbow told me, as clear as day, that the world needs a whole lot more singing in the rain!

May 30
◇ THE ALL-KNOWING DEWDROP ◇

L ike pretty much every human who has ever lived, I often struggle to fully embrace the glory of each moment.

But Ollie helps me with that.

This morning, Ollie was walking me around the impeccably manicured corporate gardens near our home.

I was preoccupied with to-do lists and errands I needed to run, and I wasn't present to the beauty around me.

However, Ollie really caught my attention when he sniffed a eucalyptus leaf with a big, fat dewdrop on it.

My precious Ollie took me to that eucalyptus leaf on purpose. He wanted to share with me the spiritual realm that he is much more privy to than us humans.

Ollie pointed out to me that somehow, that dewdrop contained all that there is to know about life.

At that moment, I got to remember that there is so much more going on here than what meets the eye.

And as you go about your day, I hope that you, also, get to encounter the all-knowing dewdrop.

May 31

◇ YOU CAN'T GET NEW OLD FRIENDS ◇

The most important friendship I had as a teenager was sealed by a hush-hush bond. And while my friend's secret had a nine-month expiration date, she kept mine until I was ready to share it with others.

My dad's brain went haywire once I shared my secret with him, and one of the zanier ways he tried to control the situation was by going out and buying my dream car, a brand-new white Ford Mustang convertible.

My dad believed that somehow, some way, the magical qualities of this all-American muscle car would convince me to conform to his will while simultaneously calming his uncomfortable emotions.

Unfortunately for my dad, his plan didn't work, but we sure did enjoy our newfound ticket to freedom!

Whether we were heading to the mall, to our church, or prom, we loved making the rounds through our teenage stomping grounds with the top down; therefore, I'll refer to this friend throughout the book as Mustang Sally!

We took regular trips to the concert amphitheater about an hour away, and all the way home, we'd take the back roads, singing country songs at the top of our lungs!

Once I went to college, things changed. I needed a fresh start and I didn't know any other way than an 'all or nothing' approach, so I regrettably cut ties with Mustang Sally.

But what I never told her is that I covered half of my freshman dorm room with pictures of our misadventures.

Although I no longer talked *to* her, everyone in my dorm knew her by name.

Luckily, in my late twenties, I felt strong enough to start reintegrating the best parts of my past without feeling like I was losing myself. And the most rewarding part of that process has been reuniting with Mustang Sally!

When we talk on the phone each week, our inner teenagers get to see that we made it to adulthood. We each got a little bruised and scraped along the way, but we stayed true to ourselves and created lives that make sense for us.

Mustang Sally and I know each other in a way that no one else really does, and we're now mature enough to understand just how precious it is to have each other.

Because no one in this life will ever be able to get new old friends.

◇ JUNE ◇

June 1

◇ WELCOME, EVERY GUEST! ◇

Just minutes ago, I waved hello to our High Ambassador of Cuteness as he processed by me in his stroller-chariot.

With great pride, he showed me the drawing he made at school and asked, "Where's Ollie?" in his cute toddler voice.

And at that moment, my heart was stolen!

Minutes later, as I took the keys out of my pocket at my apartment door, I heard Ollie's little nails furiously scratching the door as he eagerly demanded a reunion.

Upon opening the door, he panted and danced on his hind legs to greet me, and my heart was stolen yet again!

And while I fed Ollie a treat, I considered the qualities that make him and our High Ambassador so darn welcoming.

First, they are both completely comfortable being themselves.

Second, they are proud of who they are; they aren't trying to be anything other than who God made them to be.

And finally, they deeply like themselves, and as a result, goodwill and cheer toward others radiate out of them.

And I realized that if these are the qualities that make a person affable, then hospitality must be a leading indicator that we are well on our way to becoming who we truly are!

June 2

◇ REMEMBERING THAT I'M NOT GOD ◇

As my body jettisons out of bed, my heart rams six inches out of my chest like a 1980s cartoon character.

Once again, without any immediately apparent reason, I have emerged from slumber in an anxious state.

So, I head to the fjord to take my cure of fresh air and sunshine.

I sit down on the grass and take out my journal, and my pen liberates me with words depicting sheer terror at my human state.

Finally, three words emerge that burst the dam of my ego: *I'm not God.*

Remembering I'm not God means I don't have to have all the answers; rather, I'm only responsible for doing my small part to recreate the world.

Anxiety comes from a need to control difficult situations and have all the answers.

Peace comes from remembering that all I *really* need to do is trust God and be my authentic self.

The difference between anxiety and peace is simple in theory, but hard in practice.

And the difference is remembering that I'm not God.

June 3

◇ THE RAINBOW BRIDGE ◇

E very once in a while, my emotions back me into a corner and I need something greater than earthly aid.

Luckily, *The Honest Guys* gave me a tool for accessing the one person who understands moments like these.

And of course, that person is Zuzu.

In these moments of intense emotional suffering, I lie down, close my eyes, and turn my palms face up.

Rainbows come out of my hands, creating a bridge for Zuzu to arrive.

We meet at the rainbow bridge, smile at each other, and I immediately feel soothed and understood.

Although we are in a realm beyond words, she transmits energy that reminds me of the strength that lies within me.

She lets me know that she believes in me and that I am her hope for the future, and I bask in her gentle, honest smile of unconditional love.

When Zuzu is ready to return to never-never land, I go about my day, filled with the remembrance that I am worthy, that I am enough, and that I am loved.

Who is the person you'll meet at *your* rainbow bridge, and what message do they have waiting for you?

June 4

◇ THE HILLS ARE ALIVE WITH THE SOUND OF MUSIC ◇

When my Best Friend, Ollie, and I were exploring the beautiful town of Flåm in the interior of Norway, some locals suggested we go on a 'half-hour, easy hike' to see a beautiful waterfall and panoramic view of the town.

I forgot to translate from Norwegian to Texan, and the excursion, in actuality, took over two hours of traversing perilous, century-old granite steps!

When we got to the top, we were huffing and puffing, and poor little Ollie was too tired to even wag his tail! But our burning lungs and pounding chest were worth the payoff.

We sat beside a beautiful waterfall and felt the mist on our faces as we absorbed the quaint village of Flåm at the lookout from on high.

It felt as though we were in the opening scene of *The Sound of Music;* all we needed was a singing, spinning Julie Andrews!

Later, as we descended back down the mountain, I got to thinking that personal development is a bit like our hike to the waterfall.

When people give us directions, our minds intellectually understand it and it sounds deceptively easy.

However, *experiencing* the difficult walk to becoming who we truly are is a long, hard climb that leaves us sweaty, out of breath, and thirsty.

But if we persist, there might just be a spectacular view waiting for us after all the hard work.

And that view won't be a booby prize that indicates we can rest on our laurels. It will just be a nice, restoring moment of peace and relaxation before we head back down the mountain to do the next leg of our life's journey.

But while we're at the top of the mountain, the hills might just come alive with the sound of music to cheer us on as we become who we truly are!

June 5

◇ ICE CREAM BICYCLES ◇

Lately, I've been full of visionary creativity. It's exhilarating, but having so many ideas creates a mental swirl that leads to emotional exhaustion.

As a result, my Best Friend got fed up with my zany antics, blew his imaginary referee's whistle, and kicked me out of the house for the day!

He said, "Patrick, get out of your mind. Go to a museum, or go camping, or go read a book by the fjord. I really don't care what you do, as long as you get out of the apartment right now!"

I wanted to read him the riot act for getting into my business, but he was so playful in his injunction that I had no line of defense.

So, I decided to hop on my bike and go up to a beautiful mountaintop lake, and within five minutes of putting my feet in the stirrups, I was grateful that my Best Friend banished me from the apartment.

I could literally feel the sunshine and fresh air shoving the accumulated stress out of my mind, and the further I pedaled, the freer I felt!

Forty kilometers of huffing and puffing later, I arrived lakeside to see people playing fetch with their dogs, paddling in kayaks, feeding the swans, and building sand castles with their kiddos along the shoreline.

Mr. Magpie even made a cameo appearance on a nearby branch!

Exhausted from the uphill journey, I thanked the wind for cooling me off and relaxed beneath the shade of an evergreen tree.

Then, after waking up from an accidental nap, I walked over to a nearby ice cream stand. I closed my eyes and smiled with delight as milk and sugar lit up my mind's pleasure center like a Las Vegas casino marquis.

And in that moment, I experienced what life is all about.

It's about setting work aside to fully experience the joy of living through a fun activity.

And, in the midst of the activity, stopping.

Just stopping.

And experiencing Heaven on Earth.

June 6

◇ SPRINTING IN THE STADIUM ◇

Each year, all the companies in Norway come together and sponsor a long-distance relay race for their employees.

My Best Friend decided to sign up with his company's team, and so I biked over to Bislett Stadium, where he'd be running the last leg of his team's race.

Getting there was a pain: first, the chain on my bike broke, and I thought, "Maybe I should just go home and take Ollie for a walk. He won't be able to see me amid thousands of spectators in the stadium anyway."

But then I thought, "No, Patrick. As much as he helps you, this is the least you can do for him," so I found a bike shop and fixed the chain in no time flat.

Then, another obstacle presented itself: as I neared the city center, the streets were so packed that I had to walk my bike the last few kilometers to the stadium.

Once again, I was tempted to turn back, because I figured, "There's no way I'll ever be able to find him in this pandemonium."

Then, I realized that all the runners would be coming through a narrow entrance to the stadium, and I worked my way right up to the track barrier. And after thirty minutes or so, I saw him run past me, and I rooted him on at the top of my lungs!

He smiled and waved as he sprinted past me, trying to outpace the other runners in his orange and black company race jersey.

Now, as a kid, I never understood why my parents attended all my piano recitals and sporting events. But last Saturday, I finally understood that when you care about someone, you want to show up for the important events in their life.

I felt so much pride seeing my friend sprint down the home stretch of Bislett Stadium, and I felt a sense of joy from focusing more on what I could give to the situation rather than what was easiest or most convenient for me.

It was a powerful life lesson that I will always be grateful for!

June 7

◇ WHY HURRY OVER BEAUTIFUL THINGS? ◇

When I lived in Leipzig, I woke up every day feeling marvelously grateful to walk the same streets as Bach, Wagner, Goethe, and many others once trod.

It was as though I had taken Platform Nine and Three Quarters to Hogwarts itself!

When I visited the Schumann house, I read a wonderful quote from Clara Schumann: "Why hurry over beautiful things? Why not linger and enjoy them?"

She was talking about beautiful moments in music, but I think the same applies to beautiful moments in *life*.

Although my music career has long since ended, Clara's words continually encourage me to take time to point out—for others and myself—the beautiful moments of life.

And that is exactly what I have tried to do in this book.

I've shared personal, special memories with you so that, hopefully, you can more easily identify precious moments in your own life, linger over them, and enjoy them on this cosmic vacation of being alive and human on Planet Earth!

June 8

◇ RANGOLI ◇

During my time in my Best Friend's hometown in India, I could bet my bottom dollar that each morning, there would be many women decorating the doorway to their homes with colorful powder.

They were performing the daily Hindu ritual of *Rangoli,* most often using the *mandala* pattern, which represents our relationship to the infinite, unknowable world that extends past human thought and belief.

Their efforts would no doubt be swept away by the winds of time. Yet they still attended to their ritual with the same tender loving care as an artist who knows his painting will be immortalized in a museum. And, each morning, they began again, just as diligently as the day before.

While *Rangoli* might be the most visually appealing way to connect with the Divine, there are many other ways: we can pray, meditate, journal, or just lie down and stare at the ceiling for a few moments.

So, before you proceed in your day, how can you take time to honor your relationship with the infinite, unknowable world that extends past human thought and belief?

June 9

◇ GASTRONOMY OF THE EYE ◇

O n a beautiful June day in Paris, I boarded a bus to seek out da Vinci's *Mona Lisa,* which is the most famous painting in the world.

Well, life had other plans. The bus route had changed, and getting to the Louvre was going to take quite a long wait, so I decided to exit the bus and walk in the general direction of the Louvre.

If I made it, great; if I didn't, then I would spend the day honoring Balzac's sentiment that walking through Paris is "a form of science...the gastronomy of the eye."

In other words, rather than focusing on reaching my destination come hell or high water, I listened to serendipity, which was telling me to drop my plans and go with the flow of life.

And, speaking of going with the flow, I wound up walking along the River Seine and seeing an amazing montage of people, places, and things!

I spied, with my little eye, the Eiffel Tower in the distance as I walked past honeymooners sipping café au lait.

I strolled through an underground tunnel filled with graffiti art and surfaced at the Tuileries Garden, where I walked by fragrant flowers, priceless garden sculptures, and kids playing with toy sailboats in the large fountain.

Eventually, I made it to the *Mona Lisa* with plenty of time to spare, but I didn't enjoy my destination nearly as much as the unexpected journey.

So, I skipped the three-hour wait to get an up-close view of the famed lady and chose instead to wander around the Louvre with no particular plan or expectations.

Along the way, I experienced amazing works of art I had heard about for years but never experienced: the Hammurabi Code, Géricault's *Raft of the Medusa,* and Delacroix's *Liberty Leading the People,* among others.

My day of 'getting lost on purpose' taught me that making plans is great, but so is trusting serendipity and improvising!

So, rather than getting frustrated when life doesn't go according to plan, let's consider whether serendipity is asking us to take a path that has more 'gastronomy of the eye' than we could ever plan for ourselves!

June 10

◇ DO WE NEED TO UNDERSTAND? ◇

After Zuzu passed, my Friend in Paris comforted me by sending a letter that contained a beautiful, complete thought on the nature of life and death.

With his permission, I am sharing it with you as today's reflection.

My Friend wrote:

With my Mother dying when I was only eight years old, death has been a part of my life for most of the time I have been alive. I don't really know what I think about it. As I get older, I realize that life and living are great mysteries that we will never understand while we are alive. Whether we will understand after we die is another story.

But then, there is the question: do we need to understand? The part that I do understand is that our lives are short and very precious, and that we have an enormous opportunity to do something with our lives while we are here. The sooner we realize that, the more opportunity there is to accomplish what we are here to do, those things we come to realize that we must do.

June 11
◇ TRUST YOUR GUT ◇

In the French language, there are two separate verbs for describing knowledge.

The verb *savoir* denotes a logical, analytical knowing, such as the weather forecast.

On the other hand, the verb *connaître* embodies an emotional, intimate knowing, such as your child's favorite food.

There's also a third way: *knowing what you know without knowing how you know it.*

This type of knowledge, which we call intuition, is a gut feeling that comes from the unprovable yet self-evident spiritual realm of life.

If we are like the sheep on the cover of this book, then intuition is like an invisible shepherd that guides us and keeps us safe.

So, as you go about your day, listen to your body's tingles and gut feelings. Trust that the powerful unseen force we call intuition is steering you in the right direction on your journey to becoming all that you truly are.

June 12

◇ ACCIDENTAL PHILANTHROPY ◇

When I first traveled to Oslo back in 2020, a wonderful couple agreed to keep Ollie for a few days.

However, we had no idea that international travel would halt due to the worldwide pandemic as I was midway over the Atlantic!

Although my ten-day stay extended to four months, there was never a question of finding a different home for Ollie.

Our friends treated him like their grandson, spoiling him with a luxury dog bed and a special anxiety jacket to calm him during Houston thunderstorms!

As a result, my Best Friend and I became quite close to this special couple during weekly calls to check in with each other and share laughs over stories of Ollie's weekly adventures. It was a bonding experience in unprecedented times.

Eventually, I returned to Houston to reunite with Ollie and prepare to move to Oslo permanently. In that process, Ollie's grandparents helped me sell my home, and they even allowed me to store a few of my things in their storage unit.

Once I settled into my new life in Oslo, I realized that shipping my belongings from their storage unit was not worth the expense, so I told them that I was happy to donate anything of use to their church.

I know that their church is a source of inspiration and community for them. Thus, supporting their church would be the best way I could say 'thank you' for all they had done.

It turned out the church was able to use two of the rugs I had stored away: one in the nursery and the other in the church library. And that's fitting since I love books and I love kids!

Ollie's grandparents gave us something much greater than money. They gave us love and care for Ollie at a time when we couldn't do it ourselves.

In a virtuous circle, they gave to me, then I gave back to them. It was never intentional; it was just people loving people in a sort of 'accidental philanthropy.'

I share this story because I'd like you to consider: is life presenting a natural, organic opportunity for you to practice 'accidental philanthropy?'

June 13

◇ NATURAL BYPRODUCTS ◇

Ollie doesn't have any titles or measurable success. He just shows up and changes the world as a natural byproduct of who he is.

Now, that doesn't mean Ollie's life is a utopia.

He gets scared of thunder and laptop charger cords.

He gets angry at food he can't chew because he's losing his teeth.

He gently growls at puppies who don't mind their p's and q's in the neighborhood.

And while he loves the long, sunny days of Norwegian summers, he is decidedly *not* a fan of tundra winters.

But all in all, Ollie loves himself and he knows that he is beloved.

And because I have been able to give Ollie an environment that allows him to thrive, I have seen him literally change the world.

For example, today Ollie and I decided to enjoy the beautiful weather by taking a walk to the fjord.

Once we arrived, I strung up my hammock and we curled up together, dozing off as the wind rocked us like two babies in a cradle.

However, our sunbeam-sprinkled nap was interrupted when an elderly woman asked if she could take a picture because she had just received some difficult news and her day was brightened when she saw Ollie sleeping on my belly.

As I gently lowered Ollie out of the hammock so that she could play with him, I told her that Ollie is great therapy, and she said, "Yes, I can see that!"

Ollie wasn't being anything other than himself, yet that was more than enough to heal this woman's emotional pain.

And through this interaction, Ollie taught me that we'll never know just how many people we'll help, simply by virtue of who we truly are; not because of what we know, what we can do, or the title we hold, but simply as a natural byproduct of living an authentic life.

June 14

◇ YOU GET TO TAKE YOUR TIME ◇

Our home owner's association has planted hundreds of bushes that only bloom for about two weeks each year.

These bushes occupy tons of space, and for most of the year, they are not really all that appealing to look at.

But the bushes become worth their weight in gold for a few weeks each June when they bloom unbelievably fragrant lavender petals.

As I walked by the bushes this morning, I thought about how some people are meant to be practical, evergreen trees that are stable and sturdy throughout the year.

But some of us, on the other hand, are more like these bushes: we need a lot of time, space, and resources to make our contribution to the world.

Even when it looks like we aren't producing, we're actually in a stage of dormancy that will eventually yield a period of unique blooming that brings wonder and amazement to everyone around us.

And I think that if those flowers outside my apartment can take their time, then so can we.

June 15

◇ THE SUNLIGHT OF THE SPIRIT ◇

As I write this, my Best Friend, Ollie, and I are in one of our favorite places to visit: a little town called Voss in the interior of Norway.

With an awe-inspiring lake, a waterfall surrounded by hanging ferns, a gorgeous river walk, and a panoramic view of mountains, what's not to love?!

As Ollie took me out for our walk this morning, the peaceful atmosphere reminded me of an anonymous author who once wrote that life is all about standing in the Sunlight of the Spirit and living happy, joyous, and free!

Currently, I'm getting ready for sleep after a wonderful day, and in this moment, all I can think is, "This is my family. We belong together. This is exactly where I am supposed to be."

So, it isn't just being in Voss that helped me bask in the Sunlight of the Spirit today. It's being here with them.

Likewise, wherever you are in the world today, whether on holiday or at home, take time to bask in the Sunlight of the Spirit with the ones you love!

June 16

◇ FALLING FORWARD INTO GREAT SPIRIT'S ARMS ◇

If there ever was a person who had faith in God, it was Zuzu.

She once said:

What they don't tell you is that faith is bloodcurdling because it means you have to lean on Great Spirit with childlike faith. If you try to steel yourself up, it takes a lot of energy. But if you just fall forward into Great Spirit's arms, God will support you and hold you up.

Zuzu's insight was hard-won because, for most of her life, she operated under her own self-will.

Her prayers tended to go something along the lines of, "God, here's my plan, now bless it."

But this mode of operating got so painful that she finally surrendered her will, and instead of forcing herself to make an unhealthy marriage work, she fell forward into the arms of God and her life started to unfold in incredible ways.

The more Zuzu trusted God and operated under His will instead of her own, the more she began to see a compelling vision of what the world could be and how she could play a part in getting it there.

Zuzu helped me see that trusting God isn't easy because it's bloodcurdling to make ourselves vulnerable and trust a force that we can't touch or see.

However, she also helped me see that faith is the obvious choice when the only other option is to live in a self-imposed prison of willfulness.

Zuzu's life was a testament to the fact that if we can let go of our willfulness and lean on Great Spirit with childlike faith, He will hold us up and support us as we go about the process of becoming who He made us to be.

So, with all that being said, how can you consciously choose to fall forward into Great Spirit's arms today?

June 17

◇ THE BULL AND THE MATADOR ◇

A few evenings ago, one of my neighbors passed a pretty hefty judgment on how I live my life.

I was getting riled up by the conversation, so I left her company, saying I needed to prepare dinner.

Once I got home, I chopped veggies with the vengeance of a thousand mercenaries while my thoughts and emotions ratcheted up until I was seeing red.

All of a sudden, I had become a Spanish fighting bull, snorting my nose and stomping my hooves, ready to charge at a moment's notice.

Then, for a moment, time stood still.

I connected to my five senses.

I smelled the cumin, mustard, and turmeric.

I noticed the ballet of oil bubbles.

And I listened to the onions caramelize.

Tuning into my sensory experience allowed me to remove myself from the story my mind was creating.

And rather than charging at my friend-turned-matador, I decided to leave the bullring and cease fighting.

And as a result of surrendering, I lost my self-righteous ego, but I won back my wisdom, my peace, and my freedom.

June 18

◇ HOLDING CLOSE AND LETTING GO ◇

The brilliant poet Mary Oliver once wrote:

To live in this world you must be able to do three things: to love what is mortal; to hold it against your bones knowing your own life depends on it; and, when the time comes to let it go, to let it go.

I certainly held Zuzu against my bones, which is why life became very difficult for me when the time came to let go.

As I struggled through the mourning process, a friend gently let me know that remembering Zuzu was important, but if I stayed too attached, I might get stuck in grief.

Therefore, I was advised to cherish Zuzu fondly in my heart, *and,* at the same time, to look for similar energy in new places.

I think my friend's advice is relevant to almost anyone.

So, when you come across energy that lights you up and touches the authentic part of yourself—whether it is a person, a pet, a video, a book, or anything else—hold it against your bones until it's time to let it go.

June 19

◇ AT WORLD'S END ◇

This weekend, my Best Friend, Ollie, and I camped out at Verdens Ende, which translates to 'At World's End.'

Centuries ago, Vikings set sail to new, unknown lands from this harbor, which was the end of the world as they knew it.

But I experienced a second, inner reason that this harbor is called 'At World's End.

If you walk out into the sea as far as you can atop the miles of boulders at Verdens Ende, nature creates an optical illusion that challenges your perception.

When you're that far out to sea and you look forward into the ocean, it is impossible to differentiate where the sea ends and the horizon begins.

As a result, nature's sleight of hand makes it seem as though you are on the cusp of lifting a veil and entering a portal that takes you from the end of this world and into the next!

Now, I still don't know what's behind the veil, and I don't think anyone ever will in this lifetime.

But at Verdens Ende, I could almost touch the veil.

And for a brief second, I could hear the voice of Truth behind the veil, clear as a bell, and my life totally clarified.

That voice gave me marching orders, and I returned to shore in order to carry out the instructions I was given about the next steps in my life's journey.

Likewise, I hope you will find time today to leave the metaphorical shoreline of your external world and descend as deep into your soul as you can go, just as I walked out as far as I could on the rocks.

And once you plunge as far as you possibly can, I hope you'll wait for an encounter with what's behind the veil so that you can receive direction for the next right actions in *your* life's journey.

It's a worthy endeavor because when we get those instructions from Truth and then carry them out, the end of the world as we know it recedes and our reality expands.

And in that process, we recreate the world with just a little less space between everyday life and the Truth that resides behind the veil.

June 20

◇ THREE IDIOTS ◇

Last night, we celebrated the summer solstice by flocking to the fjord, barbequing dinner with our neighbors, and jumping off the pier into the freezing cold June waters.

Although we turned in around ten p.m., sleep was impossible between the sun refusing to set and the teenagers yupping it up outside.

After tossing and turning for a few hours, I decided to turn my frustration into fun by rewatching my favorite Bollywood movie, *Three Idiots*.

The movie certainly fit the moment, as it is a powerful coming-of-age comedy about three teenage friends who get into all sorts of zany antics at university.

The main character, Rancho, is a creative, fun-loving, divergent thinker. Rancho drives his professor crazy because he knows what the expected answers are, yet every time he's called upon, he challenges the status quo.

Rancho's classmates are stressed by this professor who enjoys making their life hell and reminding them that he controls their future.

But Rancho's playfulness helps his fellow students relax and enjoy life.

At one point, Rancho's rambunctious nature leads him to break out into song and dance alongside his buddies as he proclaims:

When life is out of control, then let your lips roll,
    whistle and say that all is well!
The chicken is clueless about the eggs,
    will it hatch or get fried in a pan?
No one knows what our future holds, but all is well!

Before watching the movie, I was feeling quite misanthropic toward the teenagers outside who were keeping me awake. But just as Rancho taught his professor to lighten up and think more creatively, the kids outside reminded me to loosen up and roll with the punches.

So, when we get annoyed at other people today, let's consider whether or not it's because they're having more fun than us. And if they are, then let's join them!

Because engaging in shenanigans reminds us that whatever the future holds, all is well!

Whether you hatch or get fried, all is well!

June 21

◇ CURVEBALLS ◇

My dad expected me to follow a predictable, linear equation for living my life.

I was supposed to marry right out of high school and work in the family business until I retired, and my dad even bought a plot of land on which he decided my siblings and I should raise our families.

Well, instead, I completely broke the mold!

I left home and pursued my love of classical music, which allowed me to travel the world and experience history and culture in a firsthand way.

And ironically, although classical music is a creative art form, making a living as a musician involves a very stiff, linear progression of professional development.

Although I was iconoclastic, my talent couldn't be ignored, and I could have easily ridden a wave of success until I retired.

However, life once again threw a curveball: a teenager asked for my assistance, and over the course of a year, I saw his life change through our brotherhood.

Befriending that young man felt so meaningful that I realized a life of helping others was my new calling.

So, I decided to pursue a career in psychotherapy, started graduate school, and served as a high school counselor.

Then, *another* curveball: just as I was preparing to become a licensed therapist, I met Zuzu, and she introduced me to the world of executive coaching.

I was going along the path to building a successful coaching practice in Houston when life didn't just throw a curveball, it threw a change-up!

The international pandemic hit, the whole world went topsy-turvy, and a series of serendipitous events prompted my Best Friend and I to move to Norway, where nature inspired me to write this book.

I share the twists and turns of my life story in order to point out that life is not linear. It's more like a squiggly graph full of ups and downs that make the plot line juicy!

Now, I would have never guessed life would lead me to where I am today; I just did the next right indicated thing as best I could, and the cards fell the way they did.

I have no idea what's next, and that's part of the fun!

So, as you go about your day, how can you adjust to life's curveballs and hit home runs rather than striking out?

June 22
◇ HOW CAN I HELP YOU SAY GOODBYE? ◇

When Zuzu died, I was in uncharted territory: I had never lost someone so close to me.

My emotions were intense and my thinking was haywire.

But I still had my intuition, which told me to go camp in Big Bend National Park.

Big Bend is *vast,* and the perspective of being a tiny human in a larger-than-life place was an altogether fitting way to grieve Zuzu, who was all about spiritual expansion.

I spent my days backpacking for miles along mountains and taking trails through the desert along the Rio Grande.

At night, I would look up and see billions of stars and know that Zuzu was looking down at me fondly.

Eventually, my legs turned to rubber, my senses became overwhelmed by all the beauty, and my heartstrings tugged at me to return to Ollie, who was staying with his grandparents.

As I left the park, an old country song came on the radio that perfectly fit the moment, and I started crying.

But these weren't tears of grief. These were tears of gratitude for a very special lady I'll call my Grief Guide who assisted me in grieving Zuzu's death.

The song perfectly describes my Grief Guide's role in my life when the singer tells us:

Time will ease your pain:
life's about changing, nothing ever stays the same.
How can I help you to say goodbye?
It's okay to hurt and it's okay to cry.
Come let me hold you and I will try;
how can I help you to say goodbye?

Since Zuzu's passing, I've woken up to just how many people in the world are stuck in the pain of unresolved, unfelt grief.

Therefore, I think learning how to say goodbye, and then helping others say goodbye, is just about the most expansive, liberating act of freedom we can perform in this life.

June 23

◊ THE ABILITY TO DISREGARD DISABILITIES ◊

Summer in Oslo is amazing, not just because of the weather, but because of the incredible way people live their lives here.

Of course, there are adrenaline junkies who parasail and cliff dive. But even more awe-inspiring is witnessing how disabled people here in Norway go about their day and enjoy the finer points of life just as I would.

Just in the last two weeks, I've seen a woman with no arms participate in a half marathon and a guy in a wheelchair fishing at the end of a pier.

I passed a teenage girl with Down Syndrome riding on a tandem bicycle with her father and I saw a blind man crossing a busy downtown street.

I saw a paralyzed young boy scooting around in his motorized wheelchair with his family on a beautiful Sunday afternoon.

And unbelievably, I witnessed a man that had almost no use of his hands nor feet somehow walking from the bus stop to the office building where he is gainfully employed.

Now, I'll be honest: these moments tend to humble me in a stomach-churning sort of way. It's initially uncomfortable to encounter these people because witnessing their life circumstances forces me to examine just how much I take my sharp mind and fit body for granted.

But then I look at how these amazing people figure out ways to engage with life, despite impediments I have never known, and I become inspired by their strength of character.

And speaking of inspiration, the origin of that word comes from the Latin *inspiratus,* meaning 'to breathe into.'

These people are somehow able to find ways to disregard their disabilities, and without ever knowing it, they breathe new appreciation and awareness into me.

And for that, I am grateful.

So today, let's all notice the people who make us feel uncomfortable.

And rather than turning away from them, let's allow their presence in our lives to breathe new appreciation and new awareness into us.

June 24

◇ THE GLEE OF GETTING TO SHORTHAND IT ◇

Third grade was one of the hardest years of my life. My parents moved my brother and I from a private academy to a public school, and I did not adjust well to the crowded, noisy new environment.

My saving grace was a girl in my class whose sunny disposition hung the moon. I always knew I had a chair at her lunch table, and years later, we even went to junior prom together!

She and I were one of the few people who left our hometown after high school graduation. She headed to San Francisco, and I headed, well, all over the place!

But we carried each other in our hearts, and one summer years ago, we reunited when my wandering ways took me to the City by the Bay.

We saw the seals at the harbor, rode the trolley up and down the hills decorated with colorful homes, ate truffle fries in Berkeley, and talked all night from a lookout point over the Golden Gate Bridge.

And on the flight back to Houston, I realized that she and I always get to short-hand our chats. There are no explanations needed, no misunderstandings.

For example, at present, she is a new mother and I am halfway across the world in Norway, so we aren't able to catch up all that often.

But nevertheless, when we do get a chance to reunite, we bear witness to and revel in the immutable, unchangeable, gloriously human parts of us that are just as relevant today as they were back in third grade!

The glee of getting to shorthand it is wonderful, and it's something only possible with a few people, because after all, you can't get new old friends.

June 25

◇ HALFWAY BETWEEN TWO SHORES ◇

I prepare a bed of blankets by the waters separating the shore of my neighborhood from the shore of downtown Oslo.

All is well externally: the sun is shining, there is a gentle breeze, soft blades of grass gently rub my skin, and there are kids from the nearby daycare playing along the shoreline.

Yet, there is discord in my heart, and my body is jittery like a thoroughbred on derby day.

Is it biology?

Probably.

It is pain from childhood?

I'll take two sides of that on my Plate of Fear, with salt and pepper, please.

But thinking about the cause of the pain isn't going to help, so instead of letting my mind ruminate, I close my eyes and go into my heart.

I take a deep breath.

I put my hand on Ollie's belly.

I listen to Mr. Magpie sing his song.

And I remember that all is well and that I can relax into God's hands.

Then, I open my eyes and take in the shimmering waters, and as I scan the horizon, I notice that there is a sailboat halfway between my shore and the city's shore.

Likewise, turning off my head and going into my heart propelled me halfway *from* the shore of my ego's fear—which is where I was just five minutes ago—and halfway *toward* the shore of my true self.

And halfway between two shores isn't half bad at all!

June 26

◇ EMOTIONAL STOPLIGHTS ◇

On the bike trail this morning, a guy and his preschool son were happily chattering when suddenly, their scooter hit a crack in the pavement and they took a tumble.

Score one for gravity!

As I watched the situation unfold, I saw in real time how emotions instruct us, just like stoplights instruct traffic.

Initially, the boy was feeling joy, a 'green light' which prompted him to shout, "Let's go faster!"

But upon falling, the boy's smile of gladness turned into tears of sadness. His inner stoplight light turned from green to red, telling him to stop, make sure he was okay, and rest.

Once the little boy realized he wasn't hurt, he dried his tears and the hesitant yellow light of fear told him to proceed with caution. He got back on the scooter but asked his dad to go slow and be careful.

Of course, as adults, the situations we face are much more complex than a scooter tumble; therefore, we need to combine logic with our emotions to find wise solutions.

But nevertheless, our emotional stoplight can at least give us a kernel of truth about when to move forward, when to slow down, when to shuck, and when to jive!

June 27

◇ THE SPIRITUAL INFORMATION OF THIS WORLD ◇

A landmark day in my life was visiting the ancient pilgrimage site of Chartres Cathedral.

After marveling at the spires, facades, and buttresses of this Gothic Cathedral, I walked toward the entrance, which was ornamented with sculptures depicting the life of Christ.

And as the sculptures transported me from the outside world to the cathedral within, I also traveled to my inner sanctum.

Joseph Campbell described my experience perfectly when he wrote:

That cathedral [Chartres] talks to me about the spiritual information of the world. It's a place for meditation, just walking around, just sitting, just looking at those beautiful things.

Similarly, at some point today, I hope you take time to find a place of beauty that talks to you about the spiritual information of the world, whether it is a book, or a pond, or a cathedral, or...

June 28
◇ WORK HARD, BE PROUD OF WHAT YOU ACHIEVE ◇

Each morning as I enter the gym, I pass a large mural with eight words written in the middle of it: *work hard, be proud of what you achieve.*

Something about that phrase inspires me to continue going back to the gym one day at a time.

Likewise, at this point in our year together, we're about at the halfway point, and there is no doubt that you've worked hard.

So, I'd like you to take some time today and look at what you've achieved thus far.

Have you found yourself a little more able to relax into wisdom, peace, and freedom?

Do you find yourself connected to infinity and eternity more often?

And do you feel like you have taken steps toward becoming who you truly are?

I'd love for you to take a few minutes to write an inventory of what you have done well this year so that you can go about your day feeling proud of what you have achieved!

June 29
◇ BIGGER THAN THE UNIVERSE AND BEFORE TIME ◇

Zuzu once told me that the more she treated her life as a spiritual opportunity, rather than a race to run, the more deep Truth appeared to her.

And she described this Truth as "Divine love, an energy that is bigger than the universe and before time."

She went on to say:

God is right here with me, and it's not a belief, because belief blocks critical thinking. When one has a belief without deeply examining it, it becomes a defense or law.

What I've been trying to do lately is live with principles, which are beyond rules and scripts. I try to explore daily the nature of God. I apply the resulting discoveries to my daily life. And more than anything, I try to remember that I am a child of Great Spirit and that I am loved, adored, and cherished.

So, as we go about our day, may we, also, remember that we are loved, adored, and cherished by the Truth which is bigger than the universe and before time.

June 30

◇ MY HEARTBEAT IN MY EARDRUM ◇

G lorious rays of the sun kiss my skin as we walk the path
　　we have traveled uncountable times before
　　　　while the verdant evergreens lift their branches up
　　　　to the birds flying above.

As we arrive at our sacred rock, we share the
　　joy of our life-changing good news (and our ice cream!)
　　with Ollie nestled between us on his blanket.

With the unique taste of sweat and sunscreen on my lips,
　　I take off my shirt and walk the planks
　　to the ice-cold summer waters of the tundra.

I fling my body into the freezing June waters
　　with a blood-curdling primal yell
　　in anticipation of the shock;
　　somehow I meld from human to polar bear,
　　yet it is still I, in another form.

I float on my back and know that all is well
   as I gaze at the wisps of clouds decorating
   the midsummer day's sky.

As the large, slow waves roll in,
   I feel cradled by the Universe,
   as though I am floating in outer space.

My neck releases, my body goes limp,
   I am motionless and relaxed,
   and I hear my heartbeat in my eardrum.

And as you go about your day, I wish you the same:
   to celebrate the joy and harmony of life
   until you hear the heartbeat in *your* eardrum.

◇ JULY ◇

July 1

◇ A STAR, A DOG, AND A FLOWER ◇

Earlier this year, I introduced Mustang Sally in order to illustrate the principle 'you can't get new old friends.'

Recently, Mustang Sally's family had to say goodbye to her dog of fifteen years, and her young daughter has since convinced herself that he will come back as a flower.

After all, Mustang Sally gave their dog a beautiful burial service next to the family garden, and in that garden are seeds, also buried, that will sprout into daffodils and lavender.

I told my friend's daughter that she is absolutely correct.

After all, energy is neither created nor destroyed, it simply changes form.

For example, stars died so that we can live, so who knows what our physical energy transforms into after our souls leave the Earth?

My friend gave me a deadpan look and said, "Patrick, that was really beautiful, but it went way over her head. I don't think you're ready to carry your message to kids."

I laughed and said, "Fair enough, but my point remains: if a star can turn into humans and dogs, then who's to say that we can't live on as a flower?!"

July 2

◇ PAYING NO HEED ◇

R ecently, a friend and I were comparing stories from childhood and he asked, "Patrick, did you face any adversity by growing up with your sort of personality in such a small town?"

I thought for a second, then playfully said, "Aristotle once said that 'the weak are always anxious for justice and equality. The strong pay no heed.'"

He looked perplexed, so I explained that the question of whether or not I experienced adversity in my childhood is, in a sense, a boring question.

Instead, I prefer to ask myself how the so-called 'injustices' and 'inequalities' I faced strengthened me.

For example, if I had fit into my culture of origin more completely, then I would have never left my hometown.

Subsequently, I would have never experienced other cultures, which has been such a huge part of developing into my authentic self.

So, as you go about your day, how can you pay no heed to justice and equality, but rather, embrace the pain of spiritual growth that is necessary for the continual, day-by-day, lifelong process of becoming who you truly are?

July 3

◇ "COWABUNGA, DUDE!" ◇

I'm not a Ninja Turtle, but when I jump into the ice-cold fjord on a hot summer's day, I always holler "Cowabunga, Dude!" at the top of my lungs.

Sure, I *could* stay dry on the shoreline and save myself from the pain of the intense temperature change.

But instead, I choose to dive off the pier, even as my body anticipates the shock to my central nervous system.

And although my body is in pain, my mind is at peace: there is simply no room for thinking when your body is busy surviving a semi-hypothermic state!

My teeth chatter throughout the twenty-meter swim back to the pier ladder, yet as I climb out of the glacier water and into the sun, the temperature change makes me feel fit, fine, and dandy!

I think most healthy things are kind of like jumping into the fjord. We know they'll come with some unpleasant sensations, but ultimately, we'll be glad we did it.

So, as you go about your day, consider: are there any opportunities for you to yell "Cowabunga, Dude!" as you leap into an uncomfortable activity in order to emerge with renewed well-being?

July 4
◇ DECLARING INDEPENDENCE ◇

In eighth grade, my class took a field trip to Washington D.C. to learn more about the wonderful country we were born and raised!

And I have to say that my favorite part of the trip was visiting the Rotunda of the National Archives Building, where the Declaration of Independence is on display.

Even as an eighth grader, I understood that when the signatories authored the Declaration, they were saying, "This is liberation day!"

Now, nothing changed externally at that exact moment; England didn't all of a sudden bestow sovereignty upon the Americans.

But something *within* changed.

The colonies were now cohesively bonded under a resolve to achieve a common purpose: freedom.

And since freedom is a central tenet of this book, let's look at how the Founding Fathers declared their independence.

The Preamble of the Declaration of Independence sets forth the philosophical principles and justifications for declaring independence.

The List of Grievances details the specific complaints against the British Crown.

And the Conclusion states the decision of the colonies to become independent states.

I think this formula is still relevant today. When we need to free ourselves from a person, place, or idea, we can start by thinking about philosophical reasons for our goal.

Then we can set out a course of listing the reasons we need our freedom (and of course, unlike the Founding Fathers, we don't necessarily need to share these publicly!).

And we can conclude by writing out a resolution of what we will do to change our circumstances.

Then, once we've done the inner work of reflecting and writing down our declaration, we can begin the hard work of bringing that dream into reality into the external world.

And finally, just as my nation celebrates the Declaration of Independence each Fourth of July, we can celebrate our newfound freedom in whatever way we choose!

July 5

◇ BREAKING FREE ◇

When I was a child, my family typically reserved Sunday afternoons for visiting my grandparents.

My dad's parents were just a three-minute walk away, but my mom's parents lived thirty minutes away by car, which meant time to read in the back seat!

Well, one fateful summer Sunday when I was six, I didn't want to put my book down once we arrived at Maw-Maw's house.

So, while my mom and her parents went to pick butter beans and okra from the garden, I stayed inside and read.

At some point, I must have needed to pee, but my little brain had forgotten that the bathroom door was notorious for getting stuck.

Now, if I had brought my book to the bathroom with me, it wouldn't have been a problem. I would have been so distracted by the juicy plot that I wouldn't have even noticed I was stuck.

But all of a sudden, I found myself locked in a bathroom, my tiny voice yelling for my mommy to no avail.

I was *not* free!

So, I did the only 'logical' thing there was to do.

I found a can of hairspray under the bathroom counter and proceeded to go about the noble task of knocking a hole in the door and trailblazing my way to freedom!

I had almost Shawshanked'ed my way out when my mom came back inside, laughing hysterically at my cleverness.

And over the years, I have come to see that we humans commit ourselves to accidental self-imprisonment all the time.

In adulthood, just a few potential jail cells include ego, judgment, debt, substance abuse, incompatible relationships, or careers that don't suit our natural strengths.

Usually, we've already been warned that the door sticks, but we generally have to learn from our own experiences.

We're hard-headed that way!

The trick to escaping to freedom is to remember that being in these situations is gloriously human.

Then, with a good dose of gumption, we can decide whether we want to relax and wait for someone to help us unlock the door, or if we want to weaponize the nearest can of hairspray and blast our way back to the freedom of authentic living!

July 6
◇ OPPOSITE SIDES OF THE SAME COIN ◇

Earlier today I was vetted as an external coach for a large international company, and of course, they couldn't end the call without that age-old interview question: "Tell us about your strengths and weaknesses."

So, I told them about how my greatest strength is also tied to my greatest weakness, like opposite sides of the same coin.

On one side of the coin, I'm a highly creative person. I see possibility when others see a dead end.

But because I am so comfortable in the realm of possibility, it's sometimes hard to come back down to earth and be in the realm of reality.

Therefore, I've had to do a lot of work and gain skills to learn how to attend to details: to really 'cross the t's' and 'dot the i's.'

However, with each passing year, I'm becoming more successful at keeping one foot in the infinite and eternal realm of creativity while keeping the other foot in the details and practicalities of the present moment.

The answer to this question set me apart from other people they interviewed and I ended up getting the contract, because it takes a lot of insight and acumen to really search inside ourselves and learn about our strengths and weaknesses.

So, I'd encourage you to start thinking about your greatest strength and your greatest weakness, all the while remembering that they're usually opposite sides of the same coin!

July 7

◇ HARDER THAN PUTTING A MAN ON THE MOON ◇

A few years back, I spent a remarkable week with my Friend in Paris. We spent our time cooking together from Julia Child and company's *Mastering the Art of French Cooking* while asking deep questions about life in the way that intuitive creatives do so naturally.

As I departed from his doorway after our last meal together, my friend said something about power.

I don't remember the words, but his soul was saying, "I am grateful for my simple, quiet life here in my little neighborhood away from the noise. All those people in power are fighting, and for what?"

I responded by telling him about the memoir of a woman who reacted to the grief of her partner's passing by cycling around the globe. She literally chose to circumnavigate the planet rather than sit still with her broken heart.

Similarly, I think that many times, people find it easier to dominate others and control things than simply feel their emotions. It seems to be human nature to chase external 'success' when we don't know how to process so-called 'unpleasant' emotions like sadness, anxiety, fear, and anger in healthy ways.

Yes, chasing a world record or that next promotion is difficult, but for many people, those goals are a breeze compared to the alternative of feeling 'painful' emotions.

This is why Carl Jung once said that it's easier to put a man on the moon than to get him to go inside himself and do inner work.

I told my Friend in Paris that in my view, some people just don't want to look at what their issues are, and that it's all too common for people to balk at the door of the inner journey and instead turn around and try to manage success in the external world.

But I went on to say that there will always be outliers who consciously choose to rise above the fray of power so they can ultimately dive down into love, creativity, and their true identity.

So, as you go about your day, remember that if you want to save yourself from the exhaustion of rocketing to the moon or biking around the world, all you have to do is grant yourself permission to feel.

July 8
◊ THE SPIRITUAL GENIUSES OF THIS WORLD ◊

My Best Friend attended grade school with bona fide geniuses who went on to study with Nobel Laureates and Fields Medal recipients.

He recently told me that he failed to use his own potential as successfully as his classmates, but I quickly interjected.

I said, "Look, there will always be plenty of people to solve equations and make innovations. But you use your genius to care for your family—even when there are difficult obstacles standing in the way—because that is what is most important to you."

He began to respond, but I playfully said "Hold on, I'm not finished with my lecture yet!"

I reminded him that the *Chandogya Upanishad*, a sacred book from his Hindu faith, describes a light that shines brighter than even the sun.

This light is not up in the heavens, however.

This light comes straight from the heart of man.

The inner light of each man, woman, and child is "smaller than the kernel of a grain of millet. But it is greater than the earth, greater than the sky, greater than the heavens."

I told my Best Friend that since the day I met him, his inner light has illuminated many parts of life I would have never seen otherwise, and that holding on to one's inner light is much more valuable and rare than a savant.

The spiritual geniuses of this world, like my Best Friend, teach the rest of us how to shine our inner light as brightly as they do.

And by following their example, we recreate the world with less darkness, less pain, and fewer secrets than before we arrived.

And that *has* to be just as valuable as a Fields Medal!

July 9

◇ SEMOLINA AND A SPIRITUAL EXPERIENCE ◇

One of my favorite memories from India was when my Best Friend and I stopped by his eldest sister's home.

As I enjoyed the home-cooked meal, my friend's nephew innocently asked, "Patrick, if you don't have a wife and you don't live with your parents, who cooks your food?"

I knew that in his family, eating in restaurants is taboo and that the women cook for the family. So I played with his expectations and kidded, "My mom cooks for me every day and ships my food from North Carolina to Norway."

My friend's nephew bobbed his head in jest and said, "My mom couriered food to my university hostel every day, so it's possible. You just have to ask!"

It was an evening of warm, playful ribbing at cultural differences with a family who genuinely liked each other.

I liked what I saw—and tasted!—and I became open to learning more.

Little did I know that my life was changing and I was having a spiritual experience alongside that delicious semolina-based sweet dish my friend's sister served!

And I think that's how spiritual growth happens: one bite of food, one happy chat, one day at a time.

July 10

◇ "I WISH I WAS AS CREATIVE AS YOU ARE..." ◇

In my first career as a classical musician, it never failed that after a concert someone would compliment me by insulting themselves.

Normally it went like this: "Gee, Patrick, I wish I was creative like you."

Comments like this really peeved me, because I believe that we are all creative.

The problem is not that some people are creative and others aren't; the problem is that our commonly held ideas about creativity are too narrow.

For example, a guy once told me he wished he was more creative, and just ten minutes later I found out that he had built a soccer league for thousands of kids based on fun and positivity rather than competition!

In my opinion, that man was highly creative, because he was facilitating an opportunity for kids to fall in love with a sport in an even-keeled, pleasant way.

So, as you go about your day, remember that everyone, including you, is creative in one way or another.

It's just part of being human, and we couldn't escape it if we tried!

July 11

◇ THE FREEDOM TRAIL ◇

I mentioned earlier this year that the greatest gift my mom ever gave me was our weekly trips to the library.

Well, in high school, she gave me a gift that came in close second.

I had just finished my year-long Advanced Placement United States history course, making top marks on the national exam.

My mom wanted to foster my budding love for history, so she decided I could pick any historic location in the continental United States for summer vacation.

Without even a second of hesitation, I said, "This is amazing! I know exactly where we'll go: Boston!"

My mom looked puzzled that I was able to answer so quickly and asked me why I chose Boston.

But my immediate response wasn't an impulse.

It was intuition.

I rattled off to my mom a slew of interesting things we could explore.

But ultimately, I wanted to go to Boston to learn how the land I was born in became free.

Convinced, she booked the plane tickets that night!

I was so excited to walk the Freedom Trail, a two-mile stretch that includes Paul Revere's Home, Faneuil Hall, the site of the Boston Massacre, and the Old North Church.

But there was another kind of freedom that I learned about in Boston: for the first time in my life, I saw that there are many different ways to be human and live life.

For example, when we went whale watching in Boston Harbor, I saw two guys quietly holding hands and looking out into the water.

It was something I had never seen before.

And at that moment, I realized the power behind the Founding Fathers' words and deeds.

Freedom wasn't a theory for the Founding Fathers. It was a core value, a principle for which they were willing to fight to the death.

And in the process, the Founding Fathers created a land in which we have the freedom to become who we truly are.

All we have to do is follow in their footsteps and summon the courage to walk down our own, individual Freedom Trail.

July 12

◇ THINK LIKE REMBRANDT ◇

To this day, I still can't believe I talked my mom and dad into sponsoring my enrollment in a summer art course in Amsterdam for my twentieth birthday!

And it was worth every penny, because I could feel my world opening up when I came face to face with Rembrandt's larger-than-life masterpiece *The Night Watch*.

Now, this painting holds a special place in history because it is one of the first to combine bright colors with dark shades, resulting in a level of nuance and sophistication previously thought unimaginable.

By synthesizing two supposedly incompatible color schemes, Rembrandt elevated his painting, and by proxy the viewer, into the spiritual realm of life.

And since the day I stood in front of *The Night Watch*, I have been convicted to do the same in my life.

I strive to elevate my *self* by synthesizing conflicting views and ideas; rather than seeing things in black-or-white, all-or-nothing terms, I try to find the grey area.

Likewise, how can you find a way to combine conflicting ideas and, as a result, elevate yourself into the spiritual realm of wisdom, peace, and freedom?

July 13

◇ THE ALBATROSS ◇

Childhood is an era where the Nutcracker still comes to life, where flora and fauna can take on human-like qualities, and where dreams come true when we wish upon a star.

And a key ingredient to becoming who you truly are is keeping a sense of life's magic intact as an adult!

For example, in Herman Melville's classic novel *Moby Dick*, Captain Ahab expresses childlike wonder when he describes the first albatross he ever saw:

At intervals, it arched forth its vast archangel wings, as if to embrace some holy ark...Through its inexpressible, strange eyes, methought I peeped to secrets not below the heavens. As Abraham before the angels, I bowed myself...

Indeed, when we live with childlike zest and an open, curious mind, we can learn the secrets of Heaven from an albatross, we can see infinity in a grain of sand, and we can recreate the world on our way to becoming who we truly are!

July 14

◇ PEOPLE WILL VEX US ◇

For *two years of my life* after Zuzu's passing, I did mental gymnastics trying to figure out why she didn't tell me she was sick with cancer.

But finally, my Grief Guide got my attention when she said, "Patrick, when you talk about trying to investigate Zuzu's reasons for not telling you she was dying, you sound like a chicken with your head chopped off. Can you just accept that there will be some things you will never know the answers to?"

This woman's words were like a slap across the face that I desperately needed in order to wake up from my own insanity.

And why did I need the slap?

Because I was refusing to accept that sometimes, people will vex us.

I eventually accepted that whether I liked it or not, Zuzu chose not to disclose that she was dying, and that was her choice to make.

I'll never have answers for why she did what she did, but that's okay, because I'm not God, and as a result, there are some things that I will never have the answers to.

Today, I invite you to identify a situation where *you* want to know the answers and, instead, try to embrace the mystery of the situation.

Maybe together we can curiously be in the question rather than needing to have all the answers.

Maybe together, we can accept that sometimes, people (and life!) will vex us, and that the discomfort of not having all the answers is just one small part of the beautiful path to becoming who we truly are!

July 15
◇ JUDGE NOT ◇

Movies and books teach us to see heroes as people who perform humanity-saving, death-defying feats.

However, I see a hero as an ordinary person who does the back-breaking hard work of identifying their biases and then shifting their perspective.

Case in point: my Coffee Companion once told me that in her younger years, she abhorred greedy people.

But over time, her prejudice has been replaced by a curiosity that has allowed her to see the strengths of this behavior.

She sees that people she once judged as greedy believe they are worthy of asking for what they need and want, and that she can learn to be more assertive from them.

So, as you and I go about our day, let's take after my Coffee Companion: let's identify the traits that we dislike in others, and instead of judging them, let's see the strengths of the very attributes we are so tempted to roll our eyes at.

July 16

◇ LOVE CAN ONLY BE FOUND IN THE PRESENT ◇

As I write these words, Ollie is in the background licking his breakfast plate clean, and once he finishes, he will prance over to the couch and hop onto his sheepskin blanket for a nap.

I love Ollie with my whole heart, and sometimes as I watch him live his life, I start to wonder how in the world I am going to manage the day he leaves his physical form.

Luckily, this morning, I read a passage by the Indian philosopher Krishnamurti that boils down to the idea that love can only be found in the present.

That passage helped me realize that when I'm worried about a future without Ollie, I'm not truly loving him.

A more loving approach is to focus on what he needs rather than my irrational desire for his immortality.

And so I've decided that when I get scared about a life without Ollie, I'll pause and go be in the moment with him, enjoy the pleasure that he gets from life, and fully attune myself to him.

So, as you go about your day, consider how you can really love those in your care in this moment.

Because this moment is the only place true love resides.

July 17

◇ THE LOFTY GOAL OF CLEANING THE TOILET ◇

I spent a huge chunk of my life chasing lofty, irritation-inducing goals because I didn't know just how powerful having a nice, simple, easy-going routine could be.

These days, however, I lead a very different kind of life.

I wake up early, go to the gym, then come home to walk Ollie and eat a breakfast of oatmeal.

Then I write, meet clients, clean, cook, and run errands.

In the evening, I eat dinner with friends and then we watch a sitcom episode or two.

And after a day well lived, I unplug from Earth and recharge through dreams that come from whatever it is that resides behind the mountain on the cover of this book.

So, what I'm trying to say, is that these days, I'm fully Patrick Parker.

From on high, from the peak of Mount Everest.

And that summit often looks like doing the dishes, giving Ollie a bath, changing the air filters, and cleaning the toilet.

So, as you go about your day, may you find your own mountain-top apex that is grounded in the beauty of daily routine, because that is *more* than enough!

July 18

◊ THIS SIDE OF THE DIRT ◊

In my early twenties, a coworker challenged me to expand my vision by writing my obituary.

He told me that by thinking about how I wanted to be remembered, I could take steps toward that legacy.

Back then, writing my obituary had a lot to do with people remembering my achievements.

But now, in my thirties, my idea of a legacy is much more in line with a quote from *The Book of Henry:*

Our legacy isn't what we write on our resume or how many commas we have in our bank account. It's who we're lucky enough to have in our lives and what we can leave them with. The one thing we do know: we're here now. So I say we do the best we can while we're on this side of the dirt.

Regularly revising my obituary allows me to consider the end game of my life's story, live more authentically, and make the best of it while I'm on this side of the dirt.

So, today, consider taking a step toward becoming more fully 'you!' by writing your obituary; it might just bring surprising insight into the next steps in your life's journey!

July 19
◊ THE RESTLESS PAIN OF DOING NOTHING ◊

Exhausted from anxiety-interrupted sleep, I squirm around my mattress at five a.m.

My body screams at me to jump out of bed and *just do.*

My mind makes lists of everything I need to accomplish today.

My emotions tell me to hurry up and get into action because there's too much to do and not enough time to do it in.

But instead, I perform the hard work of not doing and choose to *just be:* to wrestle with the restless pain of doing nothing.

I act opposite to my anxiety.

I sit still and breathe.

I look out my bedside window and notice the amazing hues of the Norwegian summer sunrise while Mr. Magpie sings a soothing melody outside my window.

And as I begin to calm down, I realize that I am interpreting the anxiety as a sign to work harder, when in reality, it's a plea from the child within me to stop everything and take him outside to play.

Now, the restless pain of doing nothing is not fun for Adult Patrick, but it's just the remedy that Little Patrick needs.

And I'd much rather Adult Patrick be in discomfort than for Little Patrick to feel unheard and overlooked.

So I reach down and hold Little Patrick's hand.

Together, we take Ollie outside and enjoy a beautiful morning together.

Eventually, we come back inside because Little Patrick is content, and I sit back down to work, this time from inspiration rather than anxiety.

And from this experience, I realize that Little Patrick has a lot to teach Adult Patrick.

When I care for Little Patrick, he reaches his little hand up to my big hand and directs my days, my ways, and my life.

I consider that, perhaps, Little Patrick knows who I truly am more than I do, so maybe I should let him lead the way more often.

Therefore, the restless pain of doing nothing, is, in a way, everything.

July 20

◇ DRINKING FROM A GLACIER WATERFALL ◇

My Best Friend, Ollie, and I recently took a few days off work and headed to the Naeroyfjord on the west coast of Norway for some summer fun!

It was a Heaven on Earth kind of experience, kayaking in the summer of eternal light.

Where the flowers are so vibrant it almost hurts to look at them.

Where hundreds of waterfalls cascade from ice caps as they melt in the summer sun.

Where the only sounds were Mr. Magpie singing his song, our paddles stroking the water, and sheep peacefully bleating as they grazed along the shoreline.

Where the only people around for miles were in the ten-person village we passed halfway through our journey.

And let me tell you, if there's one thing that can turn the mind off and turn the heart on, it's drinking out of a glacier waterfall on a bright summer day!

An experience like this can't be comprehended with the mind and a camera can't capture it.

But a heart: a heart can be softened and transformed by it.

So, as you go about your day, seek to have an experience like I had at the Naeroyfjord.

Something that your mind can't comprehend.

Something that a camera can't capture.

But something that your heart can absorb, be softened and transformed by.

Earlier this year, I shared with you Kirkegaard's idea of the dizzying anxiety of freedom.

And just to refresh your memory, Kirkegaard believed that when we are truly free, it's scary, as though we're standing at the edge of a precipice, look down, and get that feeling of stomach-churning vertigo.

Well, the other day I was on a lift to take me to the top of the Eiffel Tower and I just so happened to be standing beside the most beautiful family.

I overheard their boy, who must have been eight or nine years old, say "Momma, I'm afraid of falling off the edge."

She said, "Don't worry, I won't let anything happen to you," but he wasn't convinced.

All of a sudden, he looked up at me with fearful eyes, and I just had to chime in.

So, I shared a much more simple and age-appropriate version of the following sentiment:

"It's okay to be afraid. In fact, a very smart philosopher once said that when we are the most free to be ourselves in life, it's as scary as standing on the edge of the Eiffel Tower. So, that feeling of being scared is actually good, it's showing you that you're free, that you're exploring new things."

I proceeded on my tour of the Eiffel Tower and the family went their own way, but I have to admit that the very best part of the experience was connecting with that kid.

Interacting with the young man helped me remember that standing on the edge externally, *and* standing on the ledge of the inner precipice that leads to the unknown, is anxiety-provoking.

But it also leads to expansion, new experiences, and ultimately, freedom!

July 22

◇ GIVING AND RECEIVING ◇

I have a workout buddy who loves all things cars, especially Formula One racing.

When he first mentioned his passion, I asked him what kind of car he drives, because I thought it would be a good source of conversation while we worked out, but I was wrong.

He said, "I'm embarrassed to tell you because I'm afraid you'll judge me. But I actually have a racecar."

Confused, I replied, "I don't understand, why would I judge you for that?"

He said, "Well, my friends at university told me that I am privileged for having a nice car."

My impulse was to backlash against those comments, because I believe friends should celebrate each other rather than doling out jealousy-based guilt trips.

But instead, I took a breath and defused my anger (and his guilt) by playfully mocking his British accent, saying, "Poppycock! Bollocks!"

Afterward, I wanted to understand why I was so annoyed by the comments my friend received, so I took the situation to my Coffee Companion.

After hearing my story, my Coffee Companion reminded me that life is not fair, and as a result, the 'haves' are susceptible to guilt and the 'have nots' are prone to jealousy.

But she went on to say that, in her experience, there is a deeper way to understand life's unfairness.

She said, "Patrick, what if giving and receiving are intertwined? And what if, when we receive, we ultimately give back to others? If those rhetorical questions are true, then there's absolutely nothing wrong with having more than others, as long as we remain an open channel of giving and receiving."

And as my Coffee Companion shared her wisdom, I thought of her empathy, which she was given in spades above the average person, yet is also a gift that everyone around her has benefited from due to her openness.

So, I think it's high time we drop the cycle of guilt and jealousy, because, in the final analysis, that cycle is simply not serving us in our quests to grow spiritually.

Instead, let's recreate the world into a more authentic and creative place as we allow both gifts and receipts to flow through us.

July 23

◊ DO NOT COME WITH ALL THE TRUTH ◊

I recently spent a few weeks coaching leaders who work in an extremely high-stress environment. They are devoted to serving at-risk people who would otherwise fall through the cracks. Their work is rewarding, but it also takes a toll on their well-being, so I was brought in to help them recharge.

After sitting with these leaders' frustration and pain, the cumulative effect was as though a fire hose had been pointed directly at me and unleashed at full force.

So, I called up my Coffee Companion, who commended me for realizing that I was depleted and reaching out for help.

Then, she proceeded to heal me by reciting timely and relevant words by Olav Hauge, a Norwegian village-dwelling fruit farmer and poet, who wrote:

Don't come to me with the entire truth.
Don't bring the ocean if I feel thirsty,
nor heaven if I ask for light;
but bring a hint, some dew, a particle,
as birds carry drops away from a lake,
and the wind a grain of salt.

I cried as my Coffee Companion recited the poem to me, and she sat in silence while the tears discharged my stress.

When my tears came to an end, she said, "Patrick, many people were coming to you with big problems and you got overwhelmed. They were bringing you an ocean of stress when you could only handle a bucketful. They were shining a spotlight when you only needed a candle."

After pausing to collect her thoughts, she continued, "Of course, in your role, you couldn't ask them to quit sharing. But now it's the weekend and you have time to rest. You've been helping a whole lot of other people lately, and right now, the person that needs your help is you."

Since that fateful interaction, I have come to see that we all have times when we feel burdened and overwhelmed by people coming to us with the entire truth.

However, this poem has taught me that if we can identify we are being overexposed to the truth, and then take care of ourselves in whatever way makes sense for us, then all of a sudden, the overwhelming ocean turns into a manageable glass of water.

So, how can you turn the ocean into a glass of water?

July 24

◇ VOLTAIRE'S EDICT ◇

R ecently I came across a passage in Voltaire's *Treatise on Tolerance* that I'll paraphrase here as, "Think for yourself and let others do the same."

This one-line zinger really grabbed me by the jowls and shook me because it felt directed by Zuzu; as though she were giving me a wink and a nod from beyond the grave.

After all, Zuzu would often say things like:

We like to think that we are free thinkers, but in one way or another, we're all basing our lives on ideas implanted by someone else. The trick is to find ways to identify the brainwashing. That takes a lot of work, but it's the key to living life based on your values rather than someone else's.

When we want to control the way *others* think, it's a good sign that we are responding from our *own* unconscious brainwashing.

But true freedom of thought is a wide swath for everyone to think for themselves and let others do the same.

So today, let's take inspiration from Voltaire's edict to think for ourselves and let others do the same!

July 25

◇ BOBBING WITH THE WAVES AND WAKES OF LIFE ◇

Some of my favorite teenage memories involve my dad letting me drive the family boat through the waterways of North Carolina.

After all, what could be better than the sun on my face, the wind in my hair, and the power of having one hand on the wheel and the other on the throttle?!

The freedom I felt was only constrained by buoys that directed me to avoid sandbars and shallow waters.

When our boat would go by the buoys and make wakes, the buoys did not rigidly stay in place, but instead, they weaved and bobbed, dancing on top of the water.

What I realized is that stress is like the wake from the boats, and we humans are like those buoys: we can brace down and get knocked over by the force of the wake, or we can bob with the waves and wakes of life with ease and grace.

So, as you go about your day, remember that it's human nature to steel ourselves when we see the waves of stressful situations coming toward us, but a much better way is to weave and bob with the waves and the wakes of life!

July 26

◇ FORFEITING THE IMPOSSIBLE GAME ◇

One small word can change a child's life forever.

Case in point: when I was five years old, I overheard someone very close to me making a judgmental remark about certain types of people.

It was all unconscious: he was simply passing down the scripts and rules he learned from generations before him.

But it sure did create a belief in me that his love was conditional and that I had to mask my true self in order to appease him.

So, I tried to win his love by achieving external success.

But eventually, as I got stronger in my own individuality, I started asking some important 'what ifs?' that liberated me from the chains of approval-seeking and freed me to become more authentically me.

Questions like:

What would it be like to drop the expectation that I am supposed to do something great and just enjoy my life?

What if I didn't have to justify my existence?

And what if I could let go of winning the love of a person who doesn't freely give it, but only awards it based on my performance?

Eventually, as I continued to ask these questions, I realized that the only way to win an impossible game is to forfeit it.

And as I forfeited that unhealthy relationship, I had more room to receive true love from wonderful relationships with Ollie, Zuzu, my Coffee Companion, my Best Friend, and my Friend in Paris.

So, as you go about your day, consider: are the people in your life judging you when you don't live up to who they want you to be?

Or, do they radically accept and appreciate all that you truly are, warts and all?

July 27
◇ WEDDINGS ◇

In my early twenties, I served as the organist at Old Stone Church, a historic house of worship in Cleveland, Ohio's downtown Public Square.

Because of its location, as well as the sanctuary's stained glass by Louis Comfort Tiffany, the church was a popular venue for weddings.

In fact, it wasn't odd at all for us to perform a triple header of weddings on a summer Saturday afternoon.

I can only imagine that I saw close to a thousand couples take their nuptials, and it was an interesting way to observe society!

Some couples were deeply spiritual and I could tell they would probably stand the test of time (others, however, I was a bit less sure of. Like the bride who got out of her limo while pulling a pack of cigarettes out of one side of her bosom and a whiskey flask out of the other!).

Many beautiful passages about love were read at these ceremonies, but recently, I discovered a passage about love by David Kessler in *Life Lessons* that takes the cake.

And if ever I find myself up there at the altar one day, I hope these words are read:

Love, that thing we have great difficulty even describing, is the only true real and lasting experience in life. It is the opposite of fear, the essence of relationships, the core of creativity, the grace of power, an intricate part of who we are. It is the source of happiness, the energy that connects us and that lives within us.

Love has nothing to do with knowledge, education, or power; it is beyond behavior. It is also the only gift in life that is not lost. Ultimately, it is the only thing we can give. In a world of illusions, a world of dreams and emptiness, love is the source of truth.

So, as we go about our days, let's allow love to ground our relationships, inspire our creativity, and help us all access infinity and eternity.

And let's remember that ultimately, love is the only thing that we can give.

July 28

◊ RELATIONSHIPS OVER RESULTS ◊

When I graduated from high school, my childhood piano teacher sent me a card with a message I carry in my heart to this day.

With the class and sass of a proper Southern woman, she skipped all the tomfoolery of telling me she was proud of me; I already knew that.

She also neglected to tell me that I would go far in music; that was a given.

Instead, she gave me an integral piece of feedback that I needed to hear, even though I wasn't yet old enough to understand it.

In the card, she simply wrote, "Patrick, always remember, that *people* are more important than music."

Now, for those of us who have passion, drive, and ambition, the idea that relationships are more important than results can initially seem frustrating and can take a lifetime to really internalize.

But the wisdom, peace, and freedom that come from shifting our perspective from results to relationships are worth the work!

July 29

◇ TEFLON AND VELCRO ◇

The Swedish physician Hans Rosling once said that we humans tend to keep positive thoughts away as though we're Teflon, yet cling to negative thoughts as though we're Velcro.

And I can *certainly relate!*

Currently, my Best Friend is in India for three weeks, and before he left, I was really looking forward to alone time in our apartment and couldn't wait for him to leave!

However, two weeks into his trip, I am ready for him to come back.

In both instances, I have been clinging to the negative rather than seeing the positive, but today, I'm committing to changing my attitude.

I'm consciously choosing to enjoy my alone time, *and* I'm planning on appreciating him upon his return by cleaning the apartment floor to ceiling, which is definitely his love language.

Just for today, I'll try to cling to positive thoughts like I'm Velcro and repel the negative thoughts as though I'm Teflon.

Then I'll wake up tomorrow, and do the same again.

July 30

◊ INHALE INSPIRATION, EXHALE RELAXATION ◊

As I walked to the grocery store this morning, I just *could not* quit making mental to-do lists for the day.

In fact, I was so distracted from the present moment that my friend Mr. Wind came to my aid.

He shimmied through nearby tree branches as though he were trying to tap me on the shoulder and whispered, "Patrick, wake up! Get out of your head! Life is happening around you."

For a moment, I returned his bid for connection as his whispers surged the trees into a dance of delight choreographed just for me!

But, frustratingly, my mind's stress kept taking over.

Then, all of a sudden, I remembered that my Coffee Companion often says that a key ingredient to a life well lived is to inhale inspiration *and* exhale relaxation.

I'm great at inhaling inspiration, and my visionary optimism serves me well.

But the downside is that I often end up signing up for more than I can handle and forget to exhale into relaxation.

And that's when I find myself making incessant to-do lists on the way to the grocery store!

When I forget to exhale into relaxation, my quality of life suffers because I work until I burn out, then I grow resentful of the very commitments I so gladly agreed to.

And, ironically, when I forget to exhale relaxation, the inspiration I'm holding onto becomes stale, and I don't have any capacity to breathe in new inspiration.

So, like the sheep on the cover of this book, let's inhale the inspiration of the Truth that resides on the other side of the mountain.

Then, let's remember to exhale into relaxation as we abide safely amid our flock in our calm, sunny pasture.

July 31

◇ GAY NAZIS? ◇

My Best Friend and I were walking to a juice bar one evening in India when I noticed, side by side, a flag with a swastika and a flag with the colors of the rainbow.

Confused, I asked, "Um, are there gay Nazis in India?"

My Best Friend laughed and discombobulated my preconceived notions when he said, "Patrick, not everything can be seen within a Western context. The swastika is in front of a school because, for us, it is a centuries-old symbol of well-being, prosperity, and good luck. And the rainbow flag in front of the temple is not in support of any cause; it's just there because we like colors in India!"

As we laughed at my cultural snafu, I realized that we humans often get upset about our own incorrect interpretations of another person's words or deeds.

But what if, starting today, we consciously choose to live more generously?

Indeed, how would life change if we started to assume that the underlying intention behind messages we don't understand is fundamentally good?

◇ AUGUST ◇

August 1

◇ INTERWEAVING, INTERTWINING ◇

Ollie loves his noontime walks by the large corporate office where we live because he gets tons of attention and love from the employees eating lunch outside!

He dances for them on his hind legs, and they reward him with belly rubs and pats on the head.

As Ollie and I head over to do our daily ritual of 'dinner and a show,' we pass a modern sculpture by the offices that is engraved with the words *interweaving lives, intertwining features.*

Ollie and I don't know any of the people he blesses with his presence each day at lunch, yet our lives interweave with theirs in the fabric of the present moment.

And when you think about it, all of humanity is like a big patchwork quilt of people.

Some of us interweave, some of us intertwine, and that interweaving and intertwining is what makes the fabric of society.

And yet, the resulting societal quilt can only stand the test of time when each individual thread is strong in their sense of who they truly are.

August 2

◇ IT'S THE LITTLE THINGS ◇

After exploring Paris today, I boarded the train and headed to my Friend in Paris's home, anticipating the hot shower and delicious meal waiting for me!

And tonight, as I tucked myself into bed in 'my room' at their home, surrounded by beautiful antiques and a quilt my Friend's late aunt stitched by hand, I started thinking about how lucky I am to know this man and his spouse.

Together, they have taught me that it's not the grand gestures that make us feel loved, appreciated, and like we belong.

On the contrary, it's the little things.

For example, the last time I was at their home a year ago, I left my favorite water bottle. And without me asking, they kept my bottle safe in their home for a year, and as soon as I arrived today, they gave it to me.

This whole week, they have pampered me with the most delicious food: artichoke hearts, pavlova, brioche, quiche, apricot tarte, and much more!

And I know that when I return to Oslo, I will receive a message saying their house seems empty without me.

All these details are their way of telling me that I have value and that I matter.

So, it really is the little things, the little heartfelt gestures that show someone we love and value them.

And as we go about our day, I hope that you and I can be as thoughtful and respectful to others as my Friend in Paris and his spouse is towards me!

August 3

◇ THE WISDOM OF EMOTIONS ◇

One of the highlights of my musical career was performing at the Cathedral of St. John the Divine in New York City, which is the largest cathedral in the world.

As fate would have it, I just so happened to give my concert the same weekend that the famed Barberini tapestries were reinstalled after a lengthy restoration.

What struck me about these beautifully crafted works of art was how each tapestry depicted a scene from Christ's life, and collectively, the tapestries showed that Christ felt the same range of emotions that we humans feel.

Like all of us, Jesus was born an innocent child, adored by those who came to witness his birth.

He grew into his own until he was baptized, which was his proud rite of passage into adulthood.

He felt alone as he prayed in the Garden of Gethsemane.

And he felt pain as he suffered on the cross.

As I performed masterworks by Bach, Respighi, and Messiaen while looking at these scenes out of the corner of my eye, I realized that part of the reason Jesus is remembered two thousand years after he walked the earth is due to his ability to feel emotions.

After all, when we feel our emotions, process them, and clear them, we are left with an inner emptiness that makes room for clarity and spiritual direction.

And if there ever was a person who had clarity of purpose and spiritual direction, it was Jesus!

So, perhaps the wisdom of emotions was the wisdom of Jesus.

August 4
◇ THE LETTER ◇

O nce upon a time, I experienced a dark night of the soul. I was desperately in need of hope, so my Grief Guide advised me to write a letter to my present-day self from my future self.

Here's what I wrote:

Dear Patrick,

I know you are struggling right now. You're in a job that does not use your gifts, Zuzu just died, and your Best Friend lives across the world.

I know you feel as though no one understands just how uncomfortable and raw it all feels, but I get it, because a year ago, I was you. And because of the hard work you are doing to make big changes and create a life that works for you, I have so much peace and freedom in my life.

I know it feels like you are moving heaven and earth just to get through each day, and I know you are frustrated that things simply aren't how you wish them to be.

But I am so proud to watch as you keep working toward your calling: toward the life you were born to live.

Because of your bravery, I no longer feel misunderstood or like a misfit. I'm moving more and more into a line of work that matters to me, my friendships are improving, and I'm taking better care of myself. I wouldn't be the man I am today if not for the hard work you are doing now.

I won't spoil the surprise of what happens over the next year, but it's pretty dang wonderful!

And as you walk toward me over the next year, know that I'll be thinking of you with a proud smile on my face as you do what you need to do to get to me.

Love,

Patrick

Whether you are currently in a dark night of the soul, or whether your life is firing on all cylinders, consider taking the time to write a letter from your future self to your current self at some point today.

If you're anything like me, this exercise will create all sorts of visionary hope!

August 5

◇ OLLIE'S CURIOSITY ◇

Today, Ollie asked politely for a ferry ride! So, we took a bus to Oslo's main boardwalk, where the Old Fortress, City Hall, and Nobel Peace Museum reside, and we set sail for the islands in the middle of the Oslo fjord!

Ollie loved prancing around the ferry cabin and saying hello to everyone, but that paled in comparison to the joy he exuded as he explored each of the small islands.

And little did we know that on the last island, we would encounter the ruins of an ancient abbey!

As Ollie leaped over stones, burrowed under crevices, peed on the sacred stones to mark his territory, and sniffed at the aromas from the nearby bakery, I realized that curiosity is a pleasant emotion that arises when we feel safe enough to relax into life.

After all, Ollie wasn't scared about what he might discover; rather, he charged forth with bravery and self-assuredness, enjoying the element of surprise that only 'the unknown' can bring!

And just as Ollie curiously explored the abbey ruins, we can use *our* curiosity to plunge into *our* life experiences.

For example, what would it be like if, instead of judging people who live differently than us, we use curiosity to get to know them and see value in their way of life?

What if, instead of criticizing ourselves for falling short of our ideal behavior, we get curious about what happened so we can do things differently when life brings similar situations in the future?

And what if we drop all our assumptions and beliefs and experience everyday objects like stones and grass as though we are encountering them for the very first time, just like Ollie?

Today, Ollie's open-hearted curiosity encouraged him to pleasantly explore every nook and cranny of the abbey ruins.

Now, let's take a page out of his playbook and use *our* curiosity to explore every nook and cranny of *life!*

August 6
◇ CHOOSE WHAT'S BEST FOR YOU! ◇

I am certain that I have, hands down, the very best primary care physician in the entire world. And one of the many things I've learned from her is that health begins and ends with her slogan, "Choose what's best for you!"

If it's that simple, then why aren't more people happy?

Because choosing what's best for you can be a pain in the butt!

Choosing what's best for you is not always sexy. It's so much easier to turn on the television than go for a walk. And it's certainly more convenient to order a pizza than to make a home-cooked meal infused with the one special ingredient that can't be bought: love.

Choosing what's best for you is harder than instant gratification facsimiles. The payoff is rarely immediate; in fact, it often takes a lot of hard work in the short term and the dividends are only yielded slowly over time.

However, choosing what's best for you is much more structured, sustainable, and healthy than the alternative.

So, as you go about your day, how can you choose what's best for you?

August 7

◊ THE CAVERNS OF SONORA ◊

A few years back, I was driving from Houston to Big Bend National Park when I saw a sign on the side of the road for the Caverns of Sonora.

I knew nothing about this place, but with a name like that, how could I say no?!

Sister Serendipity magically steered my car toward the exit, and I made the side trip with perfect timing, just before the cavern entrance closed.

As the tour guide and I descended hundreds of feet below the Earth's surface, I was amazed at the treasure trove of million-year-old helictite shapes that seemed to defy gravity.

I stood there, amazed in the presence of such mysterious beauty, and I realized that each person's inner world is just as exquisite as the Caverns of Sonora.

And what I mean by that statement is this: we all contain an immense cavern of beautiful treasure that is truly awe-inspiring.

So, as you and I go about our daily life today, let's remember to stand amazed at the inner caverns of ourselves, and the inner caverns of others.

August 8

◇ THE GREATER JOURNEY ◇

Yesterday, the superlative orator of American history, David McCullough, joined the great cloud of witnesses rooting us on as we make history ourselves.

David's books have sold ten million copies and he was crowned with the Presidential Medal of Freedom, *two* Pulitzer Prizes, and almost fifty honorary doctorates.

How did he do it?

By leaving a secure, salaried position at *Sports Illustrated* to become a freelance writer, even while knowing he had five young mouths to feed!

And while he was building his stellar career, David was a great family man, serving as a companion to his wife while nurturing his children and grandchildren.

But David gave us much more than history lessons. His books are infused with the warmth of his heart, the wit of his mind, and a reminder of the hope and vision that is possible when we believe in the potential of the human spirit.

One of David's last books was entitled *The Greater Journey*, and the way he lived his life inspires us to go on our *own* Greater Journey: to seize the day, embark upon new terrain, and live life to the fullest!

August 9
◇ DISCERNMENT ◇

Imagine that you have a comfortable life teaching at both Yale *and* Harvard; would you give it all up to serve individuals with intellectual disabilities?

Well, that's exactly what Henri Nouwen did.

And in that process, he found personal happiness, a validating community, and a way to serve others deeply.

In the foreword to a collection of Nouwen's writings titled *Discernment,* Henri's friend Robert Jonas wrote:

Henri Nouwen's life did not follow a familiar trajectory or keep to a predictable path...he was breaking new ground with just about every choice he made. For Henri... discernment was a moment-to-moment practice, because he found no model, no pattern for what he felt called to do. He stepped into the unknown like a tightrope walker stepping into nearly thin air...

Today, let's all seek to be as discerning as Henri. Let's bravely step into the unknown when there is no conventional path for what we feel called to do, and let's break new ground all along the way.

August 10

◇ FAMILY TRADITIONS ◇

As my Best Friend tells it, he simply had the best childhood one could ever imagine. He felt extremely attached to his mom and sisters, he had a father who worked hard and provided for the family, and he loved his school teachers and classmates.

I have not come across very many people who feel the same way about their childhood, so I thought it would be interesting for he and I to dissect what family traditions he wanted to pass down to his kids one day.

He agreed to the exercise, but only if I did it along with him!

I won't share his part of the discussion, but personally, I realized that the family traditions I want to pass down regard security.

For example, I lived in the same house from the time I was born until I headed off to college, which I think is pretty rare.

I also realized that I want to pass down the experience of raising livestock, having pets, growing a garden, spending time in nature, and growing up in a quiet, peaceful setting.

One of the traditions that I *don't* want to pass down is overexposure to dogma and doctrine. Rather than telling the next generation what to think, I want to ask them questions to help them explore who they are, how the world works, and why they're here.

And interestingly enough, the more I got clear on which traditions I wanted to pass down and which I wanted to discard, the more I started living into those ideals.

For example, I started spending more time outdoors, and I started consciously choosing not to watch the news.

Consider doing this exercise for yourself at some point today. It might just give you some clarity in how you want to live now by seeing what traditions you want to pass on to the next generation.

August 11
◇ IF NOT THE ROSE, THE PETALS WILL DO ◇

The other day, I was loafing around Paris when I decided to head over to Les Invalides, which was founded by King Louis XIV as a home and hospital for war veterans.

When I arrived at Les Invalides, I went straight to the back of the building complex because I wanted to see the magnificent gold-domed church which houses Napoleon's tomb.

Well, I didn't check the timing, and it turns out that the Dome Church closed right before I arrived.

At first, I was disappointed and a little angry at myself, but then I remembered a mantra from my Best Friend's family: "If not the rose, the petals will do."

So, rather than wallowing in my missed opportunity, I appreciated the rose petals. At least I got to see the exterior of the Dome Church. Also, I spent time in St. Louis Cathedral inside Les Invalides, which I may have skipped over altogether if the Dome Church had been open.

Similarly, as you go about your day, may you appreciate even the smallest blossom that comes your way, because one fragrant rose petal is more than enough to suffuse life!

August 12

◇ THE SOUND OF YOUR SYMPHONY ◇

A composer gives a *raison d'etre* for a symphony: they are trying to portray a particular emotional effect.

The goal is to create an inner experience for the listener that they can take away from the symphony hall and apply once they go back out to the 'ordinary world.'

And in a way, your life is like a symphony, and you are the composer.

Other people see your actions, deeds, and thoughts, and they judge your personality by the composition of your days.

So, if the world is your audience, and your life is a composition, what emotional effect do you want to leave with people?

What insight do you want to impart?

Personally, I want to create a contemplative yet lush effect that inspires people to explore the most recessed parts of their inner sanctum in order to discover their true self.

What do you want the sound of your life's symphony to be?

August 13

◇ DON'T FEED THE DINOSAURS ◇

The beautiful city of Bergen on the west coast of Norway is a great way to spend a Saturday afternoon!

Today, we had lunch in the town square, strolled past the colorful houses by the harbor, and were astounded by the massive crustaceans at the Fish Market.

Then, we ascended to the top of a mountain via train and took in a bird's eye view of the archipelago.

And while we were distracted by the beautiful scene below us, wild goats tried to steal our lunch!

But the most memorable part of our day in Bergen was a jaunt through the Little Troll Forest.

At the entrance to this mossy woodland filled with intricate carvings of characters from Norwegian folklore, we were greeted by a sign that said, "Don't feed the dinosaurs."

Obviously, it was a joke, but that sign has stuck in my mind to this day!

After all, we humans are so easily suggestible.

We so often give up our freedom and submit to rules that have no bearing in the first place.

But I think it's up to us to live life the way *we* see fit.

So, if you want to feed the dinosaurs, *go do it!*

August 14

◇ EXPANDING OPTIONS ◇

As a tiny tot, I was enamored with the pianist at our small country church.

Each Sunday morning, she would sit down at the piano and play old Southern Baptist hymns in her early 90's shoulder pads and pants suit.

It wasn't the greatest concert pianist playing of all time, but she helped me realize that there were more occupations in life than farmers and mechanics, hair stylists and receptionists.

She showed me that life can be something more and touched something in me that wasn't stirred up anywhere else.

I'm sure she had no idea that she was inspiring me in such a formative way; of course, I had no idea either.

But in hindsight, I think back on those special Sunday mornings and realize that one of the greatest gifts we can give to the next generation is to expand their options for how they can live their life.

So, if we get the chance today, let's make sure to pay it forward and help the next person in line expand just like this special lady did for me!

August 15

◇ THE LITTLE LAMB ◇

As a child, my Coffee Companion was devastated by a bedtime story about a little lamb who wandered away from the flock and got lost in a briar patch.

She empathized so deeply with the lost little lamb's fear that she forgot she was resting safely in her mother's arms.

This moment was one of the first incidents where my Coffee Companion's disposition to care for others made it hard for her to be clear on where they ended and she began.

But over the course of a lifetime, she has learned to strengthen her internal borders.

And as a result of her deep inner work, she is now a gentle shepherdess who helps people integrate their mental, emotional, and physical energy so they can become who they truly are.

I think we can all take a page out of my Coffee Companion's book and figure out how to harness the unique, immutable traits we've carried since birth so that we can tend to others, and *ourselves,* with love and care.

August 16

◇ PERSPECTIVE ON THE POSSIBILITIES ◇

O ver the course of my life, I have had the good fortune of being around people from all over the world.

As a result, I have seen that each generation, language, religion, and career field creates certain mindsets.

Let's take a common object like a bridge, for example.

An engineer will look at a bridge and see either a safety hazard or a well-constructed work of brilliance.

A graffiti artist will look at the same bridge and be inspired to write 'Be Someone' on it.

A ship driver will look for the bridge operator to open the drawbridge and let him through.

And a poet will think of a metaphor for how bridges transfer people from one location to another and write a poem about life's transitions.

So, as we go about our day, let's remember St. Francis of Assisi's advice to wear life like a loose garment, with plenty of room for both our truth and others' perspectives.

After all, dropping the need to be 'right' opens us up to the freedom of new perspectives on the possibilities available to us in this wonderful life!

August 17

◇ OLLIE'S ENEMIES ◇

I really don't understand the audacity of a very rare subset of the human population who dare to dislike Ollie. For some reason, they see him as a dog rather than a human.

How could they be so *rude?!*

Now, I have to admit that Ollie and I break a lot of rules. I simply refuse to cow-tow to the ludicrous rule of putting such a good boy on a leash.

And Ollie occasionally gets excited to see a stranger and runs toward them, accidentally scaring them in the process.

Also, Ollie's favorite place to sunbathe is in the children's play area, where dogs are 'forbidden.' Well, that doesn't work for us. So we go about our business, asking neither permission nor forgiveness.

Finally, public enemy number one in Ollie's world is a nearby neighbor who shoos Ollie away anytime we come within ten feet of his yard.

Every time we get castigated by overly conscientious people who want us to obey the rules, my blood boils, because they don't realize that this is Ollie's world and they're just living in it!

But then, I realize that if I want others to honor my needs, then I need to first honor theirs.

So I try to anticipate when Ollie is about to run after someone he doesn't know for a belly rub, and we avoid that grumpy neighbor's home.

And all of a sudden, by adjusting my behavior just a little bit without compromising Ollie's freedom, all the resentment quits ping-ponging around the neighborhood, and peace is restored.

How can you, likewise, adjust your behavior (without compromising your values) in order to bring a little more peace into the world today?

August 18

◇ CORDS ◇

My Best Friend is a salt-of-the-earth, practical, reality-based kind of guy...except when it comes to his family!

He once told me that as a child, he realized that there was an invisible energy field connecting him with his family members, sort of like a spiritual umbilical cord.

He said, "That is probably childish immaturity, isn't it?"

I said, "Absolutely not. It sounds like a deep spiritual that I never knew about. I'm going to play with that idea and see what happens."

And indeed, I came to see that there really is a field of energy that connects me to certain people: I have cords connecting me to Zuzu from beyond the grave, my Friend in Paris from across international borders, and Ollie from across the living room.

So, as you go about your day, consider playing with this idea of spiritual cords. It's a stimulating and unique way to think about the special relationships in our lives!

August 19

◇ JANTELOVEN ◇

This morning I was working out with a gym buddy when he mentioned that he wants to become financially independent and get away from corporate work.

He wants to escape the dogma of *Janteloven,* an unspoken Norwegian cultural norm that means you aren't supposed to think you're better than anyone else.

Of course, humility is a wonderful value, but he feels as though *Janteloven* gets taken to an extreme where people feel embarrassed of their talent and feel pressure to hold themselves back.

After he finished venting his frustrations, I shared with him that on the opposite end of the spectrum, I was brought up in a family and society that expected me to stand out.

But, like him, I have had to work hard to find the middle ground, where success is defined individually rather than by following society's dictates.

My friend hit the nail on the head when he said, "Perhaps true success is simply living in a way that is in line with who you truly are rather than worrying about what others think."

There was nothing left to be said after that, so we resumed our deadlifts, which made us feel oh, so alive!

August 20

◇ FRISBEE GOLF ◇

This past weekend, my neighbors invited me to play my very first game of frisbee golf!

We drove to a beautiful island full of families picnicking and kids playing soccer and began our course of eighteen holes, some of which were in the middle of the open park, and some of which required us to perilously whisk our discs past trees and over water.

As we played, my neighbors' big black Hovavart was running all over the place chasing our frisbees!

Ollie, on the other hand, found a comfortable place to sit at each hole and slowly blinked his eyes while he basked in the sun.

I, too, felt rejuvenated from the sun after a long winter and was curious as to why it felt so good.

When we got home I did some research, and it turns out that when we're out in the sun, our body creates a hormone called melatonin that helps us sleep better and reduces stress.

Also, the vitamin D we get from sunlight helps maintain bone strength and keeps our immune system up to par.

Finally, the serotonin that is produced when we're in sunlight improves our mood and helps us stay calm and focused.

So, as you go about your day, I hope you take the time to bask in some delicious sunlight so that you can be re-energized on your journey to becoming, well, you!

August 21

◇ THE INTENTION BEHIND YOUR ACTIONS ◇

Like many of us, I was taught to see the world in judgmental terms of black-and-white, wrong or right.

As a result, I tended to be all-or-nothing in my behaviors.

But these days, I try to look at the intention behind my actions rather than the behavior itself.

For example, if I'm alone and turn on the TV at the end of the day, I'm probably trying to numb myself from a feeling of loneliness.

However, if I'm watching a Hindi movie with my Best Friend on a Friday night after a good meal, we'll happily chatter throughout the movie about cultural differences, and at the end, I'll have a deeper glimpse into human behavior.

Same action, totally different intention.

The trick is to go past surface-level judgments and to see the intention behind your actions so that you can see when an experience is expanding you, and when that same behavior on a different day may be diminishing you.

In the end, it's not the behavior that frees us or enslaves us, but rather, it's the intention behind the action.

August 22

◇ UNDOING THE CURSE OF ZEUS ◇

In *The Symposium,* Plato shares a fable about how humans originally had four arms, four legs, and two faces.

Our race had great strength in this form, and so the deities were in a dilemma.

On one hand, the gods could kill us humans and rid themselves of our potential to threaten their authority.

On the other hand, they quite liked our tributes and offerings!

Well, as usual, Zeus came to the rescue of the gods and killed two birds with one stone: by splitting humans in half, he weakened our power and doubled the gods' oblations.

This boon for the gods was a curse for us, and we have since been doomed to spend much of our life's energy trying to reintegrate the lost half of ourselves through dating and marriage.

But what Plato fails to mention in this fable is that we have the power to undo Zeus's curse, not by finding a spouse, but by doing our own inner work to develop a strong masculine side *and* a strong feminine side.

When we can do this, we open all sorts of new possibilities and we reclaim our full power that can rival the gods!

333

August 23

◇ THE GIRAFFE IN THE BARBER SHOP ◇

On the last day of my inaugural trip to India, my Best Friend gave me a sly look and said we should visit a proper Indian barber shop to capstone the vacation.

It was an experience and a half!

As I entered the barber shop, you could hear a pin drop: it was as though I were a giraffe that had left the zoo in order to come by for a haircut!

As I sat down in the chair, the barber was vexed and asked my friend in Hindi, "How in the world am I supposed to cut hair this thin?"

And trust me, he wasn't the only one who had questions!

It seemed as though every guy in the packed barber shop converged in a circle around my chair, asking my friend rapid-fire questions as though he were the giraffe's zookeeper.

After the barber struggled through cutting his first head of Caucasian hair, he gave me a shave with a blade that could have nicked my jugular and massaged my head with the fury of a thousand lions.

As my friend had his turn in the barber's chair, I thanked God for surviving and went next door to get an Indian snack.

When I came back and sat down in the waiting area to eat my samosas, I could see the guys curiously staring at me the way people watch giraffes eat leaves at the zoo.

I could hear them thinking: *Will the giraffe twist his arm around his head to take a bite, or go straight from hand to mouth like we do? And, what in the world is the giraffe hiding in those pink, chubby cheeks?!*

To say that the barber shop was full of curious people is an understatement, to say the least!

As they openly pointed and argued about what I was doing and how I was doing it, I took their innocent inquisitiveness in good stride.

After all, I do love feeling unique!

And, I could see that we were all becoming more open-minded as a result of the accidental cultural exchange.

I left the barbershop with a fresh haircut *and* a fresh attitude, aspiring to be like those guys and stay curious about people who are different from me.

I hope we all take a page from India's playbook and activate *our* curiosity when a giraffe shows up in *our* barbershop!

August 24

◊ IT'S A NICE DAY WHEN YOU WAKE UP IN INDIA ◊

As the birds and Indian women chanted their morning prayers outside my hotel window this morning, I went to the lobby to check my email.

I was minding my own business when suddenly, one of the young hotel cleaners was standing over me; I was the new kid on the block, and although he spoke virtually no English, he wanted to know all about me!

But that's understandable, as I suppose it's not every day that he comes across a foreigner in his small village.

In fact, I like to think that in his mind, his encounter with me was like seeing a polar bear in the rainforest!

We had a lot of fun together over the next hour as he brought his friends over to talk and take pictures with me, and in exchange, they cooked up one of the best breakfasts of my life. I brought color into their world, and they did the same for me!

And I think this is how people were meant to interact.

We weren't made to get angry over our differences.

Instead, we were made to learn from our differences, honor our differences, and *delight* in our differences!

August 25

◇ GOD'S HANDIWORK ◇

We are *all* children of God. No matter who we are, where we're from, or what we've done, we all *have* and *deserve* dignity and worth.

We're all God's handiwork.

We're all made in His image.

So I, for one, am committing to catching myself when I oh-so-arrogantly judge the progeny of the Creator of the Universe.

Who am I to say that I am right and they are wrong?

Who am I to say that I am wise and they are foolish?

Instead of judging them, perhaps I can seek to understand them so that ultimately, I can create more peace in the world.

And just as importantly, more peace within myself.

We are *all* children of God.

August 26

◇ MONKEYS IN MAHARASTRA ◇

To say driving in India is difficult would be the understatement of this entire book!

So, when my Best Friend decided we should drive halfway across the state of Maharastra so I could experience his sister's beautiful ashram, the decision to hire a driver was a no-brainer.

And, the decision to haze the tourist by putting me in the front seat, where it often seemed as though I was an inch away from a transfer truck careening into me, was *also* a no-brainer!

However, sitting in the front seat afforded me a squeal of glee when I saw monkeys in the wild for the first time in my life!

Now, my Best Friend and his mom both laughed hysterically at my novel delight over something they have seen thousands of times, but they were gracious enough to respect my pleas to stop and they sat by a beautiful waterfall as I marveled at the valley of the monkeys!

Then, a baby monkey walked towards a neighboring car, found a half-empty cup of coke, and drank through its straw!

Travelers from a neighboring car decided to give that cute little guy a cracker, and all of a sudden, droves of monkeys, young and old, converged upon us from all directions of the forest!

It felt like we were being chased by the Velociraptors in *Jurassic Park,* so we ran back to the car, and all of a sudden, being a millimeter away from a passing car didn't seem so terrifying anymore!

And, as you go about your day today, I hope that at some point you can experience life-expanding novelty and pure joy like I did with the monkeys in Maharastra!

August 27

◇ THIS IS ME ◇

Quite a few years ago, I receded from Houston's sweltering August heat into a movie theatre.

I had no particular qualms about what the movie was, I just knew that I wanted to escape into the fantasy world that films transport us to.

Well, serendipity worked her magic and sent me to a one-night-only reprise of *The Greatest Showman*.

In case you've never seen it, *The Greatest Showman* is a musical biopic about the life of circus magnate P.T. Barnum and how his quest to achieve greatness burned bridges with the very people who got him to where he was.

At one point in the movie, the so-called 'freaks' that made up his talent pool got fed up with his embarrassment.

So, they marched and sang a powerful anthem that caused me to start crying in my seat as they proclaimed:

Look out 'cause here I come
And I'm marching on to the beat I drum.
I'm not scared to be seen
I make no apologies, this is me.

Although Barnum's employees were considered societal outcasts because of the way they looked, they were actually more secure in who they were than he was, and they showed up, said "This is me," and drove home Barnum's cowardice.

After all, why should he need to impress socialites when he already had a family and artistic community who loved him?

Eventually, their self-confidence gave Barnum the courage to change his behavior and make amends, and in the final scene of the movie, Barnum's willingness to work on himself allowed him to also be able to boldly say: "This is me."

Can you say the same?

August 28
◊ INVICTUS ◊

I magine you are a teenager in nineteenth-century Britain and you have just been told that your right leg needs to be amputated.

And to add insult to injury (no pun intended!) your left leg has already been amputated due to complications from tuberculosis.

Well, that is exactly the situation William Ernest Henley found himself in when he wrote a poem he called *Invictus,* which is the Latin word for 'unconquered.'

Henley did not let his diagnosis conquer his spirit nor his leg; rather, he searched high and low until he found a surgeon who was willing to perform multiple surgeries to save his leg.

While recovering in the infirmary, Master Henley was so overjoyed that the following poem flowed from his pen:

Out of the night that covers me
black as the pit from pole to pole,
I thank whatever gods may be
for my unconquerable soul.

In the fell clutch of circumstance,
*   I have not winced nor cried aloud.*
Under the bludgeonings of chance
*   My head is bloody, but unbowed.*

Beyond this place of wrath and tears
*   looms but the Horror of the shade,*
*   and yet the menace of the years*
*   finds, and shall find, me unafraid.*

It matters not how strait the gate,
*   how charged with punishments the scroll,*
*   I am the master of my fate*
*   I am the captain of my soul.*

Today, let's take Master Henley's conviction as our own and remember that we are the masters of our fate, that we are the captain of our souls.

After all, if he could sing the song of his unconquerable soul in his circumstances, then whatever we face today is likely a cinch in comparison!

August 29

◇ THE DIARY OF A YOUNG GIRL ◇

Earlier this year, I shared about how the best birthday present my parents ever gave me was a trip to Amsterdam in my early twenties.

I loved walking along the boathouse-lined canals, eating a fried cheese dish called *bitterballen,* seeing the New Church where I would give a concert years later, and visiting the famed tulip markets!

But perhaps the most moving part of that trip was visiting the Anne Frank house.

Of course, in middle school, I read her diary, which she wrote over the course of two years while she and her family hid in Nazi-occupied Holland, but visiting the house made the diary come to life.

Although the diary began as a source of comfort for her, she began revising it and preparing it for future readers when the Dutch government asked for people to curate their diaries and letters as a testimony for future generations.

As I walked the steep, narrow, stairs to the Frank family's hiding place, I thought of how the Minister's call was a mission he gave to help people like Anne find meaning in their suffering and a will to live in difficult times.

As I touched the kitchen counter where Anne and her mother prepared food, so many powerful lines of the diary came flooding back to me.

Lines like, "I don't think of all the misery but of the beauty that still remains," or:

Human greatness does not lie in wealth or power, but in character and goodness. People are just people, and all people have faults and shortcomings, but all of us are born with a basic goodness.

And ultimately, as I left the apartment on the verge of tears, I thought of her most powerful and oft-quoted line: that, "Despite everything, I believe that people are really good at heart."

When Anne Frank wrote these words, she was a young girl hiding away from people who would send her to her death if they found her.

So, if she can believe in the goodness of people and appreciate the beauty of life, then so can we.

345

August 30

◇ EPOCHE ◇

Way back in February of this year, I shared with you that we are all jigsaw pieces in the puzzle of life.

Well, I recently posted a video about that idea and a viewer commented that "Edmund Husserl called this *epoche*."

I vaguely recalled that Husserl was a late nineteenth-entury German philosopher, but I was intrigued to learn more, so I replied, "Very interesting! I will have to check his work out. Thank you!"

The viewer saved me some research when he replied:

Epoche is similar to finding where your individual jigsaw piece fits in life's puzzle. Husserl said that every moment is like an individual music note and that we often need to zoom out from how we live our lives in order to hear the overall melody. In that process, seeing how the world spins for others often helps us reflect on our own world.

Today, let's zoom out from the way we naturally live, and instead, get curious about how the world spins for others so that ultimately, we can learn more about our own world.

August 31

◇ LEARNING ABOUT LOVE IN SALEM ◇

If ever you find yourself in western North Carolina, be sure to visit historic Salem, which dates back to 1766.

Salem portrays what life was like for the early settlers of the Moravian Church, which was a Protestant denomination that sought religious freedom in the New World.

Remarkably, over one hundred buildings from the eighteenth and nineteenth centuries still line the cobbled streets, including stores and workshops that display the industriousness of the era's blacksmiths and bakers.

But the best part of my experience in Salem was not enjoying the delicious sweet bread, nor was it delighting in the fact that I was walking the same streets as George Washington.

Rather, the impact of the historic community really hit me when I read the motto of the Moravian Church:

In essentials, unity; in nonessentials, liberty; and in all things, love.

And as we go about our day, may we remember those last four words: *in all things, love.*

◇ SEPTEMBER ◇

September 1

◇ DESPERATELY SEEKING SALVATION ◇

Zuzu had almost finished preparing her memoir for publication when she found out she had cancer.

However, rather than pushing herself to finish the book before she passed, she decided to let the manuscript die with her.

And although Zuzu chose not to speak about her diagnosis, I can look back and see that when she told me about giving up her book, she was in a roundabout way saying, "Patrick, I've worked for salvation my entire life, and I don't want to spend my last days seeking redemption through publication. I just want to live the rest of the time I have here as fully as I can."

Zuzu figured out something that is hard for most of us to realize: we don't need a sacrificial lamb.

No redemption is necessary.

All that is needed is for us to be our true selves, enjoy the ride, and accept the amazing gift we call *life!*

◇ THE ROUGHSHOD BARBER ◇

The other day a neighbor of mine asked, "Patrick, is there anything you miss about the United States?

I immediately said, "Affordable haircuts!"

He laughed because here in Norway, going to the barber is four times more expensive than my salon in Houston.

In fact, I know a woman who flies to London because it's cheaper to buy a plane ticket than to get her waxing and highlights done in Oslo!

Paying so much for my simple haircut seems ridiculous to me, so I found the one barber shop in Oslo that is reasonably priced, and I bike an hour across town a couple of times a month to get my ears lowered.

Now, this barber has never been a shrinking violet, but the last time he cut my hair, he practically gave me whiplash from his roughshod ways!

Halfway through the haircut, my mind started boiling over in anger, but I decided to stay quiet and work out what was going on inside of me rather than taking the easy way out and barking at him.

Upon reflection, I realized I was reacting so strongly to him because, in many parts of my life, I have been just like that barber, rushing through checklists and not taking my time to really care for the person in the seat in front of me.

And as I left the shop and entered the city street, I felt grateful that I sat through the pain and found the lesson to be learned from my anger: that the *process* matters just as much as the end *product*.

Sure, I walked out of his shop with a fresh haircut that rivaled the more expensive salons, but his rough treatment turned me off from future appointments.

So I took that lesson learned back to my writing today, resolving to not be so roughshod on myself. Rather, I'm choosing to finish this special project in a way that is graceful, gentle, and fun!

I think we've all had one too many roughshod barbers in our lives, and at times, have treated ourselves the same way.

So today, let's try things a different way. Let's ease up on all the pressure and rushing, and focus on enjoying the *process,* not just the outcome.

September 3

◊ GREETING OTHERS IS GREETING YOURSELF ◊

They say that energy can be neither created nor destroyed, but only transferred. Therefore, the way we greet others is the way we greet ourselves, because whatever energy we give someone, they're going to give back to us.

And there are many ways to greet someone.

For example, in English, the phrase 'hello' was originally used to grab someone's attention.

In India, saying *namaste* is a way of showing respect.

In Hawaii, *aloha* is a word for love and compassion.

In Norwegian, we cordially say *bare hyggelig,* which translates to 'only happiness.'

And in Hebrew, the greeting *shalom* expresses peace and wishes wholeness and well-being to the other person.

And while the words are important, an even deeper level of greeting is the intention and spirit behind our words.

So, in your day today, consider: are you greeting people superficially, do you greet them with disdain, or do you truly welcome their presence?

It matters because the greeting we extend to others shapes our interaction with them, and by proxy, that energy becomes the spirit we receive back.

September 4

◇ RIGHT IN FRONT OF US ◇

One of my last assignments in graduate school was to interview a wise elder on life, spirituality, and aging.

Of course, I asked Zuzu, who laughed and said, "I'm certainly old enough: in dog years, I'm almost five hundred!"

Zuzu told me that as a child, she knew she would never die, but at the same time, she found it painful to live in a world of people who didn't share her same reality, so she resolved to spend her life seeking ways to reconcile the difference.

When I asked her how she figured out how to do that, she said, "Patrick, there's always something in front of me I can't see. I try to look beneath the surface of things and think critically, examining everything."

Well, I think that Zuzu's idea is highly relevant to just about anyone.

So, today let's all pause to consider what is right in front of us that we can't see.

Let's go deeper than the surface and think critically, examining everything.

And in that process, we might just remember the Truth that is right in front of us: that we will never die.

September 5

◊ EMBRACING THE MYSTERY ◊

While we were in Lofoten Islands, where the idea for this book began, we took a ferry to a secluded island, then walked five kilometers through beautiful meadows and hiked up a steep hill until, finally, we arrived at Bunes Beach.

And there, we witnessed living, breathing, personality-filled boulders that separated us from mystically opaque waters, all on the backdrop of an intense fog that just barely showed us a nearby mountain peak.

As I beheld this mysteriously ethereal landscape, I thought of M. Scott Peck's words:

Only a relative and fortunate few continue until the moment of death exploring the mystery of reality, ever-enlarging and redefining their understanding of the world and what is true.

Bunes Beach taught me that life is a magical question that doesn't need to be answered so much as asked, and when we got back to our camper van, I wrote:

The ancient seers and wise men deeply understood that
there is more going on here than what meets the eye.
Those sages lived with their hearts, not just their heads.
They understood that life is a mystery.
For example, what about the lost colony on Roanoke,
the mysterious statues on Easter Island,
the ruins of Göbekli Tepe,
the ancient pyramids,
or Stonehenge?
And what about all that vast space between the stars
when we look up at the night sky?

At Bunes Beach, I learned that when we tap into the mysterious nature of being on planet Earth in a human body, life opens up amazing new dimensions and domains.

So, at some point today, I hope you try and find a way to step away from the everyday realm and embrace the mystery of life and the unrepeatable miracle that is you!

September 6
◇ WHAT'S IN A NAME? ◇

You know, I have to admit that my parents didn't do half bad naming me!

My first name, Patrick, means 'noble and dignified.'

My middle name, Aaron, means 'lofty and exalted.'

And although my two names are similar in meaning, there is an amusing contrast in how they were picked.

My mom saw *Dirty Dancing* during its original theatrical run way back in 1987. The lead actor was Patrick Swayze, and nine months later, a baby boy was born that would share his name.

A coincidence?

I think not!

On the other end of the spectrum, my dad is a man of strong religious convictions. When I was still in my mother's womb, he had an intuitive hunch that I would do great things and lead people. Therefore, he chose to name me Aaron, after the first high priest in the Bible.

So, you have the secular *and* the sacred right there in my name.

And I am certainly a mix of both!

I am not an angel, nor am I a demon.

I'm just a good old fashioned, for better or worse, down-and-dirty, nitty-gritty, messy human.

Now, Shakespeare once wrote that a rose by any other name smells just as sweet, but with all due respect to the Bard, I disagree.

I think our names have great power to influence our life's journey, and I believe that many times, whether they realize it or not, our parents channel divine energy when they name us.

Therefore, I'd like to encourage you to take a few minutes today to investigate the meaning behind your name.

And if you're anything like me, reflecting on the meaning of your name will give you some clues into your personality and your nature!

September 7

◊ BURDENS ◊

D uring daily morning workouts, my favorite gym buddy has regaled me with many stories about growing up in Norway, his days as a wrestler and gymnast, and insights gleaned from family vacations around the world.

When he described his time in Africa, his head dropped as he shared about seeing slave markets from centuries past, and how at that moment, he felt guilty for being white.

I have to admit that I had a knee-jerk reaction to his emotional pain. And in the process of acting on my impulses to *appear* to have all the answers, I separated myself from my pal.

My conscience convicted me all weekend, so I took the interaction to my Coffee Companion for clarity.

In her vast wisdom, she said, "You know Patrick, these issues are complicated. What if, rather than speaking reflexively, you had paused, breathed, acknowledged the pain he felt at the injustice, and silently acknowledged the discomfort you felt toward his pain?"

Her answer floored me and created the usual uncomfortable physical sensations that occur when my modus operandi is being challenged in healthy ways.

I said, "I see your point. But I can't quite put my finger on where my discomfort and his pain are coming from. Can you help me with that part?"

She took a minute to collect her thoughts before saying, "Perhaps you and he are both feeling burdened by an injustice that neither of you has done, yet an injustice that neither of you can undo."

My brain lit up and I was excited to reply, "Oh, I have an idea! Maybe the next time I'm in a situation like this, I can pause until my emotions subside. Then, I can say something along the lines of 'I can tell you are feeling burdened, and I feel burdened as well.' Of course, that's not an end-all-be-all, but it's a start."

My Coffee Companion thought that was a brilliant first step and she ended our conversation by acknowledging my willingness to learn and grow.

She said, "Patrick, I hope that more people become willing to sit in the pain of burdens rather than just shoving anger and guilt back and forth to each other."

And perhaps today, you and I can fulfill her hope!

September 8
◇ AFFIRMATIONS ◇

Who doesn't love a good compliment?! It's always nice to hear someone say "Patrick, you look good in that shirt," or "Wow, your cake is so delicious. Give me seconds!"

Well, affirmations are similar to compliments, but they are much deeper: they are a source of emotional support from people we share deep bonds with.

For example, in my first career as a musician, I often got doted on with all sorts of compliments, but my Friend in Paris once told me that I am a bold, innovative person who is full of ideas.

That affirmation went much deeper than all the compliments I received because he was noticing my true nature, not just saying 'Job well done.'

A second example is that people have often told me that I'm smart, just to qualify their compliment by more or less saying, "Would you please not be so different?"

However, Zuzu *loved* the divergent way I think, and she never once tried to change my natural way of being.

Indeed, one of the most powerful moments of my life was when she told me that she believes I'll be able to make money and be successful in unconventional ways due to the very thinking that others have judged me for.

My Coffee Companion reinforced Zuzu's affirmation when she told me that some people color inside the lines neatly, while I, on the other hand, need an entire billboard with every possible color!

I hope these examples have clarified the difference between compliments, which are everyday occurrences, and an affirmation, which is a rare gift.

So, before going about your daily life, take a few moments to consider an affirmation from someone who saw you better than you could see yourself, and as a result, shed new light onto who you truly are.

Savor their words and let their affirmations fuel you as you go about your glorious, once-in-a-lifetime day today!

September 9

◇ THE ITSY BITSY SPIDER ◇

A few years ago, a childhood friend of mine decided to grow his family by adopting a baby boy.

Heartbreakingly, just days after the infant's birth, doctors told my friend and his wife that their son was born with a terminal illness.

The newlyweds were devastated, but they summoned the courage to look grief in the eye, and they lived in a hospital with their child for almost a year until he passed.

One of the silver linings of this family's tragedy was the way my hometown supported my friend and his wife as they mourned; in fact, our little country church was filled to capacity for the memorial service.

When the casket recessed out of the sanctuary, their son's favorite song, 'The Itsy Bitsy Spider,' was played in the background, and as you can imagine, there was not a dry eye to be found.

Now, my friend's child never 'accomplished' anything. He didn't even survive on Earth for one year.

Yet, his life was *so powerful*, because that infant's brief existence reminded all of us that life is precious.

He helped us remember that it's okay to cry over things that are worth being sad about, like losing a child.

And he showed us that community life bonds us all together as a powerful healing agent.

We're often told to have a purpose, to create a legacy, to do something great. But the spiritual realm operates on its own terms and conditions, and often, by eternal standards, the weakest among us are the heavyweight champions.

So today, let's remember this little boy's message: that life is precious, that life is about love, and that we are all immensely lucky to be alive and to have this experience called 'being human!'

September 10

◇ NO ONE HAS A CORNER ON THE TRUTH ◇

At one point during my journey of grieving Zuzu's death, my Grief Guide and I digressed into a different topic of discussion, and she said, "Patrick, no one has a corner on the Truth and there is always more than one side to a story."

She went on to say that even if two people witness the exact same event first-hand, their interpretations of the event will be different.

For example, imagine it is the year 1969, you are a public servant, and your teenage daughter wants to go to Woodstock.

Well, chances are, the two of you are going to have *very* different ideas about what Woodstock is and whether or not she should go!

And since there is always more than one side to an issue, it's important to ask yourself what you are missing and to find the kernel of Truth in the other person's viewpoint.

That doesn't mean you are agreeing with them or abandoning your values.

It just means that, rather than reacting in fear-based anger, you curiously discuss differences in a way that honors and respects the other person, and by proxy, yourself.

September 11

◊ WHOOSH, WHOOSH, WHOOSH ◊

As a child, autumn meant having to rake mountains of leaves in the yard around my childhood home.

Whoosh, whoosh, whoosh went the sound of the rake as it hit the leaves (then, a final *whoosh* as I delightedly jumped into the pile of foliage!).

Well, the *whoosh* of the rake became an artifact from childhood when I moved to Houston, where fall weather only comes for about eight minutes on a Tuesday afternoon.

Imagine then my delight when Autumn greeted me at the door as I took Ollie out for his pee 'n' play this morning!

All of a sudden, the green leaves of summer are starting to fall from the trees, and Ollie and I love to run through the crisp air and crunching leaves.

And *whoosh, whoosh, whoosh* goes the tides of the leaves as we merrily kick them up into a flurry!

So, as you go about your day, I wish you the joy of experiencing whatever autumn brings to your little post-stamp corner of the world.

And I wish you a reunion with the *whoosh, whoosh, whoosh* of your childhood, of nature, and of *life!*

September 12

◇ THE HIGH AMBASSADOR'S MUFFIN ◇

Yesterday, our High Ambassador of Cuteness visited, and from the moment he entered the apartment, he owned the room and he owned my heart!

He very carefully took off his rain boots at the door, opened the closet, and put them on the shoe rack.

Then, he slowly walked around the apartment, inspecting the plants that had moved since the last time he visited.

Now, our High Ambassador knows there's always a treat for him at Patrick Parker's house, so he stuck out his hands with high hopes written across his face.

Teasingly, I said, "Oh, is there something you want?"

He grinned, nodded his head, and said "Chocolate!"

Our High Ambassador did a little dance of delight as I plated a chocolate muffin for him. Then, he carefully took it to the couch, spread his legs in a V shape with the plate in between, and enjoyed that snack with his whole heart.

And it was an absolute spiritual experience to watch!

As I vacuumed the crumbs off the couch after he left, I decided that this must be why we were put on earth: to fully love the person in front of us, one smile, one muffin, one day at a time.

September 13

◊ REVERSE SOUVENIRS ◊

About an hour from Oslo, in a town called Lillehammer which is best known for hosting the 1994 Winter Olympics, our ancestors left petroglyphs on a large rock.

Of course, life wasn't easy centuries ago in the tundra, yet despite the hardships, art emerged.

I like to imagine that as the artist carved the elk into the rock, he or she was thinking the following words:

Souvenirs are something you take with you from a place you love in order to remember it. Well, I left this reverse souvenir because I want to let future generations know that I came here to Earth to live, learn, and love. And although I will leave this place long before they arrive, maybe they will stand at this carving and be reminded how amazing it is that they, too, have the chance to live, learn, and love.

This artist's carvings were 'impractical' on a daily level of survival, yet it's the only remnant of his or her community.

Therefore, let's all consider doing something 'impractical' that is important and interesting to us, because it just might end up becoming a reverse souvenir for future generations!

September 14

◇ THE DAYS ARE LONG, BUT THE YEARS ARE SHORT ◇

Throughout the course of this book, I have shared lessons learned from daily walks with Ollie, but I wasn't open to these insights when he first adopted me.

The change agent that allowed me to really start appreciating time with Ollie was a story by the author Gretchen Rubin about spending time with her daughter.

She wrote:

Once upon a time, but not very long ago, my daughter was too little to walk to school, so we rode the city bus...I didn't particularly mind riding the bus, but I viewed a day off as a great treat.

I'd think with a ping of relief, "Phew, no bus ride today." Until one morning...it hit me. This bus ride was it. This was parenthood, this was the childhood of my darling girl, this was life itself.

One day—and that day probably wasn't too far away— we'd no longer be riding the bus together. And I was frittering this time away.

From then on, every morning, I thought, "Thank goodness, another day to ride the bus."

Now my little girl is bigger, and we walk the ten blocks to school. She still holds my hand, but I know this too will probably end soon. "Do you remember when we used to ride the bus to school?" I asked her the other day. "I remember," she said. "I loved that bus ride." "So did I," I answered.

The days are long, but the years are short.

Gretchen's beautiful words showed me that these heavenly moments I share with Ollie—these four walks and three plates of food each day—these moments are his *life*.

This is his doghood, this is my parenthood, and this is life itself.

I decided that I didn't want to miss one more second of one more day with him, so I started trying my best to pay attention to him in our precious moments together.

Because the days are long, but the years are short.

September 15
◇ GAME OF THRONES ◇

A few days ago, I was at the local Farmer's Market for my regular Saturday morning duck-egg pancake with wild berry jam when I spotted Kristofer Hivju, better known as Tormund Giantsbane in *Game of Thrones*!

I couldn't quite track him down, but once I got home, I was inspired to do a deep dive on the internet.

Hivju once said that the reason why *Game of Thrones* became so successful is that the show's creators followed the laws of life: people are born, they die, and in between they do wonderful things and also commit horrible acts. They change from better to worse, and from worse to better.

For example, Tormund Giantsbane started off as a 'tough guy' antagonist, then morphed into a helper, a funny man, a romantic partner, and at one point, he even cried.

In sharing with us about the character development of Tormund Giantsbane, Hivju is saying that people simply can't be put into a box, labeled, or categorized.

Instead, we should all be allowed the freedom to develop and transform as we grow into who we truly are.

And when we play *that* game, there are enough thrones for each and every one of us!

September 16
◇ FOR THE LOVE OF GOD ◇

O llie often convinces me to take a mid-afternoon sofa siesta, and as we wind down into the liminal space between wake and sleep, Ollie never fails to take the opportunity to show me just how much I'm loved!

He stretches from my armpit down to my hip and nestles my arm over his little body so that my hand covers his head.

And in these moments, Ollie brings to life the meaning behind an old Southern Gospel hymn which states:

Could we with ink the ocean fill,
and were the skies of parchment made;
Were every stalk on earth a quill,
and every man a scribe by trade;
To write the love of God above
would drain the ocean dry;
Nor could the scroll contain the whole,
though stretched from sky to sky.

Today, I will ask Ollie to extend his magical powers so that you, also, can experience the incomprehensible magnitude of just how much you are loved!

September 17

◇ "NO, YOU'RE THE ASSHOLE!" ◇

A few days ago, I was merrily humming as I walked into my apartment complex, when suddenly, out of nowhere, an older gentleman started yelling at me.

Although I tried not to engage, he followed me into the elevator and proceeded to get into my face about a grievance he had against the state of the lobby.

Although my heart was pounding out of my chest and my eyes were bloodshot, I tried to calmly say "I am sorry, I am not responsible for the cleanliness of the apartment grounds."

This only intensified his anger, so I pushed the button to exit the bizarre situation and take the stairs.

But before the doors closed between us, I lost my temper and got in the last word, yelling at him, "You're an asshole!"

Well, this morning, karma came to nip me in the haunches: I was coming back from my daily gym 'n' groceries routine when he confronted me once more.

In what I perceived to be a posturing, condescending attitude, he said, "You really hurt my feelings. Why did you say that about me? You're like a son to me, I'm like your father. You should respect your elders."

I laughed, said "You are *not* my father," turned around, and as I walked away, he shouted, "I'm not the asshole. No, you're the asshole!"

Part of me felt guilty; after all, I spend a good chunk of my career sharing communication skills with clients, and yet here I was in a quagmire.

Score one for hypocrisy!

On the other hand, no one is perfect. I have flaws, blind spots, and make inaccurate assumptions.

Just like everyone else.

That doesn't make me an asshole. It just makes me human. And the same goes for him.

I believe this man was brought into my life to remind me that I'm not God and that sometimes in this life there will be people I won't get along with and situations I can't fix.

Indeed, my Coffee Companion believes that the people who frustrate us and knock us off balance are like resistance training at the gym. Without them, we wouldn't grow into a strong sense of who we are.

So, today, rather than judging the people we're in conflict with, let's try to be grateful for their resistance training.

September 18

◊ WHAT DO WE DO WHILE WE ARE WAITING? ◊

H ave you ever felt completely stuck in a work project or creative endeavor?

If so, then congratulations: you're human like the rest of us!

It's easy to become discouraged about how much time it takes to bring dreams into reality, but luckily, a few years ago, I found a Bible passage that has become a metaphor for patiently waiting for dreams to manifest.

In the Book of Leviticus, Moses wrote:

When you come into the land and plant any kind of tree for food, then you shall regard its fruit as forbidden. Three years it shall be forbidden to you; it must not be eaten. And in the fourth year all its fruit shall be holy, an offering of praise to the Lord. But in the fifth year you may eat of its fruit, to increase its yield for you.

I love this Bible passage because it validates my personal experience that so much of life seems to involve waiting.

But what in the heck do we do in the meantime?

Well, we prepare for the harvest!

And to explain what I mean by that, I'll share my journey as an online content creator, which tends to take about five years for a return on investment.

The task of learning to make videos was daunting, but nevertheless, I tended to the process of planting the seeds, which looked like doing a ton of research into what goes into making a successful YouTube channel.

I continually water and fertilize the channel by posting weekly content and rooting out the weeds (in other words, deleting past videos that are off-brand).

And in between videos, I try to remember that 'the fruit is forbidden,' which means I tend to other parts of my life rather than obsessing over the number of views a video gets.

Recently, we've begun to see sprouts of sponsors, and hopefully, as the seasons pass, those saplings will turn into strong trees that yield a sustainable bounty year after year.

This metaphor has changed the game because rather than being frustrated that my crop isn't ready for harvest, I instead focus on tending tend to it while it grows to maturity.

Likewise, how can *you* use this metaphor to patiently wait for *your* dreams to emerge into reality?

September 19

◊ IF IT ISN'T LOVE, TURN THE PAGE ◊

During his ten years on planet Earth, Ollie has charmed and delighted so many people with his tiny body yet larger-than-life *je ne sais quoi.*

One of those people was an older gentleman in our Houston community who recently passed away, and Ollie and I were grateful to have the opportunity to watch his memorial service remotely, holding each other tight and sending good vibes from Oslo to Houston via the invisible internet and the invisible network of love.

It turns out that this gentleman and his wife had built a second home in Burgundy, France, near the Taizé Community, which was an important part of their spiritual journey.

At one point during the eulogy, the pastor shared this man's favorite mantra from the Taizé Community: "If it isn't love, turn the page."

And as I heard those words, I had a spiritual experience.

My mind flashed back to past friendships that went stale and jobs that soured, and I thought about how I stayed past the expiration date because I was afraid of losing the security those connections provided.

I stayed because turning the page from fear to love is never easy. We never know what's on the next page, and it's natural to be a little queasy about the unknown.

Therefore, it takes a surprising amount of psychic elbow grease (which is better known as humility) to leave behind what's not working and go to the next page.

But generally speaking, I've found that turning the page leads to new adventures, and subsequently, new insights about myself and others.

Yes, there's still conflict, still tough times, still adversity, but those things are part of any great story.

So, as you go about your day, consider: are there any parts of your life where it's time to turn the page?

It might be scary, but it's the only way to move the plot along in your life's story.

So, don't get stuck on page 27.

Instead, if it isn't love, turn the page.

September 20

◇ DO WHAT YOU LOVE ◇

For most of my life, I operated under the self-will of external motivation.

If only I could finish my doctorate, perform in the world's great cathedrals, buy a home, upgrade to a nicer car...the list went on *ad infinitum* and *ad nauseum.*

My unconscious thought process was that if I could just get the world to do my bidding, I might finally be happy and comfortable in my own skin.

Well, that was a thinking error if I ever had one!

But somehow, over the course of my life, I got back to the *internal* motivation of doing what I loved to do when I was a kid: write, read, be alone, and bake.

I quit worrying about what the rest of the world was doing, or if I'd get *my* fair share, and instead I started *living.*

I think a big part of enjoying a peaceful, free life is remembering childhood joys, embracing them, and allowing yourself to do them, no matter how much they diverge from others—or your own!—expectations of yourself.

Because reconnecting with childhood passions can often create deep meaning in indescribable and intangible, yet life-changing, ways.

September 21

◇ CHOCOLATE'S UNIVERSAL APPEAL ◇

When the conquistadors arrived in the new world, they came across a high-fat cacao drink that was quite bitter to the taste.

However, they saw redeeming value in the cacao, and did something virtually never found in nature: they added sugar to fat.

And today, we call this delicious recipe 'chocolate!'

The reason chocolate became such a worldwide phenomenon is that it is one of the few foods that has the same chemistry as our mother's breast milk.

Thus, chocolate reignites our earliest unconscious memories of food and love.

No wonder, then, that chocolate has been proven to relieve anxiety!

So, at some point in your day today, go get a nice piece of chocolate or a gourmet cup of coffee.

Really savor the taste and use the chemistry of chocolate to help you relax into wisdom, peace, and freedom.

September 22

◇ BUILDING BRIDGES ◇

One of my favorite parts of Paris is the Pont Alexandre III, a bridge that was constructed for the Paris Universal Exposition in 1900.

This stunning bridge stretches across the Seine River and connects the Champs-Élysées with Les Invalides in grand Belle Époque style: it is adorned with sculptures, golden statues, and intricate lamp posts crowned with winged horses!

To top it all off, the Pont Alexandre III offers spectacular views of some of Paris's most famous landmarks, including the Eiffel Tower, Les Invalides, and the Grand Palais!

And just as the Pont Alexandre III connects the Champs-Élysées to Les Invalides, we can be bridges in our own lives.

We all have rivers that separate us from others due to differences in values, cultural differences, and conflicting viewpoints.

So, the solution to is to build bridges by finding common ground through shared interests, similar viewpoints and goals, and coming together to solve big problems that otherwise would be impossible to overcome.

In other words, being a bridge builder means that we focus on what unites us, rather than what divides us.

And as a result, the collective well-being of society trends just a few ticks toward the direction of us all becoming more of who we truly are!

September 23

◇ THE MOZART OF CHESS ◇

Here in Norway, Magnus Carlsen, also known as the 'Mozart of Chess,' is a pop culture icon. Magnus is one of the youngest-ever Grandmasters of chess, and he is so good that he once defeated ten challengers on ten different boards, *simultaneously, without looking!*

I recently came across an interview where Magnus shared the secret to his success when he said:

Self-confidence is very important. If you don't think you can win, you will take cowardly decisions...I have always believed in what I do on the chessboard, even when I had no objective reason to. It is better to overestimate your prospects than underestimate them.

Without realizing it, Magnus was referring to the principles behind positive psychology, which are all about increasing positive emotions so that we can trend upward toward a state of flourishing.

So, as you go about your day today, how can you find ways to increase your frequency of positive emotions so that you can feel confident and believe in your prospects?

September 24

◇ WAKE UP, CLEAN UP, GROW UP ◇

My Coffee Companion believes that pain occurs when the mind, heart, and body are not integrated, and she taught me that pain can be soothed by the three-step process she calls *wake up, clean up,* and *grow up.*

Pain *wakes us up* to the fact that there is work to do: it forces us to get honest with ourselves.

After we wake up, we start *cleaning up*: we make changes that are needed in order to reduce the pain.

And as a result, we *grow up,* expanding in ways we didn't know were possible.

For example, in my early twenties, I almost lost a close friend because of mean-spirited jokes fueled by alcohol.

Hurting her *woke me up* to the fact that my drinking habits were affecting people I cared about.

Thus, I *cleaned up* my behavior by deciding it would be prudent to quit drinking.

Subsequently, a decade of replacing alcohol with personal development has allowed me to *grow up.*

So, how can you *wake up* to pain, *clean up* any conflict between your behavior and your values, and *grow up* into who you truly are?

September 25

◇ BALANCE AND MOTION ◇

My Best Friend, Ollie, and I were recently invited to a dinner party hosted by our neighbors, and at the entrance of this lovely family's home was a picture of a bicycle framed with the words 'balance and motion.'

I asked our friends what the artwork meant to them, and the wife said that it is a daily reminder that in life, we need balance *and* motion.

She went on to say that if you're just going fast without any balance, you end up crashing and burning. However, if you focus so much on safely balancing to the point that you forget to pedal, then you never go anywhere!

For example, she and her husband are both pursuing big careers, which require a lot of motion. Yet, at the end of the day, they find balance by coming home to each other and remembering the traditions of their Indian heritage.

So, as you go about your day, how can you pedal forward into who you truly are through the combination of balance and motion?

September 26

◊ THE BABY-FACED ASSASSIN ◊

When you consider the world population, Norway is a tiny fraction at just 5.5 million inhabitants. And yet, Norwegians consistently find a way onto the world stage.

Case in point: Ole Gunnar Solskjær played many seasons of soccer for Manchester United, where he was affectionately known as "The Baby-Faced Assassin."

After retiring as a player, Solskjaer became a manager, and I just love his attitude when he was asked about how it felt to come just a few points shy of a championship.

He answered:

It's not the trophies all the time that are the end-all-be-all... we know the work we put in is so important, and to get to that final [game] and to get so close, we had to make so many good decisions along the way...[therefore] I look back at every single second with pride.

So, sometimes it's about the hard work and the good decisions along the way—more than a trophy—that allows us to look back with pride.

Ole said it perfectly, and nothing more needs to be said!

September 27

◇ EMOTIONAL KRYPTONITE ◇

Earlier this year, I shared about how I was sent away from my momma to the prison they call kindergarten.

Luckily, I ended up with a cellmate that became my best buddy, and we ended up sitting beside each other through eight grades!

Then, one night, my dad called me downstairs when the local news announced my friend had died in a tragic car accident.

A good, healthy dose of denial kicked in. I said, "No that's not my friend, that's someone else," and went to sleep.

But the next morning, reality overrode my denial when my friend's passing was announced over the school intercom during first period.

Now, like many of us, I was taught the ridiculous notion that boys don't cry, so I held back my tears until I climbed into my cousin's truck after school.

And once we were out of the parking lot, I sobbed uncontrollably until the exact moment we hit the driveway of my childhood home.

Then I sucked it up, dried my eyes, and that was the end of that.

In fact, I learned to push my sadness down *too* well, because for the next *twenty years,* I went to extraordinary lengths to avoid sadness, sometimes to great consequence.

But everything changed when Zuzu died and my Grief Guide taught me how to invite sadness in.

Every evening, I went to the bathroom, drew myself a hot bath, and opened myself up to sadness.

Some days I was emotionally constipated, but on other days, a monsoon of healing tears flowed.

At the time, I was terrified that the sadness would swallow me whole, but as a result of finally learning to grieve, I now have a much healthier relationship with sadness.

Zuzu's passing taught me that sadness isn't emotional kryptonite after all; on the contrary, it has actually been my friend all along.

And as a result of my emotional reintegration, I'm one step closer to living as my fullest, most authentic self.

So, before you go about your day, consider: do you have a particular emotional kryptonite that you need to reclaim in order to become your best self?

September 28

◇ A PRAYER OF ENCOURAGEMENT ◇

I have a wonderful friend in Houston who, despite his meekness, prides himself on being an encourager.

Naturally, then, when I come against roadblocks in bringing my dreams into reality, I call up this friend.

And I have to say that the very best part of these conversations is the last few minutes, when he ends the conversation by saying a prayer for me that generally goes along the following lines:

God, help Patrick believe, with every fiber of his being, that he is here for a reason and that you have a plan for his life.

Encourage him, lift his spirits, and lighten his emotional load.

Give him clarity about what to do next, then give him the willingness and the strength to carry that out.

Help Patrick remember that You love him, that he is an amazing man, and that he has a lot to give.

And may I just say that I look forward to saying 'I told you so!' after he keeps the faith and it all works out!

Now, I don't know what you might be facing in your life today, but I do know that life is hard and that we all have pain points.

So, I'd like you to reread my friend's prayer of encouragement, and this time, imagine that I am the one praying it, and replace my name with yours.

I hope you receive as much comfort and peace from this prayer as I do, and I hope that despite the roadblocks you face, you will find the inspiration to continue bringing your dreams into reality!

September 29

◇ ASKING THE UNIVERSE FOR HELP ◇

F̲ive weeks before this book went to press, I felt like I was sprinting down the home stretch in grand fashion!

I had revised several drafts of the manuscript and began preparing the audio recording to be released alongside the hard copies.

Then, as I approached narrating this last quarter of the book, I hit a major snag.

For some reason, the material that I was once proud of now felt trite and bland.

It was fine enough, but in that 'saltless french fry' sort of way.

And I wanted to give you, the reader, something better than that!

So, I decided to completely toss out a quarter of the book I had been writing for almost three years, take a break for a week, and come back to it.

I thought the week away would help, but when I came back to my task of rewriting, the mission felt impossible and my emotions went into DEFCON 1!

I realized that I was not in my wisdom, so I put on a tape by *The Honest Guys* and serendipity struck.

Midway through the guided meditation, the speaker instructed me to ask a question to the universe about anything I needed help with.

I took a deep breath and said to the ceiling, "Universe, how in the *world* am I supposed to finish this book in the next five weeks?"

After a pause in the tape, the speaker praised my willingness to ask the question and said that the answers would start to arrive in unlikely places like a book, a dream, a message from a friend, or a television show.

I went to sleep, and indeed, the next morning I woke up with all sorts of new ideas!

I once again charged forth into rewriting the book, but this time, I wasn't coming from a place of urgency or dread.

Rather, I knew that the Universe was guiding my pen to the pages, and all I had to do was let the words flow.

So, before you continue your day today, consider what question you need to ask the universe.

Then, as you go about your day, remember the answer will come in unlikely places; all you have to do is take notice!

September 30

◇ COMES AUTUMN TIME ◇

If there ever was a place that had four distinct, unique seasons, it's Oslo, Norway!

The winters are quiet and dark, which creates an ability for the citizens of the city to go within themselves for a period of quasi-hibernation.

Spring is full of life, teeming with daily new blossoming delights!

The midnight suns of summer lends well to time outdoors with friends, camping, and escaping the heat by jumping into ice-cold glacier water.

And, at present, autumn has arrived in full glory, creating vibrant hues of purple, orange, and yellow foliage that carpet the forest floor.

So, as we go about our autumn day today, let's reflect upon and appreciate the miraculous rhythm of the four seasons which shape our life's journey.

Comes autumn time: have you noticed?

Really noticed?

◇ OCTOBER ◇

October 1

◇ MANAV PARIVAR ◇

Somehow, I woke up from a kindergarten nap and found myself twenty-seven years old, sitting cross-legged in front of an Indian woman at a meditation retreat!

She and I were asked to hold hands and look into each other's eyes as the retreat leader asked, "What if you can access God through this person's eyes?"

Needless to say, both of us started to tear up as we experienced the intense vulnerability of our eye contact.

After the exercise was over, I told her that somehow, looking into her eyes connected me to a greater human family.

She smiled and said, "Yes, Patrick, that's right. In Hindi, we have a phrase for that: *manav parivar.*

I've tried to remember this life-changing concept of shared humanity since the retreat.

And what I've found is that, when I can practice *manav parivar,* well, that is when I can most relax into wisdom, peace, and freedom.

So, as you go about your day, I hope that you, also, can connect to the greater human family of *manav parivar.*

October 2
◇ GIVERNY ◇

When I lived in Cleveland in my early twenties, I would often walk through the always-free Cleveland Museum of Art in between classes and see one of Claude Monet's paintings from his famous *Water Lilies* series.

And fifteen years later, my Friend in Paris, his spouse, and I went to Giverny, which is the small village where Monet made his home, constructed his very own Garden of Eden, and created some of his greatest paintings.

First, we toured Monet's home: we saw the studio where he created many of his famous works, as well as a stunning yellow dining room, an expansive kitchen with copper cookware, and bountiful windows which filled the house with sunlight and offered beautiful views of the gardens just outside.

The first garden, called the Clos Normand, is characterized by winding paths, arches of climbing roses, and a colorful array of flowers including flowering garlics, poppies, purple sage, dahlias, snapdragons, daylilies, foxglove, roses, and much more!

Finally, we arrived at the Water Garden, which features a Japanese-style bridge, water lilies, weeping willows, and a pond filled with various aquatic plants.

Now, I was totally enamored and enchanted with the beauty of the gardens, but my Friend in Paris brilliantly pointed out that there weren't any exotic or rare plants.

The beauty wasn't in the ingredients, but in how the flowers were planted to either complement or contrast each other, and of course, in the overall volume of the gardens.

And all of a sudden, I had an 'aha!' moment.

When I think about the best days of my life, they're like Monet's garden. There isn't anything 'big' that happens on those days. Rather, it's a day where all the basic ingredients like a good night's sleep, healthy eating, doing a good job at work, and being around people I love all come together so that the overall effect is astounding in fulfillment, well-being, and beauty!

In other words, Monet's gardens at Giverny gave me a great mental picture of the principle that life is lived one day at a time and that the very best days are full of basic elements of life placed in optimal ways.

October 3

◊ THE LUCKY ONES ◊

My guilty pleasure is the a capella group Pentatonix! Their Christmas music helps me deck the halls, their sad songs helped me grieve Zuzu, and, more than anything, they inspire me to dance, sing, and have fun!

A few years back, Pentatonix started doing original songs alongside their popular a capella covers, and their song *The Lucky Ones* gets stuck in my head quite often.

The verses talk about growing up in a small town and trying to blend in by putting up walls around your vulnerabilities so that you don't get hurt.

I can relate to that!

But the chorus feels like a message from Adult Patrick to Little Patrick when they sing:

Look how far we've come, and it was all so unexpected.
We were broke and we were young,
*   but somehow we stayed connected.*
So we hold on to our better days,
*   'cause easy come, easy go away.*
Still can't believe we were the lucky ones.
Look how far we've come.

Indeed, if there is one message that I could give my teenage self, it would be, "Patrick, you will one day be amazed at just how far you've come."

After all, who could have guessed that my life would take me from a town of two thousand people to a career in classical music or living in Norway?

In many ways, I wake up most days feeling like I hit the lottery. But I couldn't have won the lottery without buying a ticket, and in this case, the ticket was willingness.

A willingness to leave my small town and expand into a bigger life.

A willingness to work on my personal development when my best efforts to succeed in the world left me lonely.

And a willingness to trust my intuition and take chances, even when others thought I was being foolhardy.

So, as you go about your day, use the ticket of willingness to hit the jackpot of life so that you can eventually look back and say, "Wow, look how far we've come! I still can't believe we were the lucky ones."

October 4

◇ THE POWER OF CROWDED PLACES ◇

Many years ago, I celebrated giving a concert at St. Thomas Church Fifth Avenue in New York City by going to the top of the Empire State Building.

Now, crowds are my personal version of being waterboarded, but I wanted a view from the top to physically embody the joy of this special moment in my career!

As I stood in line, I just so happened to be waiting in front of a woman who was with her family.

And, bless her heart, she kept going on and on about how she went to the Luis Vuitton store and after waiting for two hours in line, they didn't have the handbag she wanted.

Her husband said, "Why don't you order it online?"

She said, "Because when my friends ask me where I got it, I want to say 'Oh, I got it on my trip to New York!'"

Now, I'll be honest, I rolled my eyes and scoffed before quickly catching myself.

Why did I think I was better than her when we were both standing in line to have the same experience, and when we both once stood in the same line to have the experience of being human before we came down here to Earth?

Instead of judging her, I started to think, 'Okay, what is it about the Empire State Building that has all of us gathering to it? What's so special that we'd pay good money, and wait in line for hours, just to be so crowded at the top that we can barely even experience the view?'

Well, Siân Lloyd-Pennell of *The Honest Guys* would tell me years later that perhaps humans are here on Earth to help the universe grow into consciousness as we ourselves grow into who we truly are.

And I started thinking: 'What if these crowded places, whether it's a theme park, a rock concert, the Mona Lisa, or the Eiffel Tower, are places that have a certain *je nais se quois* that draws us to them because just being in their presence raises our consciousness?'

I have no way of proving whether or not I'm right about this observation. But, it sure did help me quit judging the people around me and enjoy the view!

October 5

◇ CALLING TIME OF DEATH ◇

J ust the other day, I walked past the Place de la Concorde and descended the Champs-Élysées to meet my Friend in Paris at La Madeleine, a beautiful nineteenth-century church designed after Greek temples.

Of course, I had to stop for macarons at a nearby tearoom and bakery called La Durée, and I munched on my delicious treats as I waited for him on the steps.

Well, I realized that I was about thirty minutes early, so I walked inside, and serendipitously, a wonderful high school choir just happened to be giving a concert.

As I listened to the teenagers sing, I thought about how when I left music, I had four years of concert bookings lined up, including at Notre Dame and La Madeleine, both of which were considered the apex of opportunity in my former career.

Naturally, then, some of my colleagues strongly advised me not to cancel my high-profile concerts because they feared I would come to regret it.

But as I was sitting there, I reflected on those memories briefly, and I can honestly say that I did not feel even an ounce of regret.

For most of my life, music was my absolute passion, but at some point, my career had run its course and it was time to transition.

It was time to say goodbye, shed tears over the loss, and move on to something more deeply rooted in my authentic self.

Now, of course, it's always sad to give up that which has outlived its usefulness.

But, if there's something more on the other side of the grief, then is giving up what we're holding onto really that much of a sacrifice?

So, as you go about your day, may you call time of death when something or someone is no longer working in your life, so that you can get to the 'something more' on the other side!

October 6
◇ GLOW ◇

A few months ago, my path crossed with someone who knew me back when I was in my early twenties.

We talked for a while about all that had happened since the last time we saw each other, and after a while, he said, "Patrick, it's amazing how much you've changed since I first met you. Back then, it seemed as though you felt the world and everyone in it owed you something. Now, you just seem to be positively glowing!"

I paused before responding, "I'm not sure exactly what happened except that the passage of time brought into my life so many moments and friendships that the cumulative effect causes me to wake up every day grateful to be alive, thinking, 'how wonderful it is to be me!'"

When he asked me to go into more detail, I told him about all the people I've acknowledged in this book as life-changing agents of wisdom, peace, and freedom.

I went on to tell him how blessed I felt to have had an entire career by the time I was thirty, and then to have the wherewithal to grow into something more.

I also extended my gratitude list to include having the time and resources to gain a world-class education as well as the good fortune to live in different countries and take yearly trips to Paris and India.

Finally, I said, "Yes, I was suffering when you first met me, but that pain propelled my growth. And today, that glow comes from really feeling, in my bones, blood, and soul, that I am exactly who I was made to be."

I think that the reason I was able to articulate to the reasons behind my glow was because of how much time and energy I have spent putting this book out into the world.

So, I hope that you, also 'feel my glow' through these pages the same way that he saw on my face.

And, I hope that this book helps you to find so much gratitude for the special people and moments in your life that you, also, glow so bright that you stop people in their tracks!

October 7

◇ DESENSITIZING MYSELF TO THE NOISE ◇

J ust before this book was released, my YouTube channel had its first viral video.

The video featured the stories from my time in India, and it was really cool for my Best Friend and I to see the numbers roll in!

But with the newfound popularity came an interesting sort of infamy.

There were over a thousand comments on the video.

Half of them chanted "Patrick, Patrick, he's our man!"

The others got a bit nasty.

Now, throughout my life, I have been a bit of a wilting flower to criticism and judgment, but this time, I just didn't care what they had to say.

I knew that my intentions were pure, that I had made that video with as much humility as I could muster, and that we had spent a year doing everything we could to get the script as authentic, accurate, and powerful as we could.

My state of mind and heart was pure through the process of preparing, recording, and editing the video, so for the first time in my life, I just *did not care* what other people thought.

And it was liberating!

I wish I could bottle up and freely give away my 'devil may care' attitude about the reception of this video, because I think that fear of judgment and criticism prevent many people from putting their best ideas forward.

But I can say that putting yourself out there is worth it, and that the first step to desensitizing yourself to the noise of the world seems to be knowing that your intentions are pure.

Learning to desensitize myself to the noise of the world has been a real spiritual experience for me, and I wish the same for you!

October 8

◊ THE SCREAM ◊

Here in Norway, the artist Edvard Munch is a national hero. Even if you don't recognize his name, I'd bet dollars to doughnuts you've seen his painting *The Scream,* which sold for nearly $120 million in 2012.

I recently took my friends who were visiting Norway to the Munch Museum here in Oslo, where I tripped over a statue of the goddess Nike and was almost booted out!

But once they realized I was not a vandal, but just a clumsy oaf, I got to learn about Munch.

Munch's dark art was likely influenced by his mother's death when he was five and being reared by a strict father.

In fact, Munch once said, "The angels of fear, sorrow, and death stood by my side since the day I was born."

He thought that to create great art, he had to suffer, that he had to be alienated from others, and that he had to be afraid.

Munch wrote:

My fear of life is necessary to me, as is my illness. Without anxiety and illness, I am a ship without a rudder. My art is grounded in reflections over being different from others. My sufferings are part of myself and my art. They are indistinguishable from me, and their destruction would destroy my art. I want to keep those sufferings.

Munch's way of thinking is all too common among creatives: just look at the legendary stories of mental illness about van Gogh, Beethoven, and a litany of others.

However, I don't think we have to suffer to be creative. Just look at all the highly creative people behind the scenes, raising children, cooking meals with love, and mending clothes while they also mend hearts.

Living a creative life doesn't require us to scream in anguish like Munch.

Rather, true creativity comes from being comfortable with who we are and our station in life, and being content with whatever creative byproduct flows from that wellspring of wisdom, peace, and freedom.

October 9

◇ CHEERLEADERS AND PRAGMATISTS ◇

I live my life under the assumption that 'somebody has to be the first man on the moon, and it might as well be me!'

I simply can't help that intuition inspires lofty goals and then my quick tempo and sharp brain gets into action!

So, as I shoot for the moon, it's easy to appreciate the people who root me on and encourage me to go for my dreams.

On the other hand, I tend to be a bit ungrateful and defensive toward the pragmatists who force me to take pause and make sure my rocket ship to the moon is prepared so that I actually make it back to Earth safe and sound.

But what I've learned over the years is that we need cheerleaders *and* pragmatists equally.

We need the cheerleaders to help us fly.

We also need the pragmatists to help make sure we get back to the ground in one piece.

We need both energies so that we can keep one foot grounded in reality and the other in eternity as we shoot for the moon!

October 10

◇ BE PROUDLY IRRESPONSIBLE! ◇

The late great physicist Richard Feynman had a primary purpose to advance the field of science, and he did his best to avoid anything that might distract him from his mission.

Feynman once said:

To do real good physics work, you do need absolute solid lengths of time...it needs a lot of concentration...if you have a job administrating anything, you don't have the time. So I have invented another myth for myself: that I'm irresponsible...If anyone asks me to be on a committee for admissions, "no," I tell them: "I'm irresponsible."

There are times in life when we need to be team players, but there are also periods when we can take after Feynman and singularly focus on our primary purpose, letting all else fall away until we achieve what we are working toward.

So, when you're working on a special project that is coming from your deepest creativity and based on who you are, I think it's quite alright to be proudly irresponsible!

October 11

◇ SHARED HOPES AND DREAMS ◇

L ast autumn, I was wrangled into attending a men's conference in Brussels.

Now, I'm not a fan of large gatherings, and I loathe 'networking events' and 'happy hours,' which are never very happy for me.

And I knew there would be plenty of political overtones, which I am completely allergic to.

So, I went in with my guard up and I didn't even realize it!

But halfway through the weekend, it became apparent just how defensive I was behaving.

So, I decided to zip my lips, sit on my hands, and go within to examine what in the world was going on inside of me.

And as I began to do this hard work, I started being surprised that every once in a while, someone would say something that perked my ears up and delighted me.

The more I acted opposite to my emotions of repulsion and opened my heart, the less internally combative I became and the closer I moved toward an 'aha!,' which I experienced on the last morning.

Now, the 'aha!' may have been partly inspired by the almond croissants from Renard Bakery, which you simply must try if you're ever in Brussels!

But nevertheless, a participant said something that resonated with me, and suddenly, I felt a sense of equanimity and unity emanate throughout my body.

I finally understood that no matter how different we all looked, or how differently we saw the world, each person at that conference was there because we all had a similar hope and dream.

And our shared hopes and dreams made us a brotherhood.

During that weekend in Brussels, I learned so much more than the technical information I was there to receive.

I learned that if I can do the hard work of continually listening rather than shutting down through judgment, I will be more at ease and have the space to connect through shared hopes and dreams.

And when I can do that, life will go from feeling like a constricting corset to an oversized, worn-out, comfortable old hoodie!

October 12
◇ THE BASICS ◇

The other day, I was up for a very large coaching contract, and I felt really good about the entire vetting process.

However, the stars aligned in a way that negated my will, and as a result, I naturally felt disappointed and frustrated.

So I called up Mustang Sally, because she knows how to bring me *down* to earth when I get too big for my britches, and she also knows how to bring me *up* to earth when I start sinking into self-pity.

Now, Mustang Sally lives in the real world, where she busts her butt raising and homeschooling three kids, so she cut right to the chase.

She replied to my whining with the loving-but-firm assertiveness of a Johnston County woman by saying:

Those things weren't meant for you. All that matters is that you do things that bring you joy and that you also do the things you need to do to be self-supporting in the world. Those are the basics.

So, today, let's play with Mustang Sally's words and see where attending to the basics of life takes us!

October 13

◇ RELAX INTO YOUR BODY ◇

Are you stressed?

If so, you might be tempted to check out of life by picking up a liquor bottle, binging a television show you don't even like, or losing your temper.

Most of us tend to default to these sorts of numbing behaviors when we get stressed, but a better way is to find relaxing behaviors like taking a shower, having a nap, exercising, playing chess, or working on a jigsaw puzzle.

When I take time to relax, my shoulders drop, my nervous system relaxes, and fearful inner voices are replaced by an assuredness that the world is a safe and loving place.

My worries fall away and I remember that I have gravity. to ground me and my breath to anchor me.

It's as though I'm a computer that restarts after a glitch.

It's a free miracle!

Now, it will always be easier to numb out, but that's all just quicksand that doesn't allow us to move forward in our life's journey.

So, today, I hope you can find a relaxing activity to reduce your stress in a way that allows you to move forward into becoming all that you truly are!

October 14

◊ THE LONELINESS THAT PRECEDES REVELATION ◊

Lying on my yoga mat during *Shavasana,* amidst a crowded session, I feel utterly alone.

No one can be with me during this time
of revelation.

Yes, they can lie on their mat alongside me,
but it's not their experience to have; it's mine.

The loneliness of *Shavasana* arises because at this moment,
I experience more of life's bigness than ever before.

It's scary because it feels like I am flailing in the open sea
with tidal waves tossing me around,
threatening to drown me,
making my belly shake in fear.

No one is coming to save me,
it's just me,
in the dark,
a tiny, helpless human.

Then, at the eleventh hour, I remember
  that I am so much more than my physical body.

And I find the courage to dive down under the waves,
  where I discover I have a fin and gills!

After plunging into the depths of the ocean,
  I summon the audacity to grow wings
  and dart through the space between the stars,
  and from the view on high,
  I see others who feel as though *they* are drowning.

I realize that I must return to my human body
  which still lies on the mat,
  so that I can help those still thrashed by the waves,
  one person at a time, one day at a time,
  as best I can.

And as the bell rings and *Shavasana* concludes,
  I feel grateful for the loneliness that precedes revelation.

October 15

◇ GIVING IT TO THE GODS ◇

I have a confession to make: I *seriously* underestimated how long it would take to write this book!

And because I wasn't quite clear on how hard writing this book would be, I severely undershot the release date and scrambled to finish on time.

Of course, it didn't help that at the same time, I saw a big uptick in the other parts of my career!

I extended the release date as much as I possibly could, and at one point, it seemed like I wouldn't be able to make the final deadline.

I was getting a little frantic, so rather than writing a book about wisdom, peace, and freedom while I was stressed out (which would have been quite ironic!) I gave myself a time-out, sat on the couch, and sent up a prayer to the gods.

Upon saying 'amen,' I felt comfort in knowing that the book was now in the universe's hands.

Thus, if the book ended up being a heaping pile of garbage, it was the universe's fault!

And since the universe doesn't produce junk, I knew I'd be in good hands.

So, I set back out to finish this book, but this time from a place of relaxation and spaciousness rather than claustrophobic stress.

And as you go about your day, what do *you* need to give to the gods?

October 16

◇ BE BOLD! ◇

Basil King once said, "Be bold and mighty forces will come to your aid."

Now, many of us are taught that the tall poppies are the ones that get cut down.

At the same time, it's hard to remember our bigness when so many things that are simply out of our control.

And it's a real pity that life's worries and stressors cause us to forget that our souls are infinite and eternal.

But when we remember the Truth about our greatness, there's no need to stick our head in the sand like an ostrich.

Instead, we can be like a buffalo and charge forth directly into the thunderstorms, because we trust that when we are bold, mighty forces will come to our aid.

So, as you go about your day, thrust yourself into life's challenges so that you can reside in the peaceful, calm weather on the other side of the storm, proud that you rose to the occasion and became a little more of your deepest self.

Be a mighty buffalo and run into the storm.

Be bold, and mighty forces will come to your aid!

October 17
◇ ATHITHI ◇

When I was in India, I learned that there is a word that teaches Indians how to treat guests with hospitality.

The word is *Athithi*, and it is the term for a guest who turns up unannounced and without appointment.

That person is equated to God.

I'll be honest: in my life, I'm often annoyed by the people, places, and things that turn up announced and derail me from my train of thought.

But perhaps a better way is to not get annoyed by *Athithi.*

But instead, to make room for *Athithi.*

To not be so overscheduled that I have to reject *Athithi.*

And to welcome and appreciate God showing up in the form of a person, which we call *Athithi.*

October 18

◇ WE ALL HAVE A SACRED SELF ◇

I shared with you earlier this year that a woman I look up to taught me that we all have an inner Lippizaner stallion that kicks up their heels and an inner rider that harnesses that energy.

Well, that same brilliant woman also taught me that we all have a sacred self: an inner world that is just as describable as our external physical body.

If we think of this inner sacred self through the metaphor of our outer physical body, then at the inner 'head' we have our morals and values.

Obviously, my values are wisdom, peace, and freedom; but perhaps your values have nothing to do with mine, and that's totally okay!

At the neck, let's consider resources like time, space, and money.

I prefer to live simply so that I can spend most of my time enjoying life and pursuing my creative calling, but you may feel driven to make lots of money.

Neither person is wrong, it's just different modes of being.

At the heart, there are feelings and emotions.

I'm a highly sensitive, artistic type, but you might be more of a steely, warrior type.

And at the feet, we have behaviors and actions.

I'm a bit of a go-getter with a pretty quick pace, but my Best Friend is a self-described sloth!

The point I'm trying to make is that my sacred self may look nothing at all like yours. But it's what's sacred to me. It's the makeup of who I truly am.

Likewise, you might like things I have no interest in, but if it's important and precious to you, then I should take the time to get to know those things as well if I want to be close to you.

If we could remember that we all have a sacred inner self that others can't see, and that we are all just trying to become who we truly are, it sure would dial down a lot of the anger and disagreements in the world.

So, as you go about your day, may you explore and honor your sacred self.

And may you do the same for others and their sacred self.

October 19

◇ MERLIN'S BEARD! ◇

Last night I was flipping through the television channels when I came across a scene from the Harry Potter series where Ron Weasley, in a moment of exasperation, lets loose the slang phrase "Merlin's Beard!"

As the movie kept playing, I left the physical reality of my apartment and went deep into my inner realm in order to think more about Merlin.

Just as Harry Potter needed Dumbledore, King Arthur needed Merlin.

And because of characters like Dumbledore, Merlin, and Gandolf in *Lord of the Rings*, the archetype of the wise, philosophical elder pervades the stories we tell.

These trusted advisors generally have a bit of a sly, sphinx-like, magical nature, which is appropriate since they represent a higher knowledge that the hero relies on to fulfill their destiny.

And the thing is, we all need our own, individual Merlin!

Each of us needs at least one sacred, private relationship with a trusted advisor who can listen to us, model values, shed light on blind spots, ask thought-provoking questions, and give tough feedback when necessary.

And I have to say that I've been quite blessed with many Merlins throughout my life!

My conversations with people like Zuzu, my Coffee Companion, and my Friend in Paris have brought me to the portal of the inner experience, allowed me to access the Divine, to touch the face of God, to stand in the sunlight of the spirit, to walk the road of happy destiny, to fully experience love and life.

Their love and care have inspired me a life worth living and a career worth having.

So, my point is this: when you meet a Merlin, grab him (or her) by the beard, hold on with all your might, and don't let go!

They might just take you on a magical ride through the universe, or even better, help you sit still and go within yourself.

October 20

◇ THE CATACOMBS ◇

The Catacombs of Paris consist of two hundred miles of underground tunnels that were created in the eighteenth century as a solution to the city's overcrowded cemeteries.

But of course, since it's Paris, they didn't just throw the bones in a big pile.

Rather, they created art from the skeletons, including walls made entirely of bones or stacked skulls, resulting in a haunting display that really makes you think about the transient nature of this life we get to live.

Indeed, at the entrance to the ossuary is a sign that translates to "Stop, this is the empire of the dead!"

As I walked past the ominous warning and entered the catacombs, I was shocked by the sheer scale of the underground graveyard.

It's easy to read that seven million people are buried in the catacombs, but to experience corridor after corridor of skulls and bones is a singularly unique experience.

At one point, I passed an engraving of Alphonse de Lamartine's poem, "Thoughts of the Dead," which translates to:

So all things pass upon the earth:
  spirit, beauty, grace, talent.
Ephemeral as a flower, tossed by the slightest breeze,
  they were as we are, dust, the wind's plaything,
  fragile as men, feeble as the void.

The poem got me thinking about the individual lives that make up the millions of bones in the Catacombs.

Perhaps some of those people were rich, and some were poor.

Maybe some were beautiful and some were practically the Hunchback of Notre Dame.

Women and men, children and the elderly, the strong and the handicapped, are all housed in the Catacombs.

And yet in the end, all that remains are dried-up old bones, and that's a great reminder that we can't take earthly riches with us.

All that we can take when this life is over is our souls.

So in that case, we might as well focus on the deep inner journey to becoming who we truly are.

October 21

◇ BOLLINGEN TOWER ◇

Before I leave this earth in physical form, I would really love to visit a village named Bollingen near Lake Zurich in Switzerland.

What's so special about this little coven of six thousand people, you ask?

Well, it's where Carl Jung built a simple two-story stone house he called Bollingen Tower.

And why did he build a home there, when he had a busy schedule lecturing and counseling clients in Zurich?

Well, Jung wanted to revolutionize our understanding of the unconscious mind, and in order to do that, he needed a distraction-free environment that allowed for repose and renewal.

Away from the busyness of city life, his time at Bollingen Tower was completely devoted to the inner journey.

Most days, Jung woke up at seven a.m. and ate a big breakfast.

Then, he wrote for two hours in his private office, which he kept under lock and key as though it was the Ark of the Covenant.

Afternoons at Bollingen Tower included meditation and long walks around the countryside, and since there was no electricity at the Tower, Jung would normally fall asleep early in the evening.

Since moving to Norway, I have taken inspiration from Jung and created my own Bollingen Tower: I live in a quiet neighborhood away from the city and I have a daily routine that involves waking up early, meditating, exercising, and long walks with Ollie.

Now, these choices aren't necessarily right for everyone, but nevertheless, I think there are times when we all need at least a little escape to solitude.

So, as you go about your day, how can you begin to intentionally create *your* Bollingen Tower?

October 22

◇ PASSPORTS ◇

Although travel is an integral part of becoming who I truly am, I definitely do *not* love airports!

But the other day, I felt very grateful when I showed my passport to the airport security agent because, for the first time ever, I truly noticed all of the beautiful pictures and quotes inside my U.S. passport.

In each American passport, there are pictures of the Liberty Bell, the Declaration of Independence, the Statue of Liberty, and other symbols of my country.

But most striking to me was a quote about freedom by Anna Julia Cooper, who wrote:

The cause of freedom is not the cause of a race or a sect or a party or a class—it is the cause of humankind, the very birthright of humanity.

Throughout this book, I've shared what freedom means to me, but as you go about your day, I'd like you to consider: what does freedom mean to *you*?

And, how can freedom help you become who you truly are?

October 23
◇ I DON'T WANT TO BE ANYTHING OTHER THAN ME ◇

As a teenager, I was terrified of being myself. But at the same time, I was allergic to the identity crises of adults who had given up their souls in exchange for a comfortably numb existence.

I consider it divine providence, then, that the same year I began to struggle with this dilemma, a new pop artist emerged with a song that gave voice to my existential teen angst:

I'm surrounded by identity crisis everywhere I turn.
Am I the only one who noticed?
I can't be the only one who's learned:
  I don't want to be anything other than me.

Now, don't get me wrong: it took almost two decades after I first heard this song to set up a life that was congruent with my authentic self and to be able to say with my whole heart, "I don't want to be anything other than me."

But these days I can honestly say that.

Can you?

October 24

◇ TURNING LIFE UPSIDE DOWN ◇

If you ever find yourself in the Latin Quarter of Paris, head on over to the tranquil atmosphere in the Church of Saint-Étienne-du-Mont, which is right next door to the Panthéon.

The facade of the church displays nuanced carvings and sculptures, and the statue-adorned portal that borders the beautiful purple doors is breathtaking.

Inside the church, you'll be stunned by the beautiful stained glass windows, the majesty of the pipe organ, and a lovely rood screen that is singularly unique in all of Paris.

One of the main attractions inside the Church of Saint-Étienne-du-Mont is the shrine and relics of Saint Genevieve, the patron saint of Paris.

Additionally, the church houses the tombs of several notable individuals, including the French writer and philosopher Jean Racine.

Now, Jean Racine has been largely forgotten by modern culture, but he had some pretty pithy one-liners in his extensive writings.

He wrote that "The more one judges, the less one loves," which I have certainly tried to drive home in this book.

Racine also talked about the value of embracing the hardships of life and using those events to fuel the deep inner journey of becoming who you truly are when he wrote:

What good is a life that has not been turned completely upside down? You must turn your life upside down at least once to find the truth.

But I think my favorite quote by Racine is, "There is only one happiness in this life, to love and be loved."

So, as we go about our day, let's remember that turning our lives upside down every once in a helps us find the truth, just like turning a purse upside down helps my mom find her keys.

And, may we remember to drop the judgment and just love and be loved.

October 25
◇ WHO DO YOU RELY ON? ◇

Henry David Thoreau once said:

I learned this, at least, by my experiment; that if one advances confidently in the direction of his dreams, and endeavors to live the life which he has imagined, he will meet with a success unexpected in common hours.

For Thoreau, the way to do this was to circumvent the trappings of society that leads to foreclosing on your dreams and who you truly are.

Thoreau believed that, just as wolves try to prey on the sheep that cover this book, the pressure to conform to society's will preys on our souls.

So, if we don't want to become enslaved to the trappings of society, which is certainly bigger than us, then we have to find something even bigger.

And most people call that something 'God.'

Now, I'm not talking about the God that other people try to program us with.

Rather, I'm talking about a God of our personal, experiential understanding.

Not a damning, authoritarian God, but a kind, loving, altruistic Higher Power that wants nothing but the best for us.

So, as you go about your day, who will you rely on:

Society, with its pressures to conform, which is like a wolf chomping at your heels?

Your own will, which can lead you to wander off and get stuck in a briar patch?

Or, a benevolent shepherd who will watch over you as you calmly graze in the pasture next to those big mountains that call us all to look upward and abide in infinity and eternity?

October 26
◇ THE BEST PARENTING ADVICE EVER? ◇

Recently, Mustang Sally texted me with three words: "Parenting is hard."

I took the bait and asked, "What's up, doc?"

She told me that she was having a hard time giving her teen daughter the space to experience the pain of young love without interfering.

I asked her, "Is that the hardest part of parenting?"

And I loved what she said next:

Well, it depends. Letting her do her own thing even when I know it's going to lead to pain is hard.

With my little girls, on the other hand, the hardest part is standing my ground, which shifts as they progress in the stages of childhood and adolescence.

In other words, the difficulty changes from making the right choices for them in their first years, to letting them experiment with making choices safely in our home in adolescence, to eventually letting go.

Now, I don't have kids of my own, so I have no idea if my friend's three-stage conception of parenting is universal, but it sure does seem chock full of common sense!

I also think this three-stage conception of parenting is useful in the manager-employee relationship, the teacher-student relationship, and perhaps many others.

After all, we all have *someone* who looks up to us, which means, whether we want to be or not, we're all mentors in some shape or form.

So, today, think about the needs of the people who consider you a role model, whether you are their boss, their parent, or their hero.

Do they need you to make their choices for them?

Do they need you to give them space to experiment with making their own decisions within a controlled environment?

Or, ultimately, do they need you to let them go, so that they can go out into the world and have the freedom to become who they truly are?

October 27

◇ LIFESTYLE ◇

As you know by now, I start every morning at a magical playground five hundred feet away from my apartment called Lifestyle Gym!

Well, today, after walking into the gym for the umpteenth time, the meaning of the gym's name finally dawned on me: whether I go to the gym or not is indicative of my lifestyle.

When I go to the gym, I feel fit and trim and I tend to eat healthier.

I feel tired but really fantastic!

When I don't go to the gym, I'm more anxious, less patient, I tend to eat more, and I feel ill at ease.

And, ironically, my creativity—the excuse for putting off going to the gym in the first place—suffers.

So, as you go about your day, I hope that you, also, prioritize the activities that will give you the lifestyle you need to keep one foot in the realities of being human and the other foot in infinity and eternity!

October 28

◇ TEMPO ◇

Each human seems to have a unique tempo. Some of us charge forth like a bull in a china shop, while others make sloths look like sprinters!

Let's take my Friend in Paris for example: he once told me, "Patrick, I was *born* tired!"

He tends to be pretty mild in his tempo; in fact, he's one of the best classical musicians in the world, and he's always enjoyed playing slow, soft music over fast music.

His spouse, on the other hand, has a speedy tempo to the point that when we take walks together during my visits, I can't keep up even though I'm half their age!

But the interesting thing is that over thirty years of marriage, my Friend in Paris and his partner have figured out how to meld together and be flexible.

Sometimes my Friend needs to speed up, and sometimes his spouse needs to slow down.

But by being flexible with their individual tempi, they have built a sustainable relationship and a beautiful home.

Likewise, how can adjusting your natural tempo yield dividends for you today?

October 29

◇ DO A GOOD TURN DAILY ◇

Some of my favorite childhood memories are from my time in the Boy Scouts of America.

Eventually, I became an Eagle Scout, which is the highest award given by the organization, but to be honest, the happiest times were at the very beginning.

As a twelve-year-old, I felt super spiffy in my brand-new uniform bought from the last old-school tailor in town.

And I loved the process of earning the first rank, called Tenderfoot, which included a ton of campouts and learning all the Boy Scout mantras, including their slogan, "Do a good turn daily."

My Scoutmaster taught us that some good turns are big, like helping out after a natural disaster.

However, other good turns are small, daily, thoughtful acts like helping an elderly person take groceries to the car or holding the door open for a mother pushing a stroller.

Well, once upon a time, a guy did his daily good turn on me!

I was in Paris, my phone had died, and although I knew the city very well, I just could not find the train station I needed to head back to the airport to catch my flight home.

I was getting a little panicky because I didn't want to miss my flight.

So, I asked a stranger if he could point me in the direction of the train, and he said, "No problem, I'll take you there because my restaurant is right beside it."

As we walked the five blocks over to the train station, I was surprised to find out that my good samaritan is the head chef of a wonderful restaurant called Le Coupe Gorge!

And although I didn't have time to thank him by dining at his restaurant, I'd like to give him a plug here.

So, if you're ever in Paris and looking for a great place to eat, look up Le Coupe Gorge and have a delicious meal!

In summary, this gentleman's good turn was more than just proper manners. It was a special act of kindness.

How can you, also, do a good turn today?

October 30

◊ IF YOU CAN DREAM IT, YOU CAN DO IT! ◊

One of my earliest memories involves a family vacation to Disney World when I was five years old.

Most of the memories are a bit hazy, but a few do stand out:

First of all, going on the Dumbo ride.

My tiny young mind literally thought I was riding on a real-life, bona fide, flying baby elephant!

Second of all, my mom bought me a popsicle from an ice cream cart, and it was so cold from the dry ice that it stuck to my tongue.

Terrified, she went berserk and spit in my mouth to unwedge the icicle from my tongue. That's a moment my family has roasted both of us over for the last thirty years!

Finally, a plaque containing the words of Walt Disney left an enduring impression on me.

And those words were, "If you can dream it, you can do it!"

So, let's remember that when we wish upon a star, our dreams come true.

That a dream is a wish the heart makes.

And, that if we can dream it, we can do it!

October 31

◇ THE CYCLE OF THE SEASONS ◇

Each year, the four seasons teach us about life and death. The bleak mid-winter is a season of stark dormancy, when animals and plants go into the earth to quietly reflect.

Spring is a time of rebirth, of vitality.

Summer is the bright, dynamic apex.

And autumn is the golden season of wisdom and reflection.

This yearly cycle of life, death, and rebirth has so much wisdom to teach us about how to be alive.

Therefore, may we all listen to the seasons, to the song of the earth.

Because Mother Nature can teach us how to be alive if we listen to her melody and then participate in the song ourselves.

◇ NOVEMBER ◇

November 1

◇ WE'RE ALL DOING THE BEST WE CAN ◇

It's hard to remember that, at every single moment, each one of us is doing the very best we can.

Even back in 2014, when I weighed 333 pounds and was eating everything in sight, I was doing the best that I could.

My life was unmanageable: I was working for a difficult boss and was struggling through a doctoral program that just didn't suit me, although I didn't know it at the time.

I had intense emotions from an environment that was not letting me be who I wanted to be, I didn't know how to get out, and food was my only reprieve.

The best I could do at the time was to smash the square peg (myself) into a round hole (life) all day.

And when that inevitably backfired, I came home exhausted and ate the entire refrigerator.

Eventually, I found skills to handle my emotions and realized that my career wasn't working for me.

But, time takes time, and before those insights came, overeating was the best skill I had.

So, if you, also, find yourself in a habit or situation that is not optimal, don't be too hard on yourself.

Because we're all doing the best we can.

November 2

◇ HAPPY DIWALI! ◇

Today, we took a thirty-minute bus ride to a temple to celebrate Diwali, the Hindu Festival of Lights.

Diwali is all about good winning over evil, light winning out over darkness, and wisdom winning out over ignorance.

As we entered the temple, I was taken aback at the men dressed in beautiful kurtas and the women in their beautiful saris and jewelry.

It was a sight to behold!

As the priest chanted sacred texts for the occasion of Diwali, an adolescent girl came around with a flame which we put our hand into and then rubbed onto our head, which symbolized purifying ourselves in front of the gods.

Then, the priest wnet around the temple and sprinkled water on all of us as a blessing.

Next, we all went up to the front of the gods to offer food and water to the avatars, then stood in line for the priest to dab a red mark on our foreheads, which is considered a sign of blessing on this auspicious day.

After the worship and prayer, which they called *pooja*, we had the most wonderful food: deep-fried paratha, lemon rice, delicioius curry made of mushroom, okra, and broccoli, and exotic Indian desserts.

Yum!

When my neighbor sitting next to me asked me if I liked Indian food, I stuttered out "Jevan chaan ahe," which meant "The food is good!"

As we left the temple, I rang the bell as is custom when leaving a Hindu temple, and we headed home!

For the last few years, the celebration of Diwali has signaled the beginning of the holiday season, which continues with Thanksgiving, Advent, Christmas, and New Year's!

As the famous Hindi actor Prabhas says, "A holiday is an opportunity to journey within."

So, as we begin to ramp up to the holidays, let's remember that this special time of the year is not just an opportunity for external celebration with family and friends; it's a chance to go deeper in our own in journeys to becoming who we truly are.

November 3

◇ OLLIE: MASTER NEGOTIATOR! ◇

Lions and tigers aggressively roar to tell the animal kingdom who's boss.

Turtles passively recede into their shell when danger lurks.

House cats can be hilariously passive-aggressive as they knock items off the counter when they don't get their way.

But Ollie, my dear Ollie, is a master of assertiveness!

In summer, Ollie knows how to stretch out a walk 'just five more minutes' through his cuteness.

He jumps up into my lap and gently puts his paw on my chest to let me know it's time to eat.

And Ollie is starting to lose his teeth, so if I don't properly grind up his food, he patiently looks up at me until I realize my error and present a proper course of food for him.

Personally, I think that we could all learn from Ollie's assertiveness, because when we find this sweet spot of relating to others, we can miraculously improve our relationships while getting more of what we want in a way that we feel good about!

November 4

◇ EXHALE STRESS, INHALE PEACE ◇

At a snail's pace—or perhaps God's timing—I am learning from trial and error to be at peace with the natural ebbs and flows of life.

The way I do that is by viewing my mind as a book and consciously choosing to 'turn the page' when I become fearful.

The best way I have found to 'turn the page' is to focus on my breath, which like the sun, is free and life-giving.

As I exhale stress and inhale peace, I become less judgmental and begin to see the subtleties and nuances of the issue that is stressing me out.

And, in that process, I reconnect to who I am and what is important and meaningful to me, allowing all else to fall away.

So, as we go about our day, let's remember that exhaling stress and inhaling peace is like a North Star that helps us stay coordinated on our unique path of becoming who we truly are.

November 5
◇ DOMINOES ◇

My Friend in Paris once told me that playing a musical composition beautifully is kind of like setting up dominoes.

If you have each domino standing and placed optimally, then all you have to do is flick the first one gently and the rest just fall with the momentum that is gained from that first small release of energy.

Well, that is one of the many lessons from my music career that I have carried over to my new life.

So here are the dominoes that I need each day: a good night's sleep, exercise, meditation, a creative activity, walks with Ollie, helping someone out in some small way, making a living doing what I love, and cooking meals at home.

If those foundational dominoes are set up in the right way, then when I flick them, they fall and set off a chain reaction for all the finer points and details of each day to tumble down in synchronicity as well.

But that's just my way.

More importantly, how do *you* need to set up the individual dominoes of your daily routine in a way that once you flick the first one, a beautiful chain reaction happens?

November 6

◇ AS GOOD AS IT GETS ◇

So many people bite the bullet and suffer through intolerable circumstances today because they hope for a return on investment down the road.

But maybe a momentary reprieve we carve out for ourselves, one day at a time, is as good as it gets.

And if emotions are God's way of talking to us, then is heaven simply cultivating the ability to experience each day's emotions without running away from them?

For example, I spent most of today editing the umpteenth draft of this book.

This morning, I was stressed about making the final deadline, and I wasn't enjoying myself, so I took a nap.

I woke up refreshed and returned to editing, and all of a sudden I could hear my Best Friend humming in the background while he cooked dinner.

I saw Ollie relaxing on his special pillow by the window.

And I saw Mr. Magpie's baby perched on the balcony railing, pecking at himself to clean under his wing!

And I realized, once again, that the all too often, the only difference between hell and heaven is adjusting my attitude.

And maybe that's as good as it gets!

November 7
◇ SPEED LIMITS ◇

If you're like me, it is easy to get so caught up in the to-do lists of life that you go faster than the 'speed limit' of peaceful living.

Breaking spiritual speed limits creates anxiety, and inevitably, the policeman better known as 'exhaustion' puts on his alarm and I have to screech to a halt so he can write me a ticket.

The fine?

A depression-like feeling of physical fatigue that forces me to slow down.

I have to admit that over the years, I have amassed a draw-dropping amount of tickets in the spiritual realm.

And those tickets have often looked like kicking ass all week at work to the point that my own ass got kicked in the process and I spent all weekend in bed recovering.

One day, I decided I was sick and tired of the consequences of my spiritual speeding tickets.

I realized that if I want to be truly free, I needed to become obedient to the spiritual speed limits.

But to obey spiritual speed limits, I often have to turn down opportunities.

That's always hard for me, but as a result, I am so much more effective at the things I do choose to do.

When I harness my energy this way, I feel as though I am living life from on high, the promised land.

So, this sweet spot of obeying spiritual speed limits is the way to live, in my opinion!

November 8

◇ LOVE OFTEN REQUIRES SACRIFICE ◇

A year or so ago, I was sharing with my Coffee Companion about a difficult crossroads I was at: it seemed that there were two mutually incompatible goals I desired equally, and I had no idea how to choose which path to take.

She simply said, "Patrick, love often requires sacrifice."

I could literally hear a 'whoosh' sound inside my brain as I started to connect the dots by thinking about a high school classmate of mine.

Years back, this classmate took some interesting turns in life and she ended up getting hooked on crystal meth.

It was a pretty horrible few years for her.

Then, she got pregnant.

Everyone was terrified for that little baby, but my classmate turned her life around the instant the pregnancy test came back positive.

My classmate wised up and realized that she was at a crossroads: she could continue to ruin her life *and* lose her child, or she could clean up her act.

Miraculously, she quit cold turkey and has been completely sober for several years now.

I'm sure it was hard for her to quit such a powerful drug, but thinking of her story perfectly illustrated my Coffee Companion's principle that love often requires sacrifice.

And with my newfound clarity, it became abundantly obvious which path I should take.

So, I sacrificed my ego and submitted myself to the requirements of reality, thinking it was the end of my creative freedom.

But actually, my willingness to make sacrifices for love allowed me to integrate my need for creative freedom *and* my need for a family in a way I didn't think was possible.

As a result, I flourished into a whole new level of fulfillment, just like my classmate did by getting sober and attending to motherhood.

So, next time you're at a crossroads, remember that love often requires sacrifice, and it might be painful to make the sacrifice in the short term.

But if you're anything like my classmate and I, the sacrifice you make might just end up giving you joy beyond fathom!

November 9
◇ FIRST THINGS FIRST ◇

As the clock struck midnight on a very special Wednesday night, the organist of Notre Dame Cathedral in Paris met me at the side entrance to the cathedral, hundreds of feet below the gargoyles and spires.

We went inside the cathedral and walked up a seemingly endless spiral staircase that seemed older than time and more magical than Hogwarts.

And at the top of that staircase was the loft that held the Grand Organ of the cathedral!

Parts of the organ are four hundred years old, and the facade of cherub angel babies watching over the organ dates back almost one thousand years.

And as the Cathedral bells rang the midnight hour, an idea came to life within me, just as the gargoyles came to life in Victor Hugo's classic novel!

And the idea was a metaphor for how Paris expanded from the very island that Notre Dame sits on.

When tourists visit the island where Notre Dame resides, very few of them realize that once upon a time, that island *was* the city of Paris!

The people who founded Paris got it right: they settled on a little island that was abundant with resources and they built a beautiful cathedral to focus on contemplation, music, and art.

And as a natural result of putting first things first, there was a gradual expansion from the island to a grand city that has influenced world history for centuries and is now home to millions of people.

So, today, how can you put first things first?

How can you create an inner island that is rich in resources for meeting your basic needs, and meeting your spiritual needs, so that you eventually expand into all that you truly are, just as Paris did?

November 10

◇ THE WITCHING HOUR ◇

In Roald Dahl's beloved story *The BGF [Big Friendly Giant]*, there's a moment each evening when all the children must be tucked in before the giants come out and have their witching hour.

In my opinion, Dahl was creating a metaphor for the dangers of staying up too late, and he wasn't just talking to children.

Think about how many of us adults stay up late into the night working, drinking, watching television, or just staring at the ceiling.

Why is that?

Well, my personal observation is that there seems to be a primal fear of the vulnerability that sleep requires.

In the external world, we more or less have to trust that the world is safe and loving enough to take care of us while we're unconscious.

And in the inner realm, it's always uncertain as to what the nether regions of the universe are going to insert into our dreams.

So then, no wonder that so many people in the world are chronically sleep-deprived!

But the problem is this: when we succumb to the fear of sleep and stay up past the witching hour, all sorts of giants come out and trick us into doing all sorts of zany things based in fear.

So, perhaps it's better to go ahead and radically accept the witching hour and figure out a comforting sleep routine.

For me, that includes taking a quick shower and then writing down all of the things I did well throughout the day.

But that's just what works for me; that's how I, personally, put myself to sleep before the witching hour.

Likewise, how can you create a sleep routine that makes you feel safe enough to surrender unto the magical nether regions of the universe that we connect to through sleep?

November 11

◇ NOTHING IS WASTED ◇

The other day, my gym buddy said, "I don't know if it's impulse or intuition, but I like to expand past what people assume I am limited to. Who knows, tomorrow I might wake up and decide to sail to Australia."

I laughed and said, "Yeah, I get it. For instance, higher education isn't emphasized in my family of origin, yet I ended up with a doctorate."

He raised his eyebrows because we've known each other for a while and I never mentioned that.

He naturally followed up by asking what my field of study was, and I shared that once upon a time, I was a classical musician.

Then he asked, "Patrick, now that you're in a new field, are there any lessons you take from your past career?"

My face lit up because the last person to ask me that was Zuzu, many years ago, when she was still alive!

I told my friend that music allowed me to travel throughout the U.S. and Europe, experience many different cultures, and gain firsthand knowledge of history.

I chased my childhood dreams, achieved them, and then got to see that no amount of external success is a substitute for the deep inner journey of becoming who you truly are.

Perhaps most relevant to my 'new life' is that music and art have taught me to develop my own perspective while also respecting and seeking to understand others' viewpoints, because in art, like in life, there is very rarely an absolute answer.

I finished by telling my friend that when I first left music, I felt guilty for wasting time, my talent, and the resources of people and institutions who invested in me.

But now I see that nothing is wasted in the spiritual realm, and thinking in interdisciplinary ways has uniquely positioned me to help people.

So as you go about your day, remember that nothing is wasted.

No matter what we've done or left undone, no matter how off track it seems we've gotten, nothing is wasted.

Because in the end, all of those experiences come together to help us become who we truly are.

November 12

◊ WHY THEN, SHOULD WE FEAR? ◊

People make handsome profits by exploiting fear and creating illusions of security through indoctrination.

It's all too easy to succumb to these authoritarian, judgmental forces that are selling fear and, as a result, numb the anxiety with a dealer's choice of vices.

But we don't have to buy into the great marketing strategy of fear.

We really don't.

And it's not turning a blind eye or being naive or ignorant.

It's simply choosing to focus our time and energy on positive, uplifting, peaceful thoughts and messages so that our impact on the world is based in love rather than fear.

And to ignore all the fear-mongering, we can desensitize ourselves by relaxing into our body, taking a breath, letting our shoulders drop, and remembering that all is well and that the world is a safe and loving place.

After all, we are all cradled in the hands of God who dwells in infinity and abides in eternity.

Why then, should we fear?

November 13

◇ GOLDEN HANDCUFFS ◇

When I lived in Houston, I woke up at five a.m. countless Friday mornings to meet a friend of mine at a diner before he began his workday.

At the time, he was CEO of a company and made a handsome salary, but his job felt like golden handcuffs.

He felt called to leave his job, shed his external identity, and find out who he really was.

Finally, over one of his weekly omelets, he said, "Patrick, I'm ready to quit, because I've realized that God is more interested in who I'm becoming than what I'm doing."

Now, the following weeks and months were hard for him: some people told him he had committed career suicide, while others assumed he had retired.

But he knew what he was doing. He was figuring out his second act, which looked like exploring various avenues until he found a line of work mentoring other CEOs.

My friend took a big risk, and it paid off because he got to trade his golden handcuffs for spiritual freedom.

So, let's remember my friend's wisdom: that God is much more interested in who we're becoming than what we're doing.

November 14

◇ COWBOYS OF THE SEA ◇

L ast night I watched an amazing documentary about a sport that requires humans to push their limitations to the max: free diving.

I was amazed to learn that free divers plunge into the mysterious, ethereal depths of the ocean without oxygen for up to nine minutes at a time!

These cowboys of the sea love the spiritual, peaceful space between life and death they brush up against, but they must mitigate perilous risks in order to survive the transcendent experience.

Fascinatingly, free divers often enter into a state of euphoria, where the sirens from *The Odyssey* try to seduce them to stay in the depths, which would obviously spell the end of their earthly life.

Therefore, they have to discipline their mind, act opposite to their emotions, and surface for air even when every single ounce of their being wants to stay in the serenity.

And as I watched the documentary, I realized that this phenomenon was a perfect metaphor for the creative process.

When we're fully in creative flow, it can feel so life-affirming. Time stands still, and a whole day can feel like thirty seconds.

Yet if we don't learn how to put limits around creative flow, then we forget to eat and sleep.

We become irritable.

And eventually, some of us lose touch with reality, which is why the trope of the 'temperamental artist' permeates personalities in the fine arts.

So, just like those free divers, it's important to pull ourselves out of the seduction of the creative process in order to make sure we don't drown in the intensity.

In other words, I'm once again beating a dead horse and saying that in order to become who we truly are, it's pivotal to keep one foot in infinite eternity and the other foot firmly grounded in reality.

So, as you go about your day, may you bravely free dive down into the depths of human creativity, and may you refuse the siren calls and come back to reality when it is time for air.

November 15

◊ THE PANTHÉON ◊

One of the stand-out features in the Paris skyline is the Panthéon's massive dome, which stretches almost three hundred feet into the heavens.

So, naturally, that dome magnetized me and drew me in to see what was inside!

I went up to the Corinthian columns at the entrance of the Pantheon, and as I stood in line to purchase my entry ticket, I was privy to a colorful Indian wedding across the street!

Once I entered the spacious nave, I was awe-inspired by the paintings and sculptures that adorn the Pantheon's interior.

I was also fascinated to learn that King Louis XIV originally funded the Pantheon as a church dedicated to St. Genevieve, the patron saint of Paris.

However, during the French Revolution, the National Assembly transformed the Panthéon into a mausoleum housing the remains of Rousseau, Victor Hugo, and Louis Braille.

These luminary figures are housed at the Pantheon as a way to honor their contributions to French history, and you can't talk about France without talking about Voltaire!

Voltaire was all about freedom, and he challenged the status quo by promoting freedom of thought, freedom of speech, tolerance, and reason.

As I mentioned earlier this year, my favorite quote by Voltaire goes something along the lines of 'Think for yourself and let others do the same.'

Well, standing in front of Voltaire's tomb reminded me of that mantra, and I recommitted to dropping the natural human instinct to judge people who are different than me.

After all, they're just exploring the world and discovering things about themselves as they become who they truly are.

That's the same thing I'm doing, even if our paths look different.

And we all deserve the same chance to go down our unique life journey!

November 16

◇ COMFORT, STRETCH, AND STRAIN ◇

During the COVID-19 pandemic, I went about as nutty as a fruitcake!

The cause, you ask?

Well, I was separated from friends, Zuzu passed away, and in general, it seemed like the world was on fire.

So, I vacillated between a stressed-out state of running around like a chicken with my head chopped off, and a state of false comfort that included sitting on the couch all day and watching sitcoms while eating cereal.

Life was straining me, and I was finding comfort in ways that numbed me rather than nourishing me.

So, I had to find the sweet spot between comfort and strain: the stretch zone.

When we're in too much comfort, we don't move forward in our life's journey.

When we get too strained, our efforts are often misplaced because we lose our mindfulness.

However, in the stretch zone, we can live into our purpose and achieve goals with energy that came from our deepest, core selves.

Now, I can't tell you specifically how to find the promised land of the stretch zone.

But I do believe that the more often you identify which of the three states you are in, the more you will be able to figure out how to get to the sweet spot of the stretch mode more often, and you'll learn how to stay there longer.

So, as you go about your day, check in with yourself and identify whether you are in comfort, stretch, or strain.

November 17

◇ THROW AWAY THE RECIPE ◇

I am fascinated by my neighbor. He has lived next door to us for two years, yet he can barely eke out a 'hello' back to me on the rare occasion we're in the elevator together.

I try not to judge, but after three years of living next door, I have some facts to evaluate that this guy is not a very happy person.

Now, he has all the makings of a good life: he is fit, he has a beautiful girlfriend, and he has a good job at a prominent nearby company.

Yet I've never seen him smile, and everything about his body language denotes that he is generally afraid of life.

So, how can it be that someone who has 'done everything right' is so scared of being alive in the world?

Maybe because his recipe for living life is someone else's rather than his own.

After all, as Jung said, "The shoe that fits one person pinches another, there is no recipe for living that suits all cases."

So, as we go about our day today, let's throw away other people's recipe for living when we don't like how it tastes, and instead, create our own recipe for living.

November 18
◇ THE ASCENT ◇

I love what I do, I love the people in my flock, and I love who I am.

Most days feel as though I live life from the top of those fog-capped mountains on the cover of this book.

Yet, I also know when it's time to come back down to the valley and graze in the pasture with the rest of my flock.

But it wasn't always this way.

For years I ran frantically around the base camp of said mountain, not realizing all those efforts would never get me to the top of the mountain.

However, I eventually had to confront my fear of heights and actually face the ascent.

And by that, I mean I had to do difficult things that I would rather have avoided: things like feeling my emotions, changing my habits with food, and learning how to restrain my anger, among many others.

I can't imagine a much better life than the one I have as a result of climbing the mountain of personal development.

Now, just like the cover of this book, I still can't see what's on the other side of the mountain.

But I feel like I am about as close as a human can get!

November 19

◊ WHY HAS GOD BROUGHT ME INTO THIS WORLD? ◊

Pablo Picasso once said, "The meaning of life is to find your gift. The purpose of life is to give it away."

Now, Picasso was magnificently flawed, but hey, even a blind squirrel finds a nut every once in a while!

Picasso's statement is very-action oriented: to find your gift and give it away.

But I also think there's an element of reflection required, so here are some questions that I had to ask myself when I transitioned careers in order to find my true gift and then give it away:

Why Has God brought me into this world?

More specifically, why am I here in this place, rather than on the other side of the world?

Why am I here in this time, rather than a past or future generation?

And what does God want from me in exchange for the privilege of being alive on this cosmic vacation?

As I started asking these questions, I realized that I want to spend my life sharing my belief that becoming who we truly are starts before we are born and continues after we die; that this marvelous experience we call 'life' is all just one big journey of self-exploration through the places we go, the people we meet, and the experiences we have.

So, take time in your day today to consider those questions, so you can get ever more clear on the unique gifts that God has brought you into this world to share with others!

November 20

◇ AMAZING GRACE ◇

My grandmother was a quiet, reserved lady; in fact, her home was practically an ashram!

The only sounds I remember from her home are her needles clicking as she crocheted, dumplings simmering on the stove, the ticking of the Sears and Roebuck grandfather clock, and, the sound of my grandfather and I quietly playing checkers on a wooden board that he'd carved.

But occasionally my grandmother would say, "Patrick, why don't you go play a hymn on the piano?"

I knew her favorite hymn was Amazing Grace, so over the years, I sort of made my own little version of that hymn, and she just loved it.

About fifteen years ago, she requested that I play Amazing Grace at her funeral when that day came.

Of course, I said yes!

Well, unfortunately, my professional and personal obligations just didn't allow that to be a possibility when the time came for her soul to leave her body.

But I did the best I could to fulfill my promise.

I went up to Holmenkollen Chapel, which is perched on a hilltop above Oslo that offers the most beautiful panoramic view of the city, and I made a video of Amazing Grace with footage from the beautiful chapel and surrounding area.

And at the end of the video, I included the text of a little-known verse of this famous hymn:

Yea, when this flesh and heart shall fail,
*   and mortal life shall cease,*
I shall possess within the veil,
A life of joy and peace.

My grandmother didn't have the easiest life. Her mother died young, and as the eldest child, she became the surrogate for five children before having a large family of her own.

And I think the reason that her home was so quiet was because she longed for peace.

So, I hope that today, she possesses within the veil, a life of joy and peace.

November 21

◇ PLACEHOLDERS ◇

O n an ordinary day that seems like both a lifetime ago and two seconds ago, an acquaintance invited me to lunch.

Well, that guy and I ended up being pals and did all sorts of fun activities together including Sunday afternoons at Houston Astros games, going to the opera, and frequent trips to Galveston Beach.

He also mischievously helped me with my fear of heights by teaching me to rock climb at the gym and shoving me down the steepest waterslide at a theme park!

One evening, we were walking Ollie in a nearby park when we came across a pickup soccer game.

He said, "Patrick, one day we'll be standing at a field like this with our spouses, watching our kids play ball together."

In other words, he intended for our friendship to stand the test of time.

But unfortunately, that wasn't the case.

Now, I could tell you that the nature of our friendship changed as we both moved away from Houston.

But I think the real reason that our friendship didn't last is that I never fully saw him as a real person.

It was as though he was a placeholder I used through a difficult career and life transition.

So, when he would tell me that I had done or said things that hurt his feelings, I wasn't really capable of listening to him, apologizing, and changing my behavior.

Instead, I would more or less tell him, "Suck it up and get over it."

As a result, he would naturally pull away and not want to spend time together, which would further annoy me.

Lather. Rinse. Repeat.

Looking back, I wish I had treated my friend as more than a placeholder, but I just wasn't capable of respecting him at that point in my life.

But I do cherish the many positive memories from our friendship, and I am grateful for the lessons learned.

And these days, I'm quick to notice when I start to treat someone as a placeholder.

Instead, I remember my previous mistakes and figure out a way to see them as a human being with their own sacred self.

And as a result, I get to keep the friendship.

November 22

◇ MIDNIGHT SUNS AND MIDDAY MOONS ◇

Ollie and I just got back from our late-night stroll. And by late night, I mean it's four p.m. and it's already been dark for hours!

Just moments ago, we were in the summer land of midnight suns; now we are bathed in noontime moons.

And where tablecloths once graced the picnic area by the playground Ollie trots through, there is now a linen of fresh snow atop the tables.

In these long dark days of tundra winters, it's eerily mysterious to watch the fog roll in over the fjord.

In other moments, the night sky clears and you can see the snow-dusted trees interlacing the homes leading up to the famous ski jump built for an Olympics that took place several lifetimes ago.

Walking through the quiet, barren forests reminds me of the long, bleak mid-winter that lulls all of the woodland creatures into hibernation.

And as you go about your days this wintry season, may you take nature's tempo.

Slow down, tuck yourself in, and go into dormancy, so that new ideas can incubate and bloom forth in spring!

November 23

◇ THE MOST IMPORTANT CAKE EVER BAKED ◇

M y great-grandparents had guns to fight with and plows to feed their family.

My grandparents had sewing machines and automobiles.

My parents had television and the age of mass-marketed goods.

And my generation was blessed with rapid progress in transportation and the internet.

Now, I don't know what advancements will happen in my child's generation.

But I hope that those resources will allow him or her to go ever deeper into the inner realm of life.

And I hope that he or she will use the insights gained from the tools they are given to recreate the world with more wisdom, peace, and freedom than they found it.

I will give my kid the ingredients he or she needs, but they will bake the cake of their life—or the pie, or the casserole—the way they want!

And, at least in my little post-stamp corner of the world, that will be the most important cake ever baked.

November 24

◇ THANKSGIVING PRIDE ◇

One of the few minor drawbacks of living my sweet, heaven-on-earth life in Norway is that Thanksgiving is obviously not celebrated here.

And since there is no one around to make my favorite dishes for me, I have had to teach myself the wonderful dishes from childhood.

So, year on year, I improve my take on classic dishes like green bean casserole, stuffing, homemade macaroni and cheese, sweet potato casserole, and a spice cake to top it all off!

And I have to say that the secret ingredient to this carb-loaded meal I prepare is a sense of pride.

After all, food always tastes better when I make it myself because I gain a sense of accomplishment and a sense of connection with the ingredients and the process.

So, as you go about your day, consider making your favorite fall dish while saying thanks to the source of our life and the source of our food.

And as you do so, I hope you feel pride that you can navigate the world successfully in all sorts of ways, including in the kitchen!

November 25

◇ FOR THE BEAUTY OF THE EARTH ◇

Quite a few Thanksgivings ago, I gave one of my last concerts at Wells Cathedral in Somerset, England.

I arrived a few days early to spend time in Bath, which you may know as Jane Austen's old stomping grounds.

I was transformed by the picturesque autumn scenes: swans abiding in pristine ponds, sheep grazing under mighty oak trees, and the magical waters of the ancient Roman baths.

A century prior to my visit, the Bath native Folliot Pierpoint mindfully described the same landscapes in his perennial Thanksgiving hymn:

For the beauty of the earth, for the glory of the skies. For the love which from our birth over and around us lies. Lord of all, to Thee we raise, this our hymn of grateful praise.

So, as you go about your day, may you notice the beauty, glory, wonder, and joy of being alive on Earth this Thanksgiving season.

November 26
◇ HOSPITALITY ◇

On a cold, dark Thanksgiving night, my Best Friend and I walked over to the American Lutheran Church in downtown Oslo to take part in a good old-fashioned pie potluck with a group of American expats.

We sat around old tables covered in cheap tablecloths and ate pie from styrofoam plates with a retired couple who could talk the ear off of an elephant.

The experience completely hit the 'home' button of childhood Thanksgivings, to say the least!

The church made it clear that all the Americans in Oslo who didn't have anywhere else to celebrate Thanksgiving were welcome.

So we all showed up and let them show us hospitality, which is actually not always the easiest thing to do.

But in giving and receiving hospitality, strangers become friends, and that is certainly a theme of the Thanksgiving season!

So, as you go about your day, how can you put a big, heaping dose of Thanksgiving hospitality out into the world?

November 27

◇ THE THINGS WE CARRY ALL THIS LIFE ◇

As I write this, I'm sitting in my airplane seat and a man twenty-five years my senior is dozing off beside me, and somehow, his presence sends me into a flurry of ideas.

I assume that man popped out of the womb wired a certain way, like we all are, and that the core of who he is hasn't changed since his birth.

His life station may have changed, but he probably had the same basic attributes from age four to age sixty-four.

I wonder if, over the years, he has been able to hold onto what made the hours pass like minutes in his childhood, which Jung said is the key to our earthly pursuits.

Similarly, I have been many places and done many things in my life, but I will always remain the little boy from North Carolina in the picture frame above my office computer.

Seeing that picture connects me to the Little Patrick I carry in my heart.

Connecting to Little Patrick and choosing what's best for him guides my days and directs my path, and reminds me of the power of the inner traits and strengths that we carry throughout this life.

November 28

◇ TULIPS IN ROSE GARDENS ◇

At the year's first snowfall, Ollie loves dashing through the fresh powder; that is, until his little feet get so cold that he sits back on his hind haunches, rubbing his front paws together for warmth like a raccoon at a river!

And as he snorts his frustration, I can't say I blame him!

After all, even with a hand-stitched sweater and top-of-the-line canine parka, the tundra is a difficult landscape for a warm-weather dog breed.

Likewise, we sometimes find ourselves in emotional environments that do not honor our true nature.

Perhaps we are dreamers but are told, "Just do your job," or perhaps we're married to a spouse who doesn't honor our uniqueness.

According to psychologist Marsha Linehan, these situations are like being a tulip in a rose garden.

Now, sometimes, it's necessary to go find a tulip garden.

At other times, we might choose to stay in the rose garden, soothe ourselves, and make the best of the situation.

But no matter which garden we choose, we should always remember that we are big, fat, wonderful tulips, and there is *nothing* wrong with who we are!

November 29
◇ THE OSLO LIGHT SHOW ◇

A t the end of each November, Oslo transforms into a week-long international light festival that infuses the city with creativity and joy!

As my Best Friend and I headed toward the festivities at the harbor promenade this evening, we walked past a beautiful holiday window scene in a snazzy toy store while the bells of Oslo City Hall chimed the hour in the background.

Advancing toward the main attraction at the Nobel Peace Center, we passed a Viking ship beautifully decorated with strings of lights.

Then, looking up, we saw beautiful lights projected onto the backdrop of a dark, starless night!

Conviviality permeated every atom of the scene: kids clutching luminescent balloons, teenagers munching on cotton candy and popcorn, and couples strolling arm in arm.

In moments like these, I feel so much inspiration and gratitude for the privilege of being alive.

And I think that as far as emotions go, that's about as good as it gets!

November 30

◇ WALKING ON WATER ◇

They say that one of Jesus' greatest miracles was walking on water.

Well, clearly Jesus didn't live in Norway, because today, my Best Friend and I joined hundreds of other people walking on water!

In Sandvika, which is a suburb of Oslo, there is a beautiful, large park and today we stopped by it on our way home.

Little did we know that there would be people of all ages walking, skating, and cross-country skiing on a fully frozen section of the fjord that stretched as far as the eye could see!

With trepidation, we hesitantly walked out to join the festive atmosphere, and before long, we were comfortably trotting all over the ice, feeling as though we had superpowers!

Walking on water is just one of the amazing features of winter in Norway, where it's an everyday occurrence to drive through a forest of snow-frosted evergreens, see kids sledding down hills, watch fjord horses carrying people in sleighs donned with jingle bells, and hear waterfalls rush through thick ice!

I can't wait to share more about winter in Norway with you over our last month together, because I believe that the holiday season is a special time of the year to savor and fully participate in.

After all, how many chances does a person get to decorate a Christmas tree in this lifetime?!

◊ DECEMBER ◊

December 1

◇ ADVENT HOPE ◇

Many millennia ago, prophets foretold the birth of a baby who would come down to Earth and teach us about how to live and how to love.

For centuries, the tribes of these prophets anxiously awaited the birth of this babe, and today we remember their hope and vision through the season of Advent, which is just as relevant today as it was back then.

For example, when we lie awake at night with dreams of how we can recreate the world, we're preparing for Advent.

When we risk the disappointment of getting our dreams dashed by reality, we're preparing for Advent.

When we refuse to lose faith, but instead wait with clear eyes and a pure heart, we're preparing for Advent.

And when we remember that hope is something to live and die by, we're preparing for Advent.

No one is clairvoyant and there is no guarantee that our dreams will manifest, but we *have* to cling to the hope of Advent.

So, as you go about your day, may you dream, envision, and bravely hope!

December 2

◇ GETTING IN LINE FOR GLUG ◇

Just the other night, my Best Friend and I were out and about in downtown Oslo when we came upon hundreds of people waiting in line outside of a church.

We had no idea what the occasion was, but a local business was handing out free Norwegian glug, which is a hot fruity soda.

So, we joined the queue for our tasty drink!

Eventually, we entered the packed sanctuary, took our seats in an old wooden pew, and enjoyed a beautiful holiday concert by a local children's choir that sang Advent anthems after the organist played Bach's "Savior of the Nations, Come."

The kids in that choir worked hard to make a beautiful contribution to their community, and through their sublime voices, we heard Truth speak to us.

And, as you go about your day, I hope that you, also, follow the stream of life wherever it leads you, whether that be a cup of glug, a children 's choir, or the Holy Grail!

December 3
◇ EVERY DAY CAN BE GORGEOUS ◇

A s I walked over to the gym on this winter morning full of moonless darkness, I was delighted that the first snowflakes of winter floated in front of my eyes!

I spontaneously began a game with the snowflakes, zigging and zagging to see if I could catch them on my tongue!

Score one for childlike glee!

The whole experience reminded me of a line from the wonderful Christmas movie *Love Actually:*

Every day has the potential, in all its simplicity, just to be gorgeous.

So, as you go about your day, may you feel free to float through life with ease and grace, just like a snowflake!

And may you find the potential for gorgeousness in the simple moments of your day today.

December 4

◇ THE WORLD CHAMPION JUST WANTS NORMALCY ◇

In Norway, we say kids are born with skis on their feet, so it's fitting that the most decorated Winter Olympian in history is the Norwegian cross-country skier Marit Bjørgen!

When an interviewer once asked Marit about her plans for the future, she said:

I'm looking forward to living a normal life and being on holiday with my family. I'm sure I will always be interested in the sport and helping the younger team to come up...but also, I think I need some years away from the sport to have the motivation to do a good job at that.

So, here we have the world champion of her sport saying that being famous has big trade-offs and that the best things in life are totally normal: just being on holiday with loved ones and having time to enjoy Christmas.

Now, maybe Marit had to become the world champion to get to that point, but I think her words contain deep Truth.

So, this Christmas season, let's enjoy a normal holiday with loved ones, because apparently, a simple, everyday sort of life is highly underrated!

December 5
◇ A TODDLER'S CHRISTMAS TREE ◇

I recently invited our neighbors over to share a homemade winter spice cake, and of course, our High Ambassador of Cuteness graced us with his presence!

But after a while, the tiny tot was getting restless sitting on the couch with the grownups.

I remembered that childhood feeling well and I knew just the trick!

I brought forth a small artificial Christmas tree from the kitchen pantry, and he was amazed when he realized that he and I would be constructing it!

When he wasn't trying to fit the ornaments in his mouth, he was taking a decidedly postmodern aesthetic to the decoration: all the ornaments were on one branch!

But hey, who am I to question a little creative genius's vision?

And as we decorated the tree, I thought to myself, *This is what it's all about: being with the ones you love in a pleasant way, and delighting in their exploration and discovery of life!*

I think that's about as good as it gets!

December 6

◇ THE WONDER OF THE CHRISTMAS SEASON ◇

I n our family, the first snowfall inspires all the Christmas traditions: carols, sitcoms, movies, tons of baking, decorating the tree, wrapping presents, the whole nine yards!

Each moment is a chance to be together, to make memories, to feel the conviviality of this once-a-year season.

And whether it's making sure the milk and cookies are out for Santa, donning your newborn with her first holiday onesie, or preparing your signature dish for the family potluck, opportunities for experiencing *joie de vivre* abound during this merry season!

Now, I must admit that it's super easy to get caught up in the Christmas season here in this Norwegian land of snow and reindeer, where we're just a stone's throw away from Santa himself!

But whether you live in the Arctic, the tropics, or any climate in between, I hope that at some point today, the Christmas season reengages your childlike wonder and takes your breath away!

December 7

◇ WHAT AM I MISSING? ◇

L ast year, my Best Friend's nephew visited for the holidays, and I was excited to take him to Oslo Cathedral for the Advent service of Lessons and Carols!

After all, I was absolutely certain he would feel the Christmas spirit as we listened to perennial scriptures, hymns, and choir anthems.

But I struck out!

The entire service was spoken and sung in Norwegian, which was just too foreign for him, so he recessed into the bowels of social media.

His behavior made my blood boil, which was ironic in a service that is all about peace and goodwill.

As I tried to dial down my anger, I asked myself: "Patrick, what do *you* miss out on because of *your* unwillingness to work hard to enter into new experiences?"

And now, every time I pass the cathedral, I remember to ask myself, "What am I missing?"

I think that's a powerful question we could all stand to regularly ask ourselves!

December 8

◇ YOUR SACRED HEART ◇

Each Christmas, people all over the world sing the "Angels We Have Heard On High," and the stirring refrain of *Gloria, in excelsis Deo!* always reminds me of my day at the Basilica of the Sacred Heart in Paris.

As I arrived at the bottom of Montmartre to climb the stairs to the basilica, there were crowds of people picnicking and relaxing, and their presence reminded me that we all want to be close to the beauty of a sacred heart.

The interior of the basilica was even more exquisite than the pure white exterior, and likewise, each of our inner landscapes is much more beautiful than the outward facade of our physical body could ever portray.

The ceiling of the basilica features a gorgeous fresco of angels looking down from on high. My soul could hear them singing *Gloria, in excelsis Deo!,* and angels within my own inner temple joined the exuberant refrain!

So, whenever the organist plays the introduction to "Angels We Have Heard On High" this Christmas season, I hope you remember these Sacred Heart metaphors.

And I hope you sing about the glory of being alive from deep within your unique, beautiful, sacred heart!

December 9

◇ WINTER WONDERLAND! ◇

When my Best Friend's nephew visited for the holidays, he wanted to try ice skating for the first time!

We took him downtown to *Winter Land,* an annual holiday festival with food booths, carnival rides, and a large ice rink just waiting for kids of all ages to try their luck.

Well, as we laced up our skates and got out on the ice, my friend's nephew was like a twenty-five-year-old toddler, grabbing at anything (and anyone!) to hold onto his balance.

So, in order to save innocent bystanders from his flailing, my Best Friend and I got on each side of him and tried in vain to help him take baby steps without crashing!

Finally, I told him to stand still, and I pushed him slowly across the rink in a hilarious comedy of errors.

Deciding he had suffered enough bruises for one day, we retired to an outdoor fire, drank hot chocolate, and recanted a play-by-play until we ended up belly-laughing!

My Best Friend's nephew reminded me that there's something magical about this time of the year that makes us more willing to try new things and laugh like little kids.

And today, I hope you get to have an amazing 'winter wonderland' experience like we did at the *Winter Land!*

December 10

◊ SKIPPING CHRISTMAS ◊

Way back in December 2012, I was driving to the airport to go home for the holidays, but somehow, my car just never quite made it to the airport.

I was exhausted from a long year of work and graduate school, and the idea of being around a bunch of people for the holidays just made me shudder.

What I really needed was peace and quiet, so I turned my car around, headed back to my little studio apartment, and skipped my favorite holiday of the year.

I was afraid I would receive a huge guilt trip, but believe it or not, Christmas happened just fine without me!

Gifts were still exchanged, food was still prepared, and carols were still sung.

Sure, they missed me, and I missed them, but taking agency over my life allowed me to visit them in the new year on my own terms and conditions, when I was well-rested, and when I was able to better relate to them.

So, as Christmas gets closer, remember that it's totally okay to thwart expectations and envision the holiday season that is best for *you*.

December 11

◇ YOUR INNER NORTH STAR ◇

According to the Christmas story, the three Wise Men were guided by the North Star to the Christ child.

Similarly, my Coffee Companion once shared with me that our personal values are like an inner North Star.

And just as there was unfathomable space between the Wise Men and the North Star, there will always be space between us and our ideal values.

But that doesn't mean we close our eyes, turn around, and run from them.

No.

Instead, we follow the inner North Star of our values with faith and anticipation, because our values are the most reliable navigational beacon to get our bearings in this life.

And just as the Wise Men followed the external North Star until they encountered the Divine Christ Child, we can be guided by the inner North Star of our values until we come to meet, well, the divinity that has been within us all along.

December 12

◇ THE CHRISTMAS ANGEL ◇

On the very first Christmas, some shepherds were attending to their flock of sheep out in a field when suddenly, an angel appeared and said, "Hey there, I've got some good news!"

Well, in December 2020, that angel had a little reunion tour and she showed up with glorious news for my own life!

Here is the back story: through a long conflux of events, Ollie and I ended up boarding a plane to start our new life in Oslo in December 2020.

I knew that because of the worldwide pandemic, we would end up having to quarantine in a hotel airport over the Christmas holiday, but what I hadn't factored in was Ollie working his magic on the nice lady at customs when we arrived in Norway!

As she rubbed Ollie's belly, she said, "Your forms indicate you will live with your friend who is here for work. Are there two separate bedrooms and bathrooms in the apartment?"

I said, "I believe there is only one bathroom."

She looked at me with a look of playful sternness and said, "I want to give you and your sweet dog a good Christmas. Please answer again."

At first I was surprised, but I quickly realized what she was up to and avoided the question by saying, "I give you my word that my friend and I will fully quarantine in the apartment for two weeks."

She winked at me and said, "I hope you and your cute dog have a wonderful first Christmas in Norway."

I replied, "Thank you so much! You have no idea what this means to me."

That nice woman at customs is proof that angels really do exist, and that Christmas miracles still abound!

December 13
◇ THE CHRISTMAS MARKET ◇

Going to a Norwegian Christmas Market is like being on the set of a Hallmark Christmas movie!

It is endearing to see pink-cheeked kiddos dressed up like Eskimos, dogs prancing around happily, and parents dressed in Nordic sweater patterns.

After hearing a girl choir sing carols in their traditional Norwegian *bunad* dresses in the village square, we grab a reindeer pelt and huddle together.

And once we warm up, we enjoy Norwegian sweet buns served by a woman who could double as Mrs. Clause!

Walking around the cabin-like *hyttes*, my senses are delighted by hand-painted ornaments, hand-knitted sweaters, jams and jellies, and candles.

And of course, taking a picture with Santa is a must!

Wherever you are in the world (and whatever holidays you celebrate), you probably have traditions that are just as delightful as Norwegian Christmas Markets.

It is these rituals that can help us really savor and participate in the moment of the season, and subsequently take that new level of attention and gratitude into all the days of our lives.

December 14

◇ SNOW GLOBE FLURRIES ◇

L ast December, our neighbors took us to Hadeland Glaswerk, a tiny glass-blowing community about an hour outside of Oslo. It was an altogether very unique day, so we brought back a beautiful Christmas snow globe as a souvenir.

Of course, every time I shake the snow globe, a flurry of snow covers the pristine landscape and characters, and as I watch the effect, I'm reminded of my Grief Guide's metaphor that emotions are like the flurry in a snow globe.

When we get shaken up by the forces of life, emotions blur our view of a situation from the cloud of 'emotional snow' swirling around.

However, once the globe is stabilized, the flurry dies down and we can see the beautiful inner scenery once again.

The snow globe helps us keep in mind that our emotions are *not* who we truly are; they simply arise when the 'snowglobe' of our mind and body gets 'shaken up' in order to let us know that things aren't quite stable.

Our *true selves* are the beautiful scenery inside the snow globe that is always there, whether shaken or calm.

December 15

◇ CHRISTMAS IN THE BAHAMAS! ◇

When I was a teenager, my family decided to spend Christmas in Nassau, The Bahamas, which to this day is one of the most beautiful places I've ever been.

After all, with sun, sand, and crystal clear waters, what's not to love?!

My favorite part of the trip was when we went to a secluded beach about an hour outside of the capital city and spent the day snorkeling and scuba diving.

I felt all sorts of joy as I plunged underwater and saw the full cast and crew from *Finding Nemo* swimming right underneath me along the coral reef!

As the initial novelty wore off, my joy turned into a peace beyond words as I watched the seaweed gently sway, gazed at a sea turtle floating past, and watched a starfish lying on the ocean floor.

Then, all of a sudden, a sting ray appeared underneath me with a wing span wider than my own; terrified, I practically broke the sound barrier on my swim back to shore!

Spending Christmas in The Bahamas was better than any store-bought gift because it was one of the first times in my life when I was able to identify exactly what emotion I was feeling in the present moment.

As a result, I went back to the drama of high school with strong mental pictures of those underwater moments of joy, peace, and fear, which helped me better navigate life.

Now, I'd like you to consider taking a few moments to go through your own memories and recall a time when *you* felt the three emotions I mentioned: joy, peace, and fear.

What were your body sensations?

What was the purpose of the emotion in the moment (in other words, what was the feeling trying to tell you)?

And how did you react to the emotion?

This exercise is important because creating a mental image of the most powerful time we felt a particular emotion helps us more quickly identify that feeling in the present day.

And, the more we can identify our emotions, the more we can understand how they are trying to help us, which inevitably leads to more wisdom, peace, and freedom.

December 16
◇ THE GREAT FELLOWSHIP ◇

Many Christmases ago, Zuzu called me up and told me about a powerful experience she had while driving down Houston's Westheimer Road.

As she sat in her car at an intersection, she saw a homeless man, and her mind decided to signify him as the embodiment of all the people who go to bed hungry, who can't afford a safe home, who feel as though they don't belong, and who will never be able to chase their dreams.

I said, "Zuzu, it sounds like your emotions hit you with the pressure of a firehose when you were only capable of drinking out of a water spigot."

She laughed through her tears and said "Yes, that's correct!"

After Zuzu cleared her throat and composed herself, she went on to tell me:

You know, Patrick, I believe that there is a Great Fellowship that is all around. We can't see it, but it's there. So, before I go into organizations and help leaders, I sing a song to help me remember why I am there. The lyrics are 'Let them know that they are loved, let them know that they are one.'

Years later, my Coffee Companion brought up the exact same concept of the Great Fellowship, and she and I delved deeper into how we could use the Great Fellowship to aid us in our life's journey.

We came up with the idea that when we get overwhelmed by all the pain in the world, we can gently put our heads on a wall to represent leaning on the Great Fellowship.

And as we lean on the Great Fellowship, we can be refueled by the knowledge that we are loved, and we can be comforted by that harmonious notion that we are one united, human race.

December 17
◊ "IF WE ALL WORKED UNDER THE ASSUMPTION..." ◊

A few years before I moved to Oslo, I read David McCullough's mesmerizing biography about the Wright Brothers, who on this day in 1903 became the first people to successfully achieve human flight.

I was so inspired by the biography that I took a week off work to visit my parents and pilgrimage to Kitty Hawk, North Carolina, where the Wright Brothers made their legendary flight.

As I walked up the historic hill, I wondered aloud to my dad, "What was it about the Wright Brothers that allowed them to solve the problem of human flight, which people had been working on since the time of da Vinci?"

Well, before he had a chance to respond, I answered my own question in a ten-minute monologue!

For starters, Orville and Wilbur's parents respected their creativity by teaching them to read voraciously and helping them explore varied interests including ornithology and the new bicycle craze.

And while a love of reading historical narrative commanded respect for the work of their predecessors, the Wright Brothers' divergent interests allowed them to tweak design flaws with a completely new approach.

In fact, the younger brother, Orville, once wrote:

If we all worked on the assumption that what is accepted as true is really true, there would be little hope of advance.

Through their fresh take on accepted facts, the Wright Brothers changed the course of human history as they recreated the world into a safer and more connected place through aviation.

Likewise, as you go about your day, how can *you* question commonly held assumptions in order to advance into more of who you truly are and what you are here to contribute?

December 18
◇ MONOPOLY ◇

One of my most memorable childhood Christmas presents was a Major League Baseball edition of the classic board game Monopoly.

In fact, I still have it to this day!

Monopoly is hands down my favorite game.

After all, what better test of friendship can there be than crushing your opponents over the course of a seemingly-never ending crusade for financial domination?!

As an adult, it's hard to find time to play an entire game of Monopoly with friends.

But luckily, I discovered a card game version that only takes about fifteen minutes to play called Monopoly Deal!

Monopoly Deal is incredibly addictive. I was immediately hooked the first time I played it, and have since shared the game with many others who have bought their own deck.

In fact, my Best Friend recently took his set of cards to India and introduced the game to his nieces and nephews, all of whom begged him to play one more round!

As I was thinking about the ripple effect of Monopoly, which has been played by a *billion* people over the last hundred years, a speech by a famous twentieth-century leader came to mind.

This leader once said that history is created from numberless courageous acts where people stand up for their values, and as a result, send out a ripple of hope.

But what if history isn't nearly as serious as this man made it out to be?

What if, instead, history is created from numberless *creative* acts (like Elizabeth Magie's invention of Monopoly) that help us relax into life as we spend time with loved ones?

And what if, as a result, ripples of wisdom, peace, and freedom are spread as we recreate the world into a more authentic place?

December 19

◇ MOOMIN IS MISSING! ◇

Today, a truly awful thing happened: our High Ambassador of Cuteness lost his Moomin!

Who is Moomin, you ask?

Well, Moomin is our High Ambssador's stuffed animal version of Ollie. Every time I see our High Ambassador, he points and looks at Ollie, smiles, and shows me Moomin.

Well, this morning as Ollie and I walked my Best Friend to his office for work, I noticed Moomin on a bench by the playground where our High Ambassador holds court.

I placed Moomin in my pocket so I could return him safe and sound, but my Best Friend said, "No, it will be okay here. His mom will come back to pick it up soon, I bet."

Well, at the end of the day, I saw our High Ambassador and asked, "Where's Moomin?"

He shrugged his shoulders and looked sad, and it was then that I realized we were in the horns of a dilemma.

First, I gave my Best Friend an obligatory "I was right and you were wrong" song and dance.

Then, I alerted a search party by posting a picture of Moomin on the community board of our apartment.

After all, I remember what it's like to lose a favorite toy as a small child, so I was determined to rectify this situation.

Luckily, by the next morning, Moomin had been returned to our High Ambassador, albeit a little worse for wear (there had been a major assassination attempt on his life by a neighborhood dog!).

Although Moomin had clearly suffered a traumatic brain injury, a broken nose, and a severed leg, our High Ambassador didn't care. He was just glad to be reunited with his safety object, a symbol for him that the world is a safe and loving place.

Returning Moomin to our High Ambassador was an important mission because trust is the first developmental task of childhood, and in many ways, trust is the foundation upon which our lives are built.

Therefore, what can you do today to help someone see that sometimes, cherished items do return, that a wilted rose can rebloom, and that a phoenix can rise from the ashes?

In other words, how can you go about your day in a way that creates just a millimeter more trust in the world?

December 20

◇ UPENDING SERIOUSNESS ◇

One of the many reasons I love the Christmas season so deeply is because society as a whole tends to upend the seriousness of the adult world.

Knowing that the Christmas season only lasts a short part of the year generally inspires us to be more childlike, to be swept up in wonder, to have special experiences, and to be just a little more alive than the rest of the year.

And *that's* a true Christmas miracle!

In this special season, there are so many opportunities for memories, connection, fun, family, and love.

So, as you go about your Christmas season, may you upend seriousness and allow yourself to be captivated by friends, family, and yuletide cheer!

December 21

◊ THE SECRET OF LIFE ◊

During her last Christmas in physical form, Zuzu called me up and said:

Patrick, it's an infinite and eternal project we're in, and the project is called life! And I, for one, am not ever going to do another single thing unless it's God's will.

Zuzu's words reminded me of Henri Nouwen's idea that we belong to God from eternity to eternity, and our life here on Earth is only part of our total cosmic life.

However, while we're here, we can do our little part in recreating the world and bringing the universe to a higher consciousness by becoming who we truly are.

And in our efforts, we are saying "Thank you, thank you, thank you!" for this amazing privilege of life we have been given.

December 22

◇ GOD'S PLAIN-CLOTHES OFFICERS ◇

I used to admire world-famous artists, musicians, and inventors, but now I'm just as impressed by the hidden heroes that are interwoven into the everyday fabric of life.

For example, the Virgin Mary was never trying to be famous, but two thousand years later we still remember her because of her faithfulness and devotion.

Like Ollie, Mary wasn't trying to seek renown.

But by virtue of her authentic, pure heart, she changed the world by doing the best she could to nurture her child one day at a time.

I think people like Mary and Ollie are 'God's plain-clothes officers,' and I aspire to join their ranks!

December 23
◇ JUSTICE AND LOVE ◇

When I was twelve years old, I had the great fortune of hearing the poet Gloria Gaither share why the Christmas season is so important.

According to Gloria's Christian faith, God tried to share with us all throughout history what He wanted us to know.

And we got *part* of the message: the part about justice, about how when we do bad things we have to rectify the situation and make amends.

But we had a difficult go of understanding the other part of what God wanted us to know: that we are *loved beyond measure.*

Therefore, God sent love right down to Earth in the form of a tiny, vulnerable baby so that we could see love, touch love, and know love.

Two thousand years later, we humans have justice figured out well enough, but we could still stand to use a few lessons on the ease and grace of love.

So, this Christmas season, let's remember that this holiday is about spreading *love, love, love,* so that there is peace on earth and goodwill toward all people.

December 24

◇ WHEN WE GIVE EACH OTHER GIFTS... ◇

A few days ago, I was perusing the bookshelves of the public library when I just so happened to discover the early twentieth-century Norwegian writer Sigrid Undset.

As I scanned through the book to decide whether or not I wanted to borrow it, I came across a beautiful passage about giving Christmas gifts that I'd like to share with you.

Undset wrote:

When we give each other Christmas gifts in His name, let us remember that He has given us the sun and the moon and the stars, and the earth with its forests and mountains and oceans—and all that live and move upon them. He has given us all green things and everything that blossoms and bears fruit...[and ultimately] He came down to earth and gave us Himself.

So, when we give and receive gifts, whether on Christmas or any other day of the year, let us remember that we are symbolizing our appreciation of much greater gifts: gifts from the Truth which created us and gave us this wonderful privilege of being alive.

December 25

◊ LOVE CAME DOWN AT CHRISTMAS ◊

Each Christmas, my Friend in Paris sends a beautiful card with the words of his favorite carol.

His yearly message reminds me that giving and receiving love is what Christmas, and *life*, are all about.

The lyrics he shares are by the nineteenth-century British poet Christina Rossetti, who wrote:

Love came down at Christmas, love all lovely, love divine,
Love shall be our token, love be yours and love be mine,
Love to God and all men, love for plea and gift and sign.

As we go about our Christmas Day, I hope that love shall indeed be our token: love be yours and love be mine.

Merry Christmas!

December 26

◇ YEAR AFTER YEAR ◇

The Estonian composer Arvo Pärt wrote a piece of music called *Annum per Annum* (meaning *Year After Year*) to celebrate the 900th anniversary of Speyer Cathedral in Germany.

This composition tries to aurally capture the rituals of the church, which have been offered throughout the world day after day, year after year, millennia after millennia.

Naturally, then, I used to perform this piece of music for audiences at the end of each December to help them transition from one year to the next in an intentional way.

And as we begin to end our year together, I want to be similarly intentional in letting you know that it has been a true honor to travel around the sun with you, day after day, this *annum*.

And also, I hope our time together will help you in your future *annums*.

December 27
◇ DID I LIVE, LOVE, ENJOY, MAKE MEMORIES? ◇

As we wind down our year together, I'd like to circle back to a conversation I once had with Siân Lloyd-Pannell of *The Honest Guys.*

When I cheekily asked her what the meaning of life is, she laughed and said something along the lines of:

I think the meaning of life is just to live as best as you can and to be able to satisfactorily answer the following questions: Did I live? Did I love? Did I enjoy what I was doing? Did I make wonderful memories?

As I prepare to bid you adieu as you sail off into the sunset, I hope that you live, love, enjoy what you do, and make wonderful memories.

And I wish you a best and most wonderful life!

December 28

◇ REFLECTIONS ◇

As I reflect back on this year we have spent together, it's impossible to not have hope about certain outcomes you may have received from our friendship.

First, I hope you feel more confident in your ability to intuitively notice where life naturally wants to take you.

Second, I hope you've gained insight into the long arc of life; after all, what we do today will incrementally build up to a life of rich fulfillment or a life of regret.

Third, as Robert Louis Stevenson once said, I hope that you are able to focus on the seeds you plant more than the harvest you reap.

Fourth, I hope you have been steered in the direction of wisdom, peace, and freedom.

And finally, I hope that in some small way, our time together has helped you become a little more of who you truly are.

December 29

◇ HAPPY FEET ◇

There is a smart, lovely, lively, little girl in the Indian state of Maharastra who once made my feet very happy.

To give you a little context, for centuries it has been customary for Indian kids to bid farewell to elders by touching their feet as a sign of respect.

And when this sweet preschooler followed the custom, I was overwhelmed.

She was so open, so available, and so *herself*.

She freely and innocently shared her energy with me, and it was one of the great honors of my life.

I share that story because I want to let you know that the respect you have given me by spending your time with me this year is like that little girl touching my feet.

And I hope that in some small way, I have returned the sentiment and given *you* happy feet.

December 30
◇ THE PENULTIMATE DAY ◇

O ver the last year, I have shared with you stories from my life's journey of seeking Truth.

And although I only know a little bit about dwelling in eternity and abiding in infinity, perhaps some of these stories have helped you find your own way to experience the spiritual realm of life that is impossible to put into words.

Now, maybe after you finish this book tomorrow, our paths may never cross again in this life.

I hope that's not the case, but nevertheless, if that's the way the cards fall, then I will look forward to reconnecting with you on the day after forever in the space between the stars.

December 31

◇ BLESSINGS FROM THE HEART ◇

R ight before she passed away, Zuzu said a benediction upon our friendship, and upon my life, with four words. *Blessings from the heart.*

A *blessing* is an infusion of holiness, divinity, and well-being.

The *heart* is the center of personality, intuition, feeling, and emotion.

As we come to the end of our very special year together, I would like to say farewell by wishing the same benediction upon you.

Blessings from the heart.

As a coach, speaker, and author, Patrick Parker has helped people around the world flourish into lives and careers that align with who they truly are.

Patrick lives with his family by the fjord of Oslo, Norway. He can often be found between the pages of a good book, baking up a storm in the kitchen, writing, filmmaking, or enjoying nature with his prancing dog Ollie!

Connect with Patrick at www.patrickaaronparker.com.

Made in United States
North Haven, CT
04 January 2024

47045119R00300